MORE
FINISH LINES
TO CROSS

MORE FINISH LINES TO CROSS

Notes on Race, Redemption, and Hope

CARY CLACK

MAVERICK BOOKS / TRINITY UNIVERSITY PRESS
San Antonio, Texas

Published by Maverick Books, an imprint of Trinity University Press
San Antonio, Texas 78212

Unless otherwise stated, the columns in this book originally
appeared in the *San Antonio Express-News*, reprinted courtesy of
the Hearst Corporation. "Voices: What Can Be Found in the Stacks"
appeared in the *Smart Set*, "Back to Denver Heights" appeared
in the *San Antonio Heron*, and "The Bout" appeared in *Truly
Adventurous.*

Book design by BookMatters, Berkeley
Cover design by Anne Richmond Boston
Cover image courtesy of Cary Clack
Author photo by Carl Booker

978-1-59534-271-3 paperback
978-1-59534-272-0 ebook

Trinity University Press strives to produce its books using methods
and materials in an environmentally sensitive manner. We favor
working with manufacturers that practice sustainable management
of all natural resources, produce paper using recycled stock,
and manage forests with the best possible practices for people,
biodiversity, and sustainability. The press is a member of the Green
Press Initiative, a nonprofit program dedicated to supporting
publishers in their efforts to reduce their impacts on endangered
forests, climate change, and forest-dependent communities.

The paper used in this publication meets the minimum requirements
of the American National Standard for Information Sciences—
Permanence of Paper for Printed Library Materials, ansi 39.48–1992.

CIP data on file at the Library of Congress

28   27   26   25   24 | 5   4   3   2   1

For

Jenny V. Clack, the best mother and my first reader so many years ago

Theresa Canales and all who didn't cross the finish line but whose lives pushed us closer

Laiana and Mikai and the hope that their generation crosses all the finish lines

CONTENTS

Contents   ix

FOREWORD

JOE HOLLEY

Think of San Antonio, the old intriguing city that Texans—indeed, all Americans—love to visit, and you think of the tried and true: the Alamo, of course, and its string of sister missions downriver; the lush and beautiful River Walk; King William, Monte Vista and other graceful historic neighborhoods; and, yes, the best Tex-Mex food in the Lone Star State.

I can think of another San Antonio essential: my old friend Cary Clack, he of the euphonious name, infectious laugh and discerning eye. For years now, readers of the *San Antonio Express-News* have turned to Clack's regular column to find out what he's thinking, what he's feeling, what he's discovered recently about their city and beyond. They laugh with him, shed tears with him, share his hopes and disappointments. He breathes life into the community he and they call home. In this book we're fortunate to have a sampling of the several thousand columns he's written—and, fortunately, continues to write.

Clack is a lifelong San Antonian. Like the late Studs Terkel's Chicago, the late Pete Hamill's New York or Margaret Renkl's Nashville, the Alamo City is his city. He knows her streets and neighborhoods, her people. He knows her pain and problems, her dreams and unexpected delights. He's privy to her secrets. Clack reminds me of Kierkegaard's categories of rotation and repetition; instead of endless novelty (rotation), he stays rooted in one place, digs deeply (repetition) and discovers.

He gives credit to the late Maury Maverick Jr., another quintessential San Antonian, for opening the door to his distinguished career in journalism. Scion of the pioneering Texas family that bequeathed its name to the American vernacular, Maverick was a crusading state representative, a fearless ACLU attorney and a columnist himself. Telling Clack that Black people needed another Malcolm X, he introduced the young man to his *Express-News* editors. They became Clack's editors. In a few years, Clack would become the first African American on the editorial board of any San Antonio daily newspaper, as well as the first metro columnist.

Knowing Maverick from my days at the *Express-News*, I laughed and nodded in agreement when I read Clack's description of the curmudgeonly, deeply caring columnist on his morning constitutional along Broadway past Brackenridge Park. Clack calls him "nature's child and freedom's apostle striding to the drumbeat in his head, on the lookout for stray dogs in need of care, and thinking about life's underdogs and the marginalized who need a voice to amplify theirs. Maybe his voice."

And Clack's. My friend grew up in Denver Heights, a predominantly African American neighborhood on San Antonio's East Side. Remarkably, one of his white ancestors fought for the Confederacy; a Black ancestor was a lynching victim. (The white forebear was the last man known to have been killed by Wild Bill Hickok in a gunfight.)

"The first time I wrote about race I was in the third grade," Clack recalls, "and we had some free time in the afternoon. I wrote a one-page essay titled 'Black People Are People Too.'" Still a resident of now gentrifying Denver Heights, he says he writes about race much less often than his detractors insist he does, and yet this former speechwriter for Coretta Scott King, the esteemed widow of Martin Luther King Jr., invariably has something to say on the subject. He offers insights and a perspective that are a bit unusual for San Antonio, a city with a relatively small African American population.

I'm walking along with him, for example, as he describes setting out to vote one morning. Although I can't see them as I read, Clack informs us that he's always accompanied by ghosts when he votes—the ghosts of Black people who tried and were denied when they attempted to cast their ballots, who were beaten and gassed and thrown in jail, who died. "I never vote alone," he writes.

Clack also introduces us to people many of us would never have known had he not brought them back to life. I think of I. H. "Sporty" Harvey, a San Antonio boxer who in 1954 won the right—with the legal assistance of thirty-two-year-old Maury Maverick Jr.—to further his career by fighting integrated matches. (In addition to a column, the collection includes a long, fascinating piece about Harvey, who lost more often than he won inside the ring but won his most important victory in the courts.)

Until I read Clack's column, I had never heard of San Antonio native Jesse Belvin, a velvet-toned singer—imagine a Johnny Mathis / Sam Cooke amalgamation—whose set-to-soar career was cut short at age twenty-five when he died in a car accident.

I should point out that these columns are not always sober and somber. You're as likely to read about Sinatra and Raskolnikov, Clack's six-toed cats, as you are his take on the latest Trumpian outrage. Did I mention that he has no use for the former president? He doesn't like figgy pudding either, or at least the earworm Christmas carol that sings its praises.

Reading these columns, which are insightful and often deeply personal, I think of the memoirist Patricia Hampl. "For we do not, after all, simply have experience," she has written. "We are entrusted with it. We must do something—make something—with it. A story, we sense, is the only possible habitation of our witnessing."

My friend Cary Clack knows, intuitively perhaps, that he has been entrusted with experience. In these columns, these stories, he shares what he has made. We, his readers, are recipients of a gift. We are the richer for it.

Introduction

Fifteen years separate the publication of this book from that of my first collection, *Clowns and Rats Scare Me*. For most of that time, I was away from the *San Antonio Express-News*, away from journalism altogether. This new collection is possible because I leapt at a completely unexpected opportunity to return to the paper.

I drifted into journalism at age thirty-four, having never taken a journalism class or worked for a newspaper. I drifted back the second time at age fifty-nine. My return was as unconventional and inexplicable as my entry.

I was nineteen years old the first time I walked into a newsroom, that of the *San Antonio Light*. I didn't go looking for a job, and I didn't leave with a fire to write for newspapers. My purpose was to advocate that the *Light* publish more Black writers on their op-ed page, but I wasn't one of them. I'd yet to think of myself as a writer or aspiring journalist, much less did I know any Black writers or journalists.

It was March 1980, and I was home for spring break during my first semester at the University of Houston. I'd transferred there after three semesters at San Antonio College, which had one of the country's top community college journalism programs and newspapers. If I knew this during my time there it meant nothing to me, since I had no interest in journalism.

Not that I didn't love newspapers. When I was growing up, San Antonio had three dailies—the *Express* in the morning and the *Evening News* and *Light* in the afternoon. On weekends the *Express* and *Evening News* combined as the *Express-News*.

They were no better than the *Light* when it came to publishing Black people. I chose to approach the *Light* because it had recently profiled an up-and-coming young Black leader. Since I didn't know any Black writers, he was one of the Black community leaders whose names I'd scribbled on a sheet of paper as people the *Light* could ask to submit opinion pieces.

With a boldness uncharacteristic of me, I called the editor of the *Light* and met with him and the publisher in their offices in the second-floor newsroom. They must have been bemused with this teenager and his handwritten list of people he thought they should let write for them. But they listened graciously and took my list.

I walked out feeling I'd done what I could and gave it no more thought. My first inkling that I might want to write on an op-ed page came a few years later.

I was a student at Saint Mary's University, studying political science, when the *Express-News*, in January 1983, published on its Sunday op-ed page a piece I'd written advocating that Martin Luther King Jr.'s birthday be a national holiday. It was the first time my work appeared in print.

In 1984, my junior year in college, I began writing unsolicited columns for a Black East Side newspaper, the San Antonio *SNAP*. I wrote about things happening in San Antonio and across the country, whatever interested me and came to mind. Because I was painfully shy and didn't want anyone to see me, I would drop my manuscript, sometimes handwritten, over the transom, and miraculously they'd appear in print each Thursday.

I didn't get paid a dime, but the paper's publisher, Eugene Coleman, wanted me to give the column a title along with my photo. Again, because I was too shy, I declined. Still, he published every piece I submitted, allowing me to write and try to discover my voice.

That summer, before my senior year, I went to Atlanta to study at the Martin Luther King Jr. Center for Nonviolent Social Change. At my grandmother's suggestion, I'd sent the piece I'd written on MLK to the King Center. They sent back an application to their scholar-internship program where college students learned about the philosophy of nonviolence as a way of life and a tool for social change. I applied and was accepted.

As part of the program, students worked in the area they were studying. Lili Baxter, the program director, who became a mentor and remains a close friend, declared me a writer and placed me with Steve Klein, the center's communication director and Coretta Scott King's speechwriter.

In that capacity I was able to write some of the commentaries Mrs. King delivered on CNN. That experience made me want to be a journalist, but I had no journalism experience and few writing samples.

For the next nine years after graduation, I sent my resume and clippings to publications across the country with no success. Another local Black newspaper, the *San Antonio Informer*, owned by Tommy Moore, gave me an outlet to write columns and expand my portfolio. I also had op-ed pieces published in the *Express-News* and *Light*, but except for $150 for an op-ed published in the *New York Times* in 1989, I wrote for free.

A door opened for me in fall 1993 when I met Maury Maverick Jr., a legendary civil rights lawyer and Sunday *San Antonio Express-News* columnist, in a typewriter shop. He was the son of a former San Antonio mayor and congressman and a descendant of the family who gave us the word "maverick."

When he learned that I was an aspiring journalist, he brought me to the attention of Bob Richter and Lynnell Burkett, the associate page editors of the *Express-News*, and Sterlin Holmesly, the editorial page editor. Sterlin invited me to submit op-eds, and over the next few months he published them, paying me $100 for each.

He then offered me a column, at the same rate, that began in June 1994. The column ran every other Wednesday. By November it became weekly.

In March 1995 the *San Antonio Express-News* gave me a try-out in the newsroom before hiring me part-time in April. I was paid by a temp agency. In June I was hired full-time as a general assignment reporter but didn't have to relinquish my column. Four days a week I was paid by the newsroom as a reporter, and the other day I was paid by the op-ed page for my column.

I became a full-time opinion writer when I joined the editorial board in 1998. In 2000 I became a three-times-a-week metro columnist. The column was moved to the features section in 2005 but remained what it had been since 1994, a general interest column in which I was allowed to write on anything I wanted, with the freedom to experiment and use different styles and voices.

I don't think I'd have left the *Express-News* if that hadn't changed. In my last couple of years there, however, for reasons neither I nor anyone else understood, the paper's editor put restrictions on what I could write. I could no longer write humor columns or about politics and national issues. The editor wanted me to write only about local topics. I was the only columnist who couldn't write about politics. This editor overall did more good for my career than bad and was largely responsible for me getting the contract for *Clowns and Rats Scare Me*, which was published in 2009. I called him the book's godfather.

But the irony is that under his new restrictions, most of the columns in that book wouldn't have been allowed. It was ridiculous and petty bullshit. I never knew when he would be upset with a particular column, but after one that upset him ran, he'd relay his displeasure through a third party.

The most nonsensical example was when I wrote a column about the Rev. Claude Black, a former city councilman, fierce civil rights activist and one of the most admired leaders in San Antonio. I grew up across the street from him and saw him as a surrogate grandfather.

Reverend Black had been hospitalized, and I went to see him. He was semicomatose and would die three months later. His hospital room looked out on the city's East Side, where he'd been born and raised, and it made me reflect on his life and service. So I wrote about it.

The editor didn't like the column because I hadn't talked to Reverend Black. He said that he had visited Reverend Black, sat on his hospital bed, and laughed with him; but that was during a previous hospital stay when Black was alert. I didn't talk to him when I visited because, again, he was semicomatose!

The editor's "punishment" was to make me, a columnist, cover the upcoming Martin Luther King Jr. Day march. Aside from the fact that no columnist in the country had written more about King and nonviolence than me, what does it say when you order the paper's only Black columnist to cover the MLK Day march—the same columnist you've restricted from writing about politics?

When I learned that the editor had written me up—I think it was over something different—I countered with a response. And when state representative Joaquin Castro asked me in 2011 to become the communications director for his first congressional campaign, I was ready to listen. I'd been friendly for years with Castro and his identical twin, Julián, who was mayor of San Antonio. With a couple of exceptions, they were the only politicians not named Obama for whom I'd consider working.

On a Monday in September I met with Joaquin and his campaign manager. I was offered the job and given until Friday to give them an answer. The next day, Tuesday, the *Express-News* editor unexpectedly resigned.

After the resignation was announced, a colleague came into my office and said, "You've been emancipated." He was right. The latitude I'd enjoyed writing about anything I chose would be restored. But by then I was ready to leave, and I did so in October.

When Castro was elected to Congress, I became his district director. From there I went to work as communications director for Ivy Taylor, San Antonio's first Black mayor, and then for the nonprofit Merced Housing Texas.

Each job, with each year, lengthened my time away from the newspaper. I missed it, and after a few years I began to hope for a way to return—though I eventually gave up on that.

Then, in October 2019, I received an email from Josh Brodesky, the *Express-News* editorial page editor, saying there was an editorial board opening for an editorial writer and columnist. I thought it was a coy way to get me to apply, but it turns out he'd sent the email to other former editorial board members asking if they knew someone qualified and interested.

I was the only one who answered yes, me. I returned to the *Express-News* in December 2019 after an eight-year absence.

I had been at the paper, in the eight-story art deco building on the corner of Avenue E and Third Street, for three months when COVID-19 locked down the city and country. Then George Floyd happened. Racial reckoning happened. So much kept happening—the 2020 presidential election, the awfulness of Trump, the election of Joe Biden, the insurrection; Ukraine, Uvalde, race (which is always happening), and life itself.

This book is about those happenings and how I saw them as they happened. Apart from a few guest op-eds and several long-form pieces included here that I wrote while I was away from the paper, these columns and editorials were written after my return to the *Express-News*.

One of the long pieces is about I. H. "Sporty" Harvey, the Black boxer who successfully challenged Texas's law banning interracial professional boxing matches. His attorney was my benefactor, Maury Maverick Jr. Another piece is about my return to the neighborhood where I was raised. The last is a tribute to an uncle who saved my life.

To be given a second life in a career I had doubted I'd ever have a first life in is a gift. I give thanks to God each morning and night.

During the COVID-19 lockdown, the *Express-News* building was sold, and preparations were made for our staff to move into the renovated building across the street that used to house the *San Antonio Light*.

I think back to the afternoon I walked out of that building after visiting the newsroom to ask the editor and publisher to print the work of more Black writers on its op-ed pages.

Whatever I was thinking then, I know I wasn't thinking that more than forty-two years later, on a cold rainy Monday before Thanksgiving, I'd be writing these words while sitting at my desk in that same second-floor newsroom.

Five Precious Words from a Poet

When Marguerite Johnson was seven years old and raped by her mother's boyfriend, she gave name to his identity. After her assailant was found kicked to death—the vengeance of her uncles—she believed her words possessed the power to kill, and for the next five years she didn't speak to anyone but her brother.

That belief in the power of language—her language—never abandoned her.

As an adult, Maya Angelou discovered that her words could be a revelation to others. She learned that by using her voice to give names to what was beautiful and ugly, she could teach, uplift, reconcile and inspire people to overcome trauma and injustice.

For all of her enormous talents, it was that magnificent gift of voice that will endure and that was most fondly remembered when news was received that she'd died Wednesday morning at age eighty-six.

The rhythms and incantatory spell of her writing, especially in her memoirs and poetry, were distinctive. The first of her six memoirs, *I Know Why the Caged Bird Sings*, is her greatest book and an American classic. This was her bridge to humanity, her passport to the world.

When Angelou would visit San Antonio, she would stay with Dr. Joe and Aaronetta Pierce. Aaronetta was one of her "daughters." I first met Angelou about fifteen years ago, at a dinner party at the Pierces' house that featured the added attraction of the meal having been prepared by Angelou herself, the kitchen being just one of many venues for her artistry.

I picked up San Antonio poet Naomi Shihab Nye, and when we arrived, it was magical seeing these two word sorceresses meet for the first time.

Aaronetta, a longtime family friend, made sure I was seated next to Angelou, who turned to me and said, in that deep and regal voice, "And you are a poet."

While this makes for a nice, self-aggrandizing story that paints a picture of me being anointed by Maya Angelou, the more I've thought about it, the more I realize it may have been more of a question than a declaration. Still, they are among the five most precious words anyone has ever said to me. In 2010, shortly before Angelou was to return to San Antonio for a speech, I interviewed her by phone for a column.

I asked her about those five years as a child when she didn't speak. She said her grandmother told her, "Sister, Momma don't care that other people call you an idiot, a moron because you don't talk. Momma know when you and the good Lord get ready, you're going to be a teacher. You're going to teach all over the world."

When I asked if she'd fulfilled her grandmother's prophecy, she answered: "I'm fulfilling it. I'm working at it. I hope I haven't fulfilled everything because, if so, you'll be the last voice I'll be talking to."

I'm glad I wasn't the last voice she talked to. But, along with millions, I'm fortunate she shared that voice with us for so long.

This phenomenal woman knew why the caged bird sang. And my, how she could sing.

It's What Jesus Said That Matters

In my house is a painting of one artist's depiction of Jesus, which I bought years ago on the South Side. I give it extra attention during Holy Week and the celebration of Easter, a special day that is on a different date each year and is commercially symbolized by a giant rabbit carrying a basket of brightly colored hard-boiled eggs it hides from children.

It's a beautiful painting that's sparked conversations and comments from people who've seen it because the Jesus in the painting is Black. He looks like the late, great singer-songwriter Nickolas Ashford.

I'm not especially concerned about what Jesus looked like. His teachings and the ideal of how we should live and treat each other are transcendent. There's a reason Muslims view him as a prophet and Thomas Jefferson created his own version of the Bible consisting chiefly of comments attributed to Jesus.

But the prevailing image of Jesus I grew up with in school and church was of one who looked like Kris Kristofferson. I love Kris Kristofferson and have a cloth calendar with a depiction of Kris—I mean Jesus—but that shouldn't be taken as the standard. That is, unless someone produces a photo of Christ stamped 30 BC on the back. I'd like to have a collection of images of Jesus representing all the world's cultures.

Once someone seeing my painting asked, "Who's that?"

"Jesus," I answered.

"But that's not what he looked like."

"What did he look like?"

"Well, you know."

"I do," I said. "And it doesn't matter what Jesus looked like. It's about his teachings and what his life and death mean to us."

"That's right," my guest said. "It doesn't matter what color he was. It's about what he taught us."

"And it doesn't matter that he could have been Black."

"But he wasn't!"

I speak with some authority on the multicultural image of Jesus because I played him in a fifth-grade Easter play at Our Lady of Perpetual Help. A substitute teacher named Mrs. Baldwin arranged the play. I started with a small role—Simon of Cyrene, the man forced to help Jesus carry the cross to Golgotha. I would later learn that my role was historically accurate since Simon was of African descent. (But, of course, all of us are of African descent.)

The boy originally cast as Jesus couldn't remember his one line: "Father, forgive them, for they know not what they do." Mrs. Baldwin, either seeing a star quality in the way I bore my cross or feeling guilty for confiscating my Roger Staubach autograph, elevated me to the role of Jesus.

As someone who has portrayed the Son of God, I cannot lie. I cannot put a bushel over the bright light of my performance. I was great. After I slowly and wearily recited my one line, dropped my chin to my chest and died, there was stunned silence in the room before my classmates erupted in applause. For several days I was treated like the star that my one performance had made me. Even Mrs. Baldwin was nicer than usual, although she never returned my Staubach autograph.

My performance was so powerful and talked about that all these years later, people still identify me with that role. I can't tell you how often people around me say things like, "Jesus, what do you want now?" and "Christ, can't you do anything right?"

I've noticed that when I call women they are aware of that performance because I get a lot of, "Jesus! Not you again!"

I love my Black Jesus painting, and it doesn't matter whether Jesus looked like Nick Ashford, Kris Kristofferson or anyone else. Not knowing what he looked like, maybe this time we'll refrain from crucifying him and doing harm to others.

Ali Taught Us about the Courage of Convictions

On Friday evening, June 3, 2016, I called the man who was my introduction to Muhammad Ali—my father, who lives in Houston and has significant health issues. I wanted to see how he was doing. He was in pain and heading for bed, he said, and I could tell that he knew nothing about the news reports on Ali's condition. I hesitated in telling him but knew he'd want to know that this would probably be the last night on earth for Muhammad, the athlete my father loves more than any other.

"I sure hate to hear that, son," he said, before saying good night and going to bed.

I'm less than three weeks older than the gold medal won by eighteen-year-old Cassius Clay in the 1960 Olympics in Rome. I don't ever remember not being aware of Muhammad Ali and not having him for a hero.

Before I knew anything about the civil rights movement, Martin Luther King Jr. or Malcolm X, I knew about Ali. Before I heard that Black is beautiful and learned about Black pride, I heard the voice of Ali, and it was more than the boasting with a twinkle in his eye. I heard him declare that he, and no one else, would define him.

"I know where I'm going and I know the truth, and I don't have to be what you want me to be. I'm free to be what I want."

If you were a Black kid growing up in the 1960s and 1970s,

Ali's words, his style and his audacity were liberating and uplifting. Because so many people despised and rooted against him for reasons that had little to do with boxing, he didn't just have to win; he had to win so we'd be free to be what we wanted. His major fights were almost as much about politics and culture as they were about sports.

It hurt when one of my favorite sports teams lost, but I hurt when Ali lost because he meant more to me than athletic competition. When he lost to Joe Frazier in the "Fight of the Century," I got nauseous and didn't want to go to school.

But one of my happiest memories is having my mom wake me up to tell me that not only had Ali beaten George Foreman; he'd knocked him out.

Ali was heroic because he was larger than the sport he dominated, and he was willing to abandon the sport rather than abandon his convictions. His death last Friday is allowing us to repeat and reaffirm what we've known for decades about him.

No athlete of any time or era has occupied a larger cultural presence, consumed more attention, stirred larger controversies, evoked more hate, or become a larger symbol of love and peace than Muhammad Ali. Had he just been a boxer of unsurpassed physical gifts, one who transformed a brutal sport into artistry, he would still be a memorable figure and mythologized athlete. In his prime, Ali was one of our best orators and one of our best comedians, a man of rare physical and verbal gifts. He was the most famous person on earth and one of its most revered, celebrated because he could jab and dance in the ring but could also take a punch and hold his ground outside of it.

The length of Ali's journey and the magnitude of his accomplishments are astonishing, from his birth in the segregated South to his death and its global coverage on a scale reserved for only a handful of world-historical figures.

Ali brought us joy with his boxing artistry, his humor, his compassion, his love of life. Yes, he taught us about having the courage of our convictions and having the freedom to be who we want. And he inspired pride in many of us.

But more than anything, he made us smile. Repeat this chant and see what happens: "Ali...Ali...Ali."

Thanks, Champ.

As Humanity Suffers, What Will We Choose?

For a few years, the third week of July was the appointed time for those searching how to love and not hate, to nurture and not destroy, to visit Sweet Auburn.

Hundreds of adults and high school students from across the United States and beyond came to Atlanta's historic Sweet Auburn District for the Martin Luther King Jr. Center for Nonviolent Social Change's Workshop on Nonviolence. The workshop, like the King Center, was created by Coretta Scott King to continue her husband's legacy of teaching the philosophy of nonviolence as a way of life and social change.

This wasn't a gathering for theoretical musings but a week of engagement for teachers, administrators, law enforcement officials, community organizers and students to explore ways to use nonviolence to overcome the very real problems in their communities and personal lives.

Many who came were initially resistant to the introspection and candor that were asked. Many weren't used to imagining the lives of others and learning histories different from theirs, both necessary if walls were to be torn down and community created.

But always at week's end, in the closing ceremony in Ebenezer Baptist Church, there would be young and old participants who'd speak about how their minds and hearts had been opened by difficult and painful conversations they'd not had before.

Many would take what they learned back home in service to their communities.

Sunday, July 17, 2016—the third week of July this year—was punctuated by gunfire that killed three Baton Rouge police officers. This after Dallas, Minnesota, Baton Rouge (again), Orlando and more had already been added to our nation's atlas of datelines of violence.

Montrell Jackson, one of the slain Baton Rouge officers, wrote a Facebook post on July 8 describing the tension of being an African American policeman: "In uniform I get nasty hateful looks and out of uniform some consider me a threat."

He also wrote: "These are trying times. Please don't let hate infect your heart."

We are overwhelmed by and weary of the recurring violence, but we shouldn't be surprised by it. Violence has marked our country and our world, our history and our species. People's cruelty to each other is not new, but, as Officer Jackson understood, neither is our capacity to change nor our ability to choose love, communication and understanding over hate, retaliation and revenge.

We decide if we slur, lie about and cast aspersions against those who are different from us in any way. It's our choice if we defame and attack someone because of the color of his skin or the uniform she wears. We choose if we're to be our brothers' and sisters' keepers instead of their tormenters or silent accomplices in their suffering.

King called nonviolence "love in action." We don't have to like each other, but we should love humanity enough to respect and protect each other's humanity.

The third week in July used to be an appointed time in Atlanta to make a commitment to nonviolence and to having the difficult, open and painful conversations that are necessary in order to understand each other a little better, love each other a little more and do right by each other a little more often. If we're serious about confronting the cycle of hate and violence, we need more appointed times for open and painful conversations that are followed by acting upon what we learned.

And we better learn.

Son of Slaves Fathered Inspiring Family

The baby of the family died at eighty-nine years of age in New York City in 2009. A few weeks later, his last surviving sibling passed away in California at age ninety-three.

In distance and time, Percy and Essie Sutton were far removed from the house of their birth on San Antonio's East Side. That address, 430 N. Cherry Street, was never well-known. But it was known well by the African American legends who visited when they passed through town—people like Booker T. Washington, W. E. B. Du Bois, Mary McLeod Bethune and Thurgood Marshall.

When the next-to-last child was born, one of those guests made a request: "You give that one to me. I want to be responsible for him." The parents didn't give away their baby, but they did ask George Washington Carver to be his godfather.

Using ethnic or regional qualifiers to describe the Suttons of San Antonio marginalizes their achievement. They're neither one of the most "influential African American families in San Antonio history," nor are they "a significant South Texas family." For their number of children, range of interests, scope of talents, levels of educational attainment, personal successes and societal contributions, the Suttons are the most accomplished family produced by San Antonio and as accomplished an American family as any birthed by this nation.

The marriage of Samuel J. Sutton Sr. and Lillian Viola Smith created a home that nurtured ambition and achievement. Their twelve children (three others didn't live to maturity) would excel—and sometimes make history—in the fields of education, medicine, science, law, business, politics and social service. All of them would earn college degrees, and ten would receive post-graduate degrees.

The oldest child, John, was a respected biochemist and protégé of Carver. Oliver would become the first African American on the New York Supreme Court. Lillian Sutton Taylor educated generations of San Antonio children, including some of her younger siblings.

Garlington Jerome, better known as G.J., became the first Black in the South in modern times to win a metropolitan elective seat when, in 1948, he was elected to the San Antonio Junior College Board. The Rev. Alexander Carver, or A.C., Carver's godson, ran the family funeral home and was president of the Texas NAACP.

Percy, the baby, was born twenty-four years after John, and would become the best known. After serving in World War II as a Tuskegee Airman, Percy moved to New York City and became a powerhouse as a civil rights lawyer, Malcolm X's attorney, president of the borough of Manhattan and head of a business empire that included ownership of the Apollo Theater.

Samuel J. Sutton Sr., the son of a slave, was born in Virginia in 1863, the same year the Emancipation Proclamation was issued. His grandfather, an English captain who ran a slave ship between Africa and Norfolk, fathered three children by a young girl of African and American descent. His children were free but upon his death were pressed into slavery. One was Sutton's father, Samuel Wesley Sutton.

After slavery, the elder Sutton, with other ex-slaves, opened one of the first chartered banks in the United States. He couldn't write and was the only board member who signed his name with an X. Despite his illiteracy, Sutton started a newspaper, for which his son Samuel J. wrote.

After writing one article denouncing the racism of the local school board, an article that offended some whites, the younger Sutton heeded his father's advice to leave Richmond before harm came his way. Samuel J. went to Mexico and operated a silver mine with a friend. In 1889 he came to San Antonio to become an educator. While teaching at Guadalupe College in Seguin, he met another young teacher, Lillian V. Smith of New Orleans.

They married in 1896 and bought the house on the corner of Cherry and Dawson Streets in Denver Heights. Eventually they'd own half of the block on Cherry. Samuel would earn a master's degree in education from the University of Colorado and for nearly sixty years would be the principal of Douglass, a junior high and high school, and Wheatley High School. Mrs. Sutton taught at Riverside, San Antonio's first Black high school.

The family also owned a mattress factory, a skating rink and a funeral home and in 1912 bought an eighty-five-acre farm on Sinclair Road.

"Do right" was the motto Samuel J. expected his children and students to abide by, while teaching them that being respectful of others didn't mean being deferential. He and Lillian provided their Sutton dozen with books and travel and had them regularly memorize and recite poetry. To help with the cost of sending twelve children to college, each child was expected to help pay the way of the sibling directly behind them.

The children were taught that their responsibilities extended beyond family. A hallmark of the Sutton legacy was their public service and relentless fight against inequality.

In 1957 G.J. was forcibly removed from the gallery of the Texas House of Representatives when he protested passage of a packet of segregationist bills. Fifteen years later he became the first Black San Antonian elected to the Texas legislature.

During the 1960s, four of the siblings, Smithie, Lillian, G.J. and A.C., refused to leave Joske's department store's whites-only dining room, the Camelia Room. Counting their own children, at one point there were as many as fifteen Suttons picketing the department store before it rescinded its racist policy.

When Jackie Robinson broke Major League Baseball's color line on April 15, 1947, Percy Sutton sat in a parked car with his wife and children, listening on the radio. "The significance was that for people living in this grossly segregated society, they no longer had to be hopeless," Sutton told me in 1997. "We could say we could make it. All of our hopes are with him."

He was right, of course. But long before Jackie took the field, Percy and his siblings had Samuel J. and Lillian telling them they could make it, that they could take their hopes out of 430 N. Cherry Street to do right.

And they did. As well as any family.

What Can Be Found in the Stacks

I stand too close to the edges of curbs. Sometimes, I stand so absentmindedly and perilously close that a slight nudge, misplaced step or strong gust of wind could lean me into traffic. The whoosh and hot air of a passing vehicle startles me out of my carelessness. That's also when my Uncle Clarence's voice pulls me back.

Clarence Thompson was the oldest of my mother's siblings. I grew up in the same house they were raised in, on San Antonio's East Side. During my first twelve years, Uncle Clarence was still living there and was the most constant male presence in my life.

In his room were boxes of books and stacks of vinyl records I'd rummage through. It was an excavation of heritage and a discovery of voices that still enriches me. Among the treasures found were collections of poems by Gwendolyn Books and Langston Hughes, Claude Brown's *Manchild in the Promised Land*, and James Baldwin's *The Fire Next Time*, a small Dell paperback with a striking cover featuring Baldwin's name in yellow letters and the title in orange against a black background.

It would be a few years before I'd read, understand and make those books part of me. But I played some of the records I found in those boxes in Uncle Clarence's room, records belonging to him and my mother, within minutes and quickly fell in love with them. Albums like the Temptations' *Greatest Hits* and Aretha Franklin's *This Girl's in Love with You* and *Lady Soul*, which featured "Ain't No Way."

In that time of discovery of new and unfamiliar voices, there were only two songs I played more than "Ain't No Way," and those were from a pair of Sam Cooke 45s: "Sugar Dumpling," with its B-side of "Bridge of Tears," and "Baby, Baby, Baby," which was the B-side of "Send Me Some Lovin'."

Cooke had been dead a few years in the late 1960s when I found his records, with the famous RCA Victor label of the dog listening to the gramophone. Something about his voice—its raspy soulfulness, his phrasing, his confidence in his magnificent gift and the clear joy he felt in using it—drew me in and made me, at nine or ten years old, probably the youngest Sam Cooke fan in my neighborhood.

Those voices from pages and vinyl would awaken in me senses of identity and pride. A sense of awareness.

Uncle Clarence was a slim, elegant and eloquent man who carried himself with such a naturally aristocratic air that a family friend called him Sir Clarence. His voice was shaded in princely colors with crisp enunciation and a tone and meter I would later recognize as similar to James Baldwin's. (He went to Baldwin's funeral at Saint John's Cathedral in 1987 and sent me the funeral program.) It was a calm, beautifully modulated voice that, with two exceptions, I never heard raised in anger or excitement.

The first time was on an early morning in June 1968. My uncle was a registered nurse who worked a night shift and didn't get home until after midnight. On this morning he hadn't been home long when he broke the sleepy silence by stomping through the house, yelling, "I knew he should have kept his ass out of California! I knew he should have kept his ass out of California!"

The news had broken on television that Bobby Kennedy had been shot after winning the California Democratic presidential primary.

Uncle Clarence was a passionate liberal Democrat who loved the Kennedys. He ran for the Texas legislature in 1958 and four years later earned a mention in *Jet* magazine for becoming the first "Negro" chairman of the Bexar County Young Democrats. He would stay interested in politics for the rest of his life but would never be as active after 1968.

The other instance I heard him raise his voice in excitement was around that same time. He and I were walking downtown and came to a walk / don't walk light at the corner of East Commerce Street and Alamo Plaza, in front of Joske's department store. He was holding my hand, but I wasn't paying attention to the don't walk signal. As I was stepping into the street he said, "Child!," and pulled me back on the curb just as a car was turning into where I would have stepped.

I don't remember what or if he said anything afterward, but I know that to this day, when I foolishly stand too close to a curb, I hear his voice saying, "Child!," and it pulls me back and focuses my attention.

Uncle Clarence moved to New York in 1972 and would return home for visits each summer and Christmas. The last time we saw him was in summer 1991. By Christmas of that year, he'd been diagnosed with lung cancer and his doctor had advised against travel.

In May 1992, my grandmother, not having heard from him for a couple of weeks, called his Bleecker Street apartment. Someone from the coroner's office answered the phone, and that was how my grandmother learned that her eldest child had been dead for a week in his apartment before anyone noticed. He was fifty-six. My grandmother died two years later.

Two months after Uncle Clarence died, the Democratic National Convention opened on July 13, 1992, my grandmother's eightieth birthday. On this day, she'd receive no flowers from him and no phone call at night wishing her happy birthday.

She reflected on the coincidence that, in the year of his death, the city he'd fallen in love with and moved to twenty years earlier was hosting the national convention of the party he'd been devoted to. Were he alive, he'd have been there listening to speeches of some of his favorite politicians: Mario Cuomo, Jesse Jackson, Ann Richards, Bill Bradley, Barbara Jordan.

And the Kennedys. He'd have loved the speeches by Teddy and Joe and the film tribute to Bobby, whose shooting sent him screaming into our house's morning darkness.

My mother still lives in that house where we were raised. What was Uncle Clarence's room is now a storeroom of sorts. Recently I was cleaning it out when I came across a box of dusty vinyl records.

Flipping through them wasn't the same as more than forty years earlier when I was being introduced to unfamiliar artists and music. A few of the albums were among those I'd seen long ago, but most of these records were bought by my brother and me when we were in our teens and twenties. This was a Sunday afternoon reacquaintance with familiar, favored and some forgotten performers. These were records seen and played before.

Except for one. Hidden among the albums, a little smaller than the LPs, was a record with a cream-colored label identifying itself as an audio disc recording blank. On one side was handwritten "C. Thompson Oct. 1955," and on the other side was "C. Thompson May 1956."

The record was older than me and had probably been among the stacks I rummaged through as a child, but I don't remember seeing it before. I took it home that night and placed it carefully on the turntable. Side one of the record was chipped. The interplay of static and needle jumping each time around sounded like a jalopy chugging along in the rain on a bumpy road.

Static filled the room like an evening shower, and I waited for the drops of crackles and hisses to conjure a long-silenced voice. Then, as summoned, arising from the grave and materializing from the mists, came the voice of my Uncle Clarence.

"Brothers, classmates, I am Clarence S. Thompson. I was born in Beaumont, Texas. I've lived most of my life in San Antonio. I have divided my school years between private and public schools. My father was a bill collector and real estate broker. However, he is no longer living. My mother is a housewife. I am a freshman majoring in prelaw at Saint Mary's University. I have one brother and two sisters."

It was the first time I'd heard his voice in twenty-four years. Either technology or his not yet having grown into the full power of his voice made it sound a bit reedy, but it was unmistakable.

"At the end of this year, it is my intention to attend Yale University and to eventually attend Harvard Law School."

Uncle Clarence was nineteen years old and, presumably, practicing a speech he would give to a class at Saint Mary's University here in San Antonio. In thirty years, he'd attend my graduation from that same school. But he spoke on this recording while seeing the Ivy League in his immediate future.

He read from a speech by Adlai Stevenson, the 1952 and 1956 Democratic nominee for president: "As citizens of this democracy, you are the rulers and the ruled, the lawgivers and the law-abiding, the beginning and the end. Democracy is a high privilege, but it is also a heavy responsibility whose shadow stalks, although you may never walk in the sun."

On side two, seven months later and in the presidential election year of 1956, Uncle Clarence practiced a speech urging his classmates to vote for Stevenson, calling him "the best and most capable candidate for president of the United States of America." He criticized President Eisenhower's "sloppy" slogan of peace and prosperity when "we have no peace in the Middle East and little prosperity in the Midwest."

The record's two sides totaled less than six minutes of Uncle Clarence's voice, but that was nearly six minutes of a voice I hadn't thought I'd ever hear again. A few weeks after finding the disc, I played a recording of both sides for my mother, aunt and uncle at a family gathering in Houston. As they listened to their brother's voice, astonishment and fond remembrance mingled with sadness in their eyes.

The cliché is that the music of certain artists is the soundtrack of our lives. But the earliest, most encompassing and more enduring score in our memory is the chorus of a cappella voices of family; voices that when stilled by death won't be forgotten yet also won't again be heard.

I imagine that relatives of public figures whose voices are preserved in the public domain are used to—if never unmoved by—sometimes hearing their loved ones' voices transmitted in some way, such as on television and over radio.

For the rest of us, the voices of our deceased are recorded only in memories. We don't expect to discover one of them on a disc a quarter century after their death.

Several years ago my father told me that Uncle Clarence, his former brother-in-law, mentioned me in their last phone conversation. "Take good care of Cary," he had said. "Take especially good care of Cary."

I don't know what he meant, and I don't know if it's something he felt needed to be said because he sensed death was near. He had no children of his own but was a wonderfully doting uncle to his ten nephews and nieces.

I wasn't singled out in his generosity, but I was the oldest, was around him the most and inherited his love of books and politics. He'd take me to Inman Barber Shop, an iconic gathering place for Black San Antonians where politics were debated, civil rights actions planned and preachers' sermons rehearsed.

In college, when I applied to be a scholar-intern at the Martin Luther King Jr. Center for Nonviolent Social Change in Atlanta, I procrastinated and didn't get all three letters of recommendation I needed. The one I did get, from Uncle Clarence, was so strong that it won me acceptance into the program that became one of the most important experiences in my life.

In the family eulogy at his funeral, I said that he'd lived a graceful and completed life with nothing left undone. I wouldn't say that now. A life is completed when it's over, but who can speak for the dead and say they left nothing undone? There must have been things Uncle Clarence still wanted to do, places he longed to go, experiences he wished to enjoy.

I am now fifty-six, Uncle Clarence's age when he died, an age I don't know I'd have reached had he not pulled me back on the sidewalk curb decades ago. An age, I now know, where all thirsts aren't quenched and new possibilities can still be imagined. I know that whenever I leave this world, it will be with much left undone. I know of dreams beyond one's reach.

Until listening to his recording, I didn't know Uncle Clarence wanted to attend Yale and Harvard Law School. I don't know why his plans changed, what circumstances superseded his ambition, what—if any—regret he carried into his later years.

As I write these last lines, it's been six months since my father died, bringing the regrets of things said and not said, of visits not made or made too brief by my impatience. Before his death I'd been lacerating myself for my poor decisions and bad choices. But too much time lost in regrets is self-indulgent, self-pitying and self-defeating. It averts your gaze, draws your attention away, makes you step off curbs into danger.

The discovery of Uncle Clarence's recording reminds me that there are always voices we return to—or that return to us—when we're lost and seeking direction, voices with the strength to hold and pull us back into focus. Voices that, from the first time they've awakened us, always possess the power to rouse us out of inattention and slumber.

King's Legacy Lives,
but His Dreams Remain Unfulfilled

By the time the trigger was pulled at 6:01 p.m. on April 4, 1968, fulfilling his prophecy from the night before, Martin Luther King Jr. was already slipping into history. The thirty-nine-year-old man dying on a balcony in Memphis no longer attracted the same rapt attention as the twenty-six-year-old phenomenon who was delivered to the world stage by a bus boycott in Montgomery.

King was less than five years removed from his "I Have a Dream" speech at the March on Washington and little more than three years from winning the Nobel Peace Prize, yet to many of his detractors and admirers he was becoming irrelevant. A 1966 Gallup poll on his popularity gave him a positive rating of 32 percent and a negative Trump-like rating of 63 percent.

His frequent and impassioned critiques of the Vietnam War and poverty drew wide scorn, including from allies in the civil rights movement. Younger Black activists were impatient with King's nonviolence and fame, and their voices were rising in louder and greater numbers to challenge his. The Poor People's Campaign he was planning for Washington, DC, and his detour to Memphis to support striking Black garbage workers weren't popular even among his staff. When he walked onto the balcony of room 306 of the Lorraine Motel, King wasn't the icon whose birthday was a national holiday. He was an exhausted, beleaguered and polarizing figure.

If King was slipping into history at the time of his murder, fifty years later he's one of history's favored children. Denied longevity in this life, he's preserved as a world-historical figure, the lodestar for movements seeking justice, freedom and equality through nonviolence. That a man who was viewed negatively by nearly two-thirds of his fellow countrymen and -women would have a national holiday less than twenty years after his death speaks to his singular stature and legacy.

King occupied a special time and place in history; circumstances and his extraordinary gifts met in a perfect union of purpose and need. Thousands of courageous women and men created the modern civil rights movement, but King emerged as its embodiment—becoming, as A. Philip Randolph introduced him at the March on Washington, "the moral voice of the nation."

If, in the eighteenth century, the Founding Fathers gave life to the nation, and if, in the nineteenth century, Abraham Lincoln fought to keep the body politic together, King in the twentieth century led the struggle to redeem America's soul. He was rooted in the African American experience, found his voice in the Black church, waded in the nonviolent spiritual waters of Christ and Gandhi and devoted his life to the ideals of the Declaration of Independence and the Constitution. King's idealism made him seek to transform hearts and minds away from bigotry, injustice and suffering. His pragmatism made him understand that of more immediate importance was to change the country's unjust laws, that regardless of how people thought and felt, their behavior must align with the Constitution.

Besides King himself, the person most responsible for how we view him and honor his legacy was his remarkable wife, Coretta Scott King, who died in 2006. She created the Martin Luther King Jr. Center for Nonviolent Social Change and advocated for the national holiday, not as static memorials but as living testimonials to the philosophy of nonviolence that animated and defined King's work. Her purpose was to extend his legacy and continue his work by teaching nonviolence as a way of life, as well as a strategy for social change.

In 2018, that's how the fiftieth anniversary of Martin Luther King Jr.'s assassination should be commemorated: through living testimonials of nonviolence against the problems afflicting us. And we should pay less attention to the "I Have a Dream" King and more to the "Where Do We Go from Here?" King.

"I Have a Dream" is a masterpiece of oratory that is a gift to humanity. King's riff on his dream is as thrilling a public performance as has ever been delivered. But he said this vision he was articulating was a dream. Like the Promised Land, we're not there yet. Many people cling to the speech's dream motif and what they perceive to be the comfortable King who doesn't challenge them. Prophets are less troublesome after they've become martyrs.

King was unpopular when he died because he made people uncomfortable and because the marches, boycotts and other acts of direct action he led were inconvenient. He was a Christian minister who took seriously Christ's teachings to feed the hungry and clothe the naked. He was a Nobel Peace laureate who believed he was charged to speak out against war.

His last book, *Where Do We Go from Here: Chaos or Community?*, challenged America to be honest about its crippling legacy of racism, to stop its senseless violence, to ease the suffering of its poor, and to make better the lives of all its people. Through nonviolence. Through love. "When I speak of love," King wrote, "I am speaking of that love which all great religions have seen as the supreme unifying principle of life. . . . Let us hope that this spirit will become the order of the day. We can no longer afford to worship the God of hate or bow before the altar of retaliation."

Hatred and retaliation pulled the trigger that took Martin Luther King Jr.'s life. His place in history is assured. The redemption of this nation's soul, if those beasts continue to roam, is not.

Back to Denver Heights

In January 1944 my grandfather—a man I'd never meet—wrote a letter to my grandmother, a woman I spent more time with than any other person in my life.

"All day yesterday," my grandfather wrote, "my left eye was jumping. That is why I called you last night to ask about the children. . . . Papa may close a deal today for a place. If he does, I think the place is nice. We have a space for you and the children now at home but am waiting until a deal is closed so when you come [you] will have a place for our things."

There were four children, the youngest being my mother. The children and my grandmother—whom I called Momo—were still in Houston where my mother was born.

My grandfather had moved to San Antonio to receive treatment for tuberculosis. He was living with his father, my great-grandfather, whose nickname was Cap ("Captain") because he owned the San Antonio Black Missions, a semiprofessional baseball team in the South Texas Negro League.

The place Cap closed the deal on was a house on a corner in the East Side neighborhood of Denver Heights, which was separated from downtown by the Southern Pacific railroad tracks. He would also buy the house next to it.

Cap, who lived a few blocks away on 303 Cactus Street, was a businessman specializing in real estate and gambling. He was a skilled pool and poker player. A room in his house was set up for multiple card games and featured a service window through which my great-grandmother dispensed fried chicken, Toll House cookies and her other creations.

In a second letter, dated March 1944, the family is soon to be reunited. "The time is not long," my grandfather writes to Momo, "before we will all be together again and I will be very happy."

But that happiness and the reunion with his wife and children was brief. In that new house, he died of tuberculosis on November 5, 1944. By then Momo was pregnant with their fifth child.

Clara Ann would be born in February 1945 but died eighteen months later in the same bedroom where the father she'd never met had died. Generations of children in our family have been photographed in the front yard of that house, none more than me. But Clara Ann was the first. For decades, until recently, the password used as a security code for the homes of relatives was "Clara Ann."

A few blocks away from the two houses Cap bought was a cluster of famed East Side businesses known as the Corner, an intersection of culture and commerce at Pine and Iowa Streets. Anchoring the Corner were W. H. Leonard's Pharmacy, a movie theater, a gas station and the Keyhole, one of the first integrated nightclubs in the South.

The Keyhole was owned by the bandleader Don Albert who, with his wife and children, lived across the street from the two houses Cap bought. Visitors to the Alberts included legendary Black entertainers like Nat King Cole, on whose lap my mother sat when she was a little girl.

I was born in 1960, and raised in the house on the corner, in a neighborhood where whistles were a constant signal of transitions and passages.

Five blocks west, where the Alamodome now sits, was Alamo Iron Works. Four times a day, except for weekends and holidays, the ironworks's whistle was a neighborhood alarm clock, going off at 8 a.m. (starting time), noon (lunchtime), 1 p.m. (end of lunchtime), and 5 p.m. (quitting time). Three blocks north, workers disappeared into Friedrich Refrigeration when its whistle blew at 8 a.m. and reemerged when the 5 p.m. whistle went off.

Day and night, the Southern Pacific trains screamed their noisy arrivals and departures. At night the sound of a distant whistle followed by the muffled rumble of boxcars along the Sunset Station tracks made a child long for places he was yet to know while already missing the places he knew so well.

Back in the day, there were places like the icehouse at the corner of East Commerce and South Pine, across the street from the Friedrich Building. The icehouse was a lively gathering place for people in the neighborhood to buy snacks, tamales, sausage, soda and beer, to play dominoes and enjoy the jukebox's soulful selection. The structure was mentioned as late as 1986 in a *New York Times* story calling San Antonio the "Icehouse Capital of the World."

On the other side of the pawn shop next to the icehouse was the most popular mom-and-pop grocery store, Mon Fung Market, which everyone called "the Chinaman's." They sold moon cookies and toys and had uneven wooden floors tilting downward toward the meat market, which made it fun to walk fast.

The best sausage in the neighborhood was sold at Johnny Johnson's yellow building at Montana and Olive. Other small stores were Joe's at the corner of Pine and Montana and Piedmont Grocery at Wyoming and Piedmont.

At the corner of Pine and Dakota was Hicks Beauty School, owned by Jessie Mae Hicks, where mothers in the neighborhood got their hair done at night while we played outside and drank tall bottles of Nehi soda from the machine at the top of a steep driveway.

These places weren't just businesses offering services to customers; they were community gathering places, extensions of our front porches where people dropped by to visit, talk and reconnect.

As time rolled through decades, the train whistles sounded like a dirge for a dying neighborhood, especially during the 1980s and 1990s when heightened gang activity earned San Antonio the moniker "Drive-by Capital of Texas."

Friedrich Refrigeration closed, leaving a vacant, brooding building, upon which were projected serial fantasies of resurrecting it into a catalyst for economic development for Denver Heights and the East Side.

Alamo Iron Works moved. The Alamodome, which replaced it, has been a success but never the engine of economic development for the East Side as promised. To be raised on the East Side, familiar with its history and long immune to the disappointment of broken if well-intentioned promises, is to tire of constantly hearing it referred to as the "long-neglected East Side."

The icehouse was torn down. The little grocery stores closed. Hicks Beauty School burned down the same night O. J. Simpson took the nation on a slow-speed freeway chase.

My mother still lives in the house she moved into in 1944. The second house, next door, bought by my great-grandfather Cap, was always used as a rental.

When I was three years old, a newborn baby girl was found alive one morning in a neighbor's garbage can. She was nicknamed Elizabeth Taylor because of her black hair. It was soon learned that her mother was the teenager who lived with her family in the rental house.

When I was four, a husband and wife moved into the rental. One day a gunshot rang out of the house. My father, a Bexar County sheriff's deputy, ran next door and took the gun from the man who'd just murdered his wife.

We sold the rental in 2014. By then I'd long been living in a house I had built on the far South Side. I loved that house and the area, but it was far from the rest of my life. I sold it in 2016 and moved into an apartment on the East Side off Interstate 35.

The apartment was all right, but I missed living in a house and after a year was wanting to rent one. I never really got around to looking for one and was about to reup on my lease. The man who'd bought our family rental had done some refurbishing on it. My brother asked him if he was looking for a renter. He was, and in December 2017 I became that renter.

It's a small house with work still to be done and not one I'd buy. But it serves my purposes for now. I call it my "writing cottage," and it's intriguing to be back on the corner in the neighborhood where I was raised.

The Friedrich Building still looms over it with dark empty eyes, and Southern Pacific trains still whistle their way through Sunset Station depot several times an hour. My next-door neighbor, my mother, was three years old when she moved into her house and is now the neighborhood matriarch—although most of the neighbors wouldn't know because they are new to the neighborhood.

I call my daily walks "memory walks" as I pass houses and remember families who used to live in them, the children I played with, the conflicts and celebrations that spilled out of those households. I remember the interiors of the homes, the meals served and the yards we played in. Those families no longer own these houses. Old folks died and the young ones moved away, never to return—except me.

In Denver Heights, I can walk for blocks in any direction and count on one hand the number of houses owned by the families who owned them when I was growing up. The near absence of generational continuity in home ownership is startling. I walk through a neighborhood of ghosts, feeling like a ghost myself, haunting streets I've tread a million steps on. I nod to unfamiliar faces in front of familiar houses and realize it's only the streets that know me, so familiar are they with my footsteps.

When I was growing up the neighborhood was predominantly Black, with a good percentage of Latinos. It wasn't unusual to stand outside and hear R&B and Tejano music being played. A mix of middle-class and poor, of nice houses and rundown ones, it wasn't anything close to being a slum or ghetto. But it says something about the mentality of my friends and me that as children, we'd feel sorry for the rare white folks who moved into our neighborhood.

We believed that no white person, if they could afford to live elsewhere, would choose to live near us, the Black and the brown. That had to mean a huge fall from the paradise we imagined all white people lived in. They never stayed long before moving on.

Today the largest demographic in the neighborhood, like the East Side itself, is Latino, and there are more whites. In my first months back I could identify the white people I saw as one of two kinds: heroin addicts and new homeowners. Fortunately the heroin addicts have disappeared. The new homeowners are planting roots. It used to be that whites lived in Denver Heights because they had to. Now they live here because they choose to, like they choose to live in Dignowity Hill and other East Side communities.

Never in my lifetime has Denver Heights—just minutes from downtown—attracted so much investment. Houses that have been refurbished are on the market for $300,000 to $400,000. Even small nondescript homes needing work are in the $100,000 to $200,000 range.

My mother's home, which was paid for decades ago, is one no member of my family could afford to buy. Expensive but unattractive condos and townhouses whose designs are out of sync with the neighborhood's older houses are popping up, as are bed-and-breakfasts. Even the Friedrich Building is to be awakened and turned into a 174-unit apartment project, which could stimulate business development along the Commerce Street corridor, east of the railroad tracks.

New retail shops and businesses are soon to open or break ground, and restaurants like Mark's Outing and Tony G's Soul Food and hangouts like the Dakota East Side Ice House and the Cherrity Bar are becoming community gathering places not only for the neighborhood but for people throughout the city.

For months I've walked these streets with an embarrassing resentment that my new neighbors don't have the memories I do and are unfamiliar with the stories I know—embarrassing because of my self-absorption and knowing that one generation can't be held hostage to another generation's memories or be held accountable for things they've been given no account of.

No one is the sole custodian of a neighborhood's memories, especially a neighborhood as old as mine. Each generation produces its own custodians. Neighborhood history is preserved in stories told and retold until they become legend and myth. But when the storytellers pass or move away, when the front porch is less crowded, and when the stories stop being told and the memories no longer shared, who remembers the history?

The places of my youth are being supplanted by new places. My old and fading memories compete with new experiences of people, and one day these new experiences will become old memories that they'll stalk while haunting these streets like ghosts.

The word "corner" appears several times in this essay, what with corners being where so many of the places I've written about stood or still stand. Street corners are intersections, a confluence of traffic where directions can be changed. The neighborhood of my childhood and—for now—my middle-age years is turning a corner. So are my initial concerns about this turn, even within the course of this writing.

On a recent Friday afternoon, days after I'd written the passages about the custodians of a neighborhood's memories and history, I went, for the first time, to the Dakota East Side Ice House on—here comes another one—the corner of Dakota and South Hackberry. I ordered brisket biscuits, which, I assure you, will make me a regular customer.

As I waited for my order I looked at the black-and-white photographs covering one wall. Within seconds I was smiling, almost laughing, and shaking my head. They were an homage to history, pictures from the 1940s and 1950s of Alamo Iron Works, the Friedrich Building, Sunset Station and the Corner, and several of Don Albert and his Keyhole club. My favorite was of Albert and Duke Ellington standing near the bar. Sitting at the crowded bar, looking back at them with a huge grin, is the unforgettable Nat King Cole. I took a picture of the image to show to my mother. This icehouse, little more than a year old and thriving, is already a custodian of its neighborhood's history.

This Denver Heights neighborhood is in transition. Yes, the sound of gunshots is frequent enough that you don't jump, while streets are in such disrepair that your car *will* jump. But it's a neighborhood slowly becoming more prosperous and inviting to new families wishing to plant roots, people who, as my grandfather wrote seventy-five years ago about a house on a corner, "think the place is nice." I hope families who've known this for decades, because they helped make it a nice place, remain part of it. Families like mine.

Returning to the Paper Felt Right

Now, I can look at you, Mr. Loomis, and see you a man who
done forgot his song. Forget how to sing it. A fellow forget that
and he forget who he is. Forget how he's supposed to mark
down life.
    —Bynum, in *Joe Turner's Come and Gone*,
      by August Wilson

Outside my front door a gray calico cat named Orphan meows, singing lead to the background chorus of a Southern Pacific freight bellowing through downtown. While it's not Gladys Knight & the Pips singing "Midnight Train to Georgia," there's some harmony between the cat's tinny whine and the train's plaintive whistle and rhythmic rolling along the tracks.

Their song is better than the daylong cacophony I've muted, the one preceding this night's impeachment of the president of the United States. I'd have preferred this "first" column be about that or some other issue or crisis obsessing and troubling me. Or, on this Sunday before the holiday, I'd love to write about Christmas.

But this is my first column the second time around, and too many people whose opinions I respect have convinced me that an unexpected return after so long an absence deserves a little explanation.

It's like leaving home, staying away for eight years with no word of your whereabouts and then unexpectedly walking through the door and asking, "Baby, what's for dinner?"

So, baby, before serving you dinner, dessert or whatever other high- or low-calorie meal you'll be offered on Sundays to come, let me give you an appetizer of an explanation. This also allows me to clear up a couple of things.

I left the *Express-News* in October 2011 of my own accord to work for Joaquin Castro's first congressional campaign. It's a decision I've never regretted, and one of the great honors and experiences of my life was to be the congressman's first district director.

Three things about this: Being Joaquin's district director meant I didn't move to Washington but stayed in San Antonio (my decision, his assent). Being Joaquin's district director meant I worked for Joaquin, not Julián. Finally, since I didn't work for Julián, I didn't go to Washington with him when he became President Barack Obama's secretary of Housing and Urban Development.

I also worked for Mayor Ivy Taylor and, for the past four years, for Merced Housing Texas. But I never stopped writing, whether in those jobs or on my own time.

Returning to the *Express-News* was something I didn't pray for or pray over. I didn't pray for it in the same way I've never prayed to return to my fifth birthday party, playing football at Saint Gerard High School or teaching nonviolence workshops during summers in Atlanta at the Martin Luther King Jr. Center for Nonviolent Social Change—all happy and memorable experiences that couldn't be revisited.

And once the possibility arose that I could return as an editorial writer and columnist, I didn't pray over it, because I instinctively knew this was where I wanted to be, this was how I wanted, as Bynum says, to mark down life.

There are areas in my life where I've become tone deaf and struck discordant notes, but when it comes to writing, to journalism, I've not forgotten my song. Sometimes my voice was tinny, even muted, but the song was there.

In my farewell column on October 8, 2011, I wrote, "The newsroom that I leave is an astonishing blend of gifted youngsters and talented veterans committed to producing quality journalism." There are different faces, but that still describes the newsroom I walked into last week: one of journalists passionate about producing the quality journalism essential to communities and democracy, of newspaperwomen and -men providing a forum for community voices often ignored.

Journalists are not the enemy of the people. They are of the people. They—we—are from the people. Journalists are among the "we the people" that begins the Constitution, a document brilliantly explained by the trio of Alexander Hamilton, James Madison and John Jay in newspapers through eighty-five pieces known as the Federalist Papers.

What we do may not rise to that level, but I'm excited to be joining the chorus of voices at the *San Antonio Express-News*.

It's now past midnight. Orphan the cat has gone for the night while another train noisily passes through.

Christmas is closer, so let there be peace on earth, but let there also be justice. Let there be goodwill to all, but deepened with understanding and appreciation. Let there be joy to the world, especially for the dispossessed and neglected.

When we possess little to share or think we have nothing to give, we still have the power to lighten a burden, brighten a mood or do something right that corrects a wrong. It's our greatest and least used power.

Merry Christmas, baby. I'm home.

Sometimes a Mystery
Is Part of the Family

All families have secrets, all houses hold mysteries, and at no time are they discussed and pondered more than when families gather in those houses during the holiday season.

There were mysteries in my grandmother's house in Highland Hills, including these: Was there a ghost as Mama Clack and others insisted? What happened to her beloved cat, White Socks, who left the house one day never to return? Who are those white people on the fridge?

Like many of us, Mama Clack used her refrigerator as a magnetized bulletin board or scrapbook, covering it with family photos, newspaper clippings, her list of medications, reminders and other things.

Fifteen or so years ago, I noticed a snapshot of a smiling, attractive young white family on the fridge, a husband and wife and a little girl who was a toddler. I don't know how long they'd been there, and since no other pictures of attractive young white families moved onto the fridge, there was no concern about gentrification. They'd moved in quietly, without any controversy, fanfare or "Hey, remember us?"

I didn't recognize them and was curious about who they were, but I didn't ask and simply accepted them as people Mama Clack knew. They became such a natural part of our family that their presence wasn't questioned. We'd go to get something out of the fridge and see the white family smiling at us, and we'd smile right back.

But over time—as in years—it became clear that no one knew who these people were. There were occasional mentions of the picture. A couple of people would be in the kitchen talking about different things, there'd be a lull in the conversation, and eyes would wander to the picture.

"By the way, who are those white people on the fridge?"

"I don't know. Been wondering that for years."

The conversation would move to the next topic.

When her grandchildren would bring new dates over to meet Mama Clack, we'd introduce them to the white family on the fridge, if asked. "There's my nephew, those are my cousins, there's—"

"And who are these people?" the guests would say, a finger pointing at the smiling trio.

"Ah, we don't really know but they've been here for years, like family."

The white family on the fridge could have been family members we'd never met. Their complexion wasn't much lighter than Mama Clack's. On my father's side, we not only knew the surnames of the families who owned our ancestors in Gonzales—the Talleys and Coes—we also knew first names. We knew them as if they were our own family because they were family. Such is the blended blood of the owner and the owned, of slave masters and slave women; so intertwined are the roots of American history and genealogy, of white and Black.

Older Black folks put up pictures of blue-eyed Jesus, and John and Bobby Kennedy next to Martin Luther King Jr., but they wouldn't display the younger generations of the people who owned their people.

There were often white people in Mama Clack's house, some

of whom regularly sat at the dining room table for holiday and birthday dinners.

The way folks expect all Black people to know each other, I was tempted to bring white guests into the kitchen, show them the picture and ask, "Do you know who these people are?"

One day I finally asked my grandmother. "Mama Clack," I said, "who are those white people on the fridge?"

She looked at the picture quizzically, smiled and said, "I don't know, Cary. I guess I know them."

Mama Clack passed away in 2013. The white people stayed on her fridge. We'd continue to have family gatherings, and when some of us ended up in the kitchen laughing and reminiscing, there they'd be, smiling along with us, although we don't know what they were reminiscing about.

Shortly before we sold Mama Clack's house in 2016 the mystery was solved. The woman in the photo with her husband and daughter is a childhood friend of one of my cousins in Dallas. I don't know what happened to the picture.

Refrigerators are sometimes like family albums and trees. You never know what you will find and how it will relate to you.

Slavery Is Intertwined in Alamo's History

By early January 1836, a twenty-year-old named Joe had lived in Texas for three years. He was now on his way to San Antonio.

Droves of men, many of them leaving debts and unsavory pasts in their wake, were pouring into the Mexican territory to make their mark and start anew. Joe wasn't one of those men. Those men were white, and Joe was Black. His past, the mark of slavery, defined his present and future.

The Kentucky-born Joe had come to Texas as the property of one man and was headed for San Antonio as the property of another, William Barret Travis, who had purchased him little more than a year earlier for $410.

Travis, recently commissioned as a Texan lieutenant colonel of the Legion of Cavalry, was leading soldiers to reinforce the Alamo against the inevitable attack of Santa Anna's Mexican army. With them on their trek to history was Travis's slave Joe.

Travis's name and those of 186 other men he commanded killed at the Alamo are engraved on a fifty-eight-foot marble cenotaph that sits on the north edge of Alamo Plaza.

Last month, two days after Christmas, a few dozen members of This Is Texas Freedom Force gathered at the cenotaph to oppose its relocation to the southern part of Alamo Plaza, some five hundred feet away. Moving the cenotaph is part of the $450 million project to transform the Alamo and Alamo Plaza. But the Freedom Force believes that moving the cenotaph dishonors those who died there, a reasonable objection when it comes to the disturbance of any battle or burial ground. It's an objection eloquently mirrored by Ramón Vásquez and the Tap Pilam Coahuiltecan Nation when they remind us of the 1,300 mostly Indigenous remains buried on the site.

But comments made by a couple of the Freedom Force members made me think of Travis's slave Joe, because, clearly, they weren't thinking of Joe. One member, who appeared to be the youngest and who had a "Don't Tread on Me" flag draped around his shoulders, said, "I'm here to protect the cultural sovereignty of 1836."

What does that mean? I know what it means, or I think I know what it means. What I'm not sure of is if he knows what that means. If he does, that's a problem.

Cultural sovereignty means that a small group of people—elites, if you will—defines a nation's culture. Would the young man prefer we conform to the mores and values of 1836, or does he want to be among the elite of 2020?

Someone who wasn't protected and didn't enjoy the cultural sovereignty of 1836 was Joe, born into slavery, sold twice and torn from his family. Which leads to a second comment from a Freedom Force member, this one a minister from Kerrville, who told *San Antonio Express-News* reporter Scott Huddleston: "They stood and fought for my rights today. And I'm going to stand and fight for theirs."

Okay—for *your* rights, perhaps. Those men died heroically at the Alamo, but they didn't stand, fight or die that day for *my* rights, nor those of many of the other people who have since enjoyed the plaza, and they certainly weren't fighting for the rights of Joe or the other slaves in the compound.

What is ironic is that most of what the Freedom Force and all of us know about what transpired on March 6, 1836, is because of Joe. Once the Alamo came under siege, he joined Travis in taking up arms. He saw Travis get shot in the head and then fatally stab a Mexican soldier who attacked him. Joe's life was spared by the Mexicans because he was a Black slave. He was interrogated by Santa Anna and released. He and Susanna Dickinson, another Alamo survivor who gave an insider's view of the siege, made their way to Sam Houston's camp in Gonzales.

Joe then gave the Texas cabinet a full account of what he saw, and this account, which spoke of the courage of Travis and his men in battle, is the fullest and most credible report we have of what went down behind those limestone walls.

Despite Joe's testimony, he remained a slave and would be sold a third time before escaping in 1837 and making his way to Travis's family in Alabama.

As we reimagine the Alamo by telling the full history of the lives and deaths that converged in that plaza, Joe's presence reminds us how intertwined slavery is in that history.

How MLK and Coretta Scott King Changed My Life

I owe my career to Martin Luther King Jr. and Coretta Scott King—both for the opportunities they and other civil rights veterans opened for people like me through their sacrifice and in a specific way.

The first writing I had published anywhere was in these pages when I was a political science student at Saint Mary's University. My op-ed in the January 16, 1983, *Express-News* advocated for King's birthday being made a national holiday.

My grandmother suggested I send the piece to the Martin Luther King Jr. Center for Nonviolent Social Change in Atlanta, which I'd never heard of. I mailed the column, expecting nothing in return. A few weeks later I received an application for the center's scholar-internship program. I applied and was accepted for summer 1984, the transformative summer of my life.

Family friends dropped me off on the front steps of the King Center with a suitcase and footlocker filled with books. Greeting me was Liliane Kshensky Baxter, the program's director, who remains one of the most important people in my life. Lili was the daughter of Holocaust survivors. Her father was liberated from Bergen-Belsen and her mother from Auschwitz. Their son, the older brother Lili never met, died in Auschwitz. Lili was born in a displaced person's camp in Sweden.

She took me into her office and, after telling me about the

six other interns, leaned across her desk, smiled and said, "And you're the writer."

My first-grade teacher, who'd also been my mother's first-grade teacher, had told Mom I'd be a writer. By then I was writing semiregular unsolicited and unpaid columns for a Black weekly, the San Antonio *SNAP*. I dropped my submissions over the transom, too shy to hand them to the publisher, Eugene Coleman. But this moment with Lili was the first time anyone told me I was a writer. Lili declared with such certainty and enthusiasm that I was a writer that I started to reach for a pen to autograph for her the many books of mine she no doubt owned but I'd yet to write.

My intern class included three African American men, one African American woman, a Sri Lankan man, a Hindu Pakistani woman, and a white Canadian man. We lived in spare apartments a few blocks from the King Center.

We soon became joint owners of a stray black dog. In thinking of names for the dog, the white Canadian male, Dave, innocently suggested Blackie.

"Dave," I told him. "I don't think it would be a good idea for you to be going down the street in this neighborhood yelling 'Blackie.'" I named her Sheba.

Over the course of the internship program, we studied the philosophy of nonviolence not only as an instrument of social change but as a way of life. We met with veterans of the civil rights movement like the Rev. C. T. Vivian, Dorothy Cotton and James Orange. On my last night we had dinner at the home of then–city councilman John Lewis and his wife, Lillian.

On the Fourth of July, Mrs. King had us over to her house for dinner, and I sat next to Daddy King, Martin Luther King Sr.

"Where you from, son?" he asked me.

"San Antonio, sir."

"Welcome to Atlanta."

As part of the internship we were placed in a King Center department related to our individual interests. Since I was "the writer," I was placed with Coretta Scott King's gifted speechwriter, Steve Klein.

The writing I did for Mrs. King was some CNN commentaries she regularly delivered. She was a great lady who was much more than a reflection of her husband. She created the King Center and the internship program to spread the legacy and use of nonviolence. I would come to know her better over the years but never shook the awe of being in her presence.

Lili made me think of myself as a writer. Mrs. King made me believe a writing career was possible.

Through the years I would return to the King Center many times to teach workshops in nonviolence. Beyond the personal relationships developed, the three greatest gifts I received from that summer in Atlanta were a belief in the necessity and possibilities of nonviolence, a deep interest in the civil rights movement and a career.

While I've often failed and fallen short of what I intended, everything I've written since has been informed by the greatest lesson of nonviolence: our obligation to love one another.

The Bout

The mingled smell of stale popcorn, beer and tobacco clung to the octagon-shaped interior. The 4,500-seat Sportatorium, south of downtown Dallas, was a beloved venue for wrestling shows and country music programs and, tonight, a one-of-a-kind boxing match.

For the past few years this was the site of the weekly *Big D Jamboree*, a Saturday night country music radio show broadcast across the country by KRLD over the CBS network. Established and rising stars from the Grand Ole Opry like Hank Williams, Sonny James and Johnny Cash would take the stage at the center of the arena.

The barnlike Sportatorium had seen audiences even bigger than the nearly 2,400 gathered here on February 24, 1955, but maybe never one so rapt. And it had never housed an audience so evenly distributed between Black and white spectators—although, this being Dallas in 1955, Blacks and whites didn't sit together. They were segregated by alternating sections steeply rising toward the crisscrossing rafters. Tonight's crowd had sat through four preliminary matches, and now, peering through the haze of cigarette and cigar smoke curling into the glow of the lights, they looked upon a sight never before witnessed in a Texas boxing ring.

The two men below mirrored the crowd. In one corner was a white boxer, in the other a Black one. The first was the young boxer with four professional fights, the other the veteran pugilist with a losing record in seventeen professional fights.

During introductions, Reagan "Buddy" Turman, the young high-flying white boxer, drew the louder applause. He was a familiar face who'd fought two weeks earlier in the Sportatorium. But the applause for I. H. "Sporty" Harvey, veteran journeyman boxer, was generous, recognizing his long and incredible fight to enter that ring. It was an outpouring.

Late in the third round Turman slammed an anvil disguised as a left hook into the right side of Harvey's face, dropping him to the canvas and sending the crowd to its feet, some with cheers, others with hearts dropping as hard as Harvey had.

The referee's voice cut through the roar and groans. "One! Two!"

This was the end that had been predicted, even preordained. Turman was more skilled and powerful than Harvey. "Three! Four!"

In a story running that day in newspapers across the country, a UPI sportswriter, previewing this fight, noted Harvey's battles to make the fight happen. But tonight, at least, he might wish he had never launched his campaign. For the twenty-year-old had been expected to make short work of the veteran. "Five!"

Searching for clarity and his legs, Harvey struggled to get off the canvas. Short work of the veteran indeed. Watching, holding their breath and trying to will him to his feet were entire sections of Black people not ready to give up a dream. "Six!"

Harvey wasn't the first Black Texas boxer to imagine that he had a chance to fight for the title of champion. But he was the only one who imagined it to the point of forcing that image into existence. "Seven!"

Ding! The bell ending the round would give him another chance if he could get up. Few thought he had fight left in him. Their mistake.

Two years before, during the 1953 session of the Texas legislature, Maury Maverick Jr., a young white civil rights attorney and state representative from San Antonio, introduced a bill he knew wouldn't pass.

A thirty-two-year-old who'd served in the Marines during World War II, Maverick, in his second term in the legislature, was already one of the leading liberals in that chamber and in the state. It was a position he came by through intellect, convictions and heritage. The sad eyes on his oval-shaped face were often offset by a wry remark that always seemed ready to spring from a mouth pulled back just shy of a smile.

During the 1960 presidential campaign, Maverick Jr. was giving John F. Kennedy a tour of the Alamo when Kennedy, late for another appointment, asked him to lead him out the back door.

"There is no back door," Maverick said. "That's why there were so many heroes."

Because of Maverick's great-grandfather, Samuel Augustus Maverick, the word "maverick" has come to apply to anyone independent and willing to think in unconventional ways. A signer of the Texas Declaration of Independence and a wealthy landowner, Samuel Maverick didn't brand his longhorns, a strange choice at the time. When one of his animals strayed from the herd it was called a maverick by cowboys.

Maury Maverick would always remember being a teenager and hiding with his parents and sister with family friends after their home was surrounded by an angry mob wanting to lynch his father. Maverick's father, a two-term New Deal US congressman and San Antonio mayor, had allowed a Communist Party rally to be held in Municipal Auditorium in 1939. That memory seemed to animate his father's advice: "When you've got a famous name, you've got to use it to speak up for people who can't speak up for themselves."

Maverick's proposed 1953 bill would repeal the ban on interracial boxing and wrestling matches, declaring, "it is discrimination and unfair to deny a boxer or wrestler the right to make a living by reason of his race, color or creed."

The two-decades-old ban wasn't popular with the boxing and wrestling communities. After Maverick's bill was filed, the *Austin-American Statesman*'s Buster Haas wrote, "We have talked to every leading boxer in the state, in addition to all fight managers, and have heard no dissenting vote against allowing Negro and white fighters to box.... In fact, most boxers and managers, in addition to promoters who predict an upswing in boxing popularity if the bill passes, say that 'mixed' bouts are the only salvation for boxing in Texas."

The prehistory of Maverick's bill went back to February 25, 1901, in Galveston's Harmony Hall, when a white veteran fighter from California named Joe Choynski slammed a right hand into the face of a Black Galveston fighter in the third round. Knocked cold, the young fighter fell into the arms of Choynski before hitting the floor. That fighter was Jack Johnson, who in seven years would become boxing's first Black heavyweight champion of the world and one of the sport's most gifted fighters in history.

Texas Rangers arrested Choynski and Johnson for fighting not because theirs was an interracial prize fight but because it was a prize fight with money on the line, which was illegal in Texas. The two men were jailed for three weeks and sparred every day in prison, often before an audience, with Johnson playing student to Choynski's teacher. Upon their release they left Galveston.

In 1933 the Texas legislature banned boxing matches between white fighters and Black fighters. Historian Francine Romero explores the motives for the ban in "There Are Only White Champions," an essay on segregated boxing in Texas. "The significant legislation that appeared in 1933 in this regard was not the segregation of the sport, but approval of the resumption of legally sanctioned boxing in the state after a thirty-eight-year absence...it is this reauthorization that prompted legislative debate and public scrutiny, not the limit on mixed matches quietly attached to it."

The institution of segregated matches was a natural consequence of the era's raw and unapologetic racism and segregation. No matter how talented or bursting with promise, a Black fighter could never be champion of any boxing division in Texas. He could, like Johnson, become champion of the world by taking a detour out of Texas, but the road to being recognized as the best in his state would always be blocked.

The same legislation banning mixed-race matches repealed the ban on all forms of boxing in the state, which through licenses and permit fees alone would deprive the state coffers of $30,000 annually, a value equivalent to more than $500,000 dollars today.

That was twenty years before Maury Maverick's attempt to change or challenge the ban. A realist, he had an idea of how it would play out. "My bill was sent to the state affairs committee, which meant from the start that the speaker wanted it killed," Maverick recalled years later.

He got a hearing but was stung by the "good old boy humor" that led up to the bill being killed. He knew it would probably die; he didn't expect it to die as quickly as it did. Recounting the experience in a letter, Maverick wrote, "It made me feel sore." He needed to find another way to win.

That summer Maverick was in his law office on the seventh floor of the Maverick Building in downtown San Antonio when a muscular, well-dressed Black man walked in. He would change everything.

"I'm Sporty Harvey," the man said. "I could be champ of Texas in the heavyweight division, but they won't let me box."

He caught Maverick off guard. "I was bewildered at first," Maverick recalled. "I didn't quite know what to make of him."

"I want to file a lawsuit with you," Harvey explained. "I want to talk to you about dignity for my people."

Harvey was born on July 21, 1925, in Hallettsville, about a hundred miles east of San Antonio. He was the firstborn of Charlie and Rosella's six children and was named I.H. That's his name in the Lavaca County birth registry and would be his name on his headstone. What the initials stood for, if anything, has been lost to history, even among his family members.

"[I] never knew," his son, Lymont Harvey, said when asked what the "I.H." stood for. "His mother just gave him that name. I guess it was the thing to do."

As a child Harvey chopped wood and picked cotton. His formal education stopped after sixth grade. In 1937 he moved with his family to San Antonio.

Somewhere between Hallettsville and San Antonio, he began to box. His nickname, Sporty, unlike those of Joe Louis's "Brown Bomber" or Jack Dempsey's "Manassa Mauler," came not from any fighting technique but from his well-groomed style and sartorial taste outside the ring. "I. H. 'Sporty' Harvey was invariably a colorful lad," wrote Mark Batterson, an *Austin-American Statesman* sports columnist, in 1953. "He affected bright, bright ring garments which established a trademark for him."

The heavyweight championship of the world was the most coveted and recognized title in sports, and whoever was the champ was one of the most famous men in the country. Joe Louis won the title shortly before Harvey's twelfth birthday. Louis's reign lasted a dozen years, extending into the first two years of Harvey's professional career. The second Black man to win the heavyweight title, after Harvey's fellow Texan Jack Johnson,

Louis was the dominant fighter of Harvey's youth and a man who carried the hopes of Blacks each time he entered the ring.

If Louis could do that for Black people across the country, why couldn't Sporty Harvey do it for Black people throughout the state of Texas? For one thing, Harvey was the ultimate underdog. Starting off as a light heavyweight, he was knocked out in Pittsburgh in 1947, in his first professional fight. It didn't get better. He was knocked out in his first four professional fights and lost his first eight, six by KO and two by TKO. His first win came in Municipal Auditorium against a fighter making his pro debut who quit between rounds.

We will never know Harvey's actual record as a professional fighter, and he probably didn't know either. BoxRec, boxing's official record keeper, lists his record as 10-23-2. They also list him as J. D. Harvey, an alias Sporty appears to have used to score more fights.

That record doesn't include some of his fights in San Antonio's out-of-the-way East Side venues like the Ritz, a former movie theater, or at Fort Sam Houston. Nor does it include fights in Mexico where he'd challenge Mexican and white boxers. Whatever the number of fights, they probably added up to a losing record.

He was an everyman, not a superman. But by all accounts he was a popular and entertaining fighter who, years before Muhammad Ali, did windmill windups before throwing a punch.

Batterson observed: "I. H. 'Sporty' Harvey used to come to Austin to engage in his profession. Just what this profession was sometimes wasn't clear. On at least two occasions, he definitely appeared to be a boxer. On another he seemed to be an entertainer, an imitator, sort of, who was giving his comic impressions of a boxer.... A more memorable trademark in this case, however, was the way he jutted out before and aft when he scampered into battle. At times this style made him look more like a Studebaker than a boxer."

There were more talented Black fighters in Texas than Harvey, but because of the ban against matches between Blacks and whites they were no closer than he was to winning a championship or maximizing earning potential.

Neither talent nor the guts to take physical punishment from another man in the ring would be enough to change the law. Such change demanded a different type of courage, the courage to challenge an entire state's legal system and way of life and risk all the forms of punishment the state could inflict.

On that July day in 1953, Maury Maverick listened to his unexpected visitor tell his story in a drawl not so different from his own. Harvey had read about Maverick's attempt to change the laws prohibiting Black boxers from fighting white boxers, which is what brought him to the office. He quickly convinced the lawyer that he should represent him. Harvey couldn't afford an attorney. Maverick wouldn't have charged him anyway.

Change was in the air. Just a few weeks earlier a bus boycott by Blacks in Baton Rouge, Louisiana, had won concessions from that city. The slavery era and Jim Crow dictums of Blacks "knowing their place" were challenged with greater frequency and variety as "their place" became any place where they'd be afforded the same rights and opportunities as whites; those places included schools, public accommodations, voting booths and, just maybe, boxing rings.

Maverick hatched a plan. He asked his new client to write a letter to M. B. Morgan, the state's labor commissioner, whose office governed professional boxing, asking for permission to fight a white boxer. When the office predictably denied the request within a week, Maverick prepared to sue.

In deploying the legal system, often used against Blacks, to assert his right to professionally fight white men in his home state, Harvey trod uncharted and dangerous territory, inviting the threats and assaults that attended Black men and women refusing to stay in their place. Physical harm always loomed, but more common, even likely, was the economic retaliation of losing jobs and being denied credit in stores.

Harvey's family supported his quixotic lawsuit but not without reservations. "We were kind of afraid for a while but we were with him all the way," his sister, Lottie, told a reporter years later.

Potential harm to the family appears to have spurred Harvey to move his family out of state. "From what I remember my mom telling me," Lymont Harvey said, "I think he moved us to California before the fight because of fear for the family."

To help fund the case, Maverick reached out to the state NAACP, which, at its convention in San Antonio, voted to underwrite $500 in court costs. He also assembled a diverse dream team of legal talent hailing from San Antonio, including Harry Bellinger, a scion of one of San Antonio's most powerful Black families; two future judges and a future district attorney; and, most notably, Carlos Cadena, a legal scholar and future chief justice of the Fourth Court of Appeals.

On August 13 Maverick filed a lawsuit in the 126th District Court in Austin challenging the legality of banning professional boxing matches between white and Black boxers, calling it "wholly unjust, arbitrary and capricious." The suit claimed that the law denied Harvey rights guaranteed by the Fourteenth Amendment and the Federal Civil Rights Act.

Maverick's decision to file the suit in state court met opposition from civil rights advocates like the NAACP and even from his own colleague, Cadena. All believed, with history as their guide, that minority plaintiffs had greater success at the federal level than in state courts, especially southern ones.

But Maverick's devotion to justice and constitutional principles paralleled his love of his state. He wanted to show that

Texas could do the right thing. "We have a great Bill of Rights in the Texas Constitution of 1876 and no one has ever paid any attention to it," he wrote in some notes. "I do believe in State's Rights, but to have those you have to have State's Duties. Blacks, browns, poor whites in state courts always got the short end of the stick, historically, and that's why everybody went to the federal courts. But, hell, I love Texas. Why not have good Texas courts?"

As Harvey navigated the maze of the legal system, a world of opportunity was open for white boxers with similar ambitions, with fellow Texan Reagan "Buddy" Turman a prime example. Born in the East Texas hamlet of Noonday in 1933, the same year of the birth of segregated boxing in Texas, Turman was a young six-foot-one heavyweight with great promise.

He began chopping wood on the family farm when he was six, and not long after his family gathered around the radio to listen to the fights of one of their favorite boxers, Black phenom Joe Louis. After a stint in the Navy, Turman came home, worked the oilfields and began his amateur boxing career. While building a record of 20-5-1, he developed what would be his most dangerous punch: the left hook.

Turman became Texas's amateur light-heavyweight champion. He had one goal, just like Sporty Harvey, and he wouldn't let anyone stand in his way to reach it: world heavyweight champion.

On January 26, 1954, Maverick, Harvey and their team walked into Judge Jack Roberts's 126th District Court seeking an order directing M. B. Morgan, the state boxing commissioner, to allow Harvey to fight any professional fighter, no matter his ethnicity. They also sought a ruling on the constitutionality of the segregated boxing law.

Testifying for the state, Morgan, age sixty-three, argued that banning professional boxing contests between Blacks and whites prevented hostility and race riots and that the law should stand as a bulwark against those threats. He claimed that "the people of Texas, from the conversation I have had with folks, are of the opinion that the customs and habits and traditions of the citizens of Texas are satisfied with our present law and think it would be best to keep the law on our books."

Contradicting Morgan's position, Maverick's witnesses included longtime Texas sportswriters who had attended countless mixed-race sporting events, including amateur boxing matches, without observing racial tension, much less violence, rising from the competition.

Then came the star of the proceeding. Wearing a dark double-breasted suit and thick black-rimmed eyeglasses, Harvey said he would never have the chance in Texas to win a championship because of his race. "The guys I want to fight I can't fight because I'm a Negro," he testified, even though he worked out with white boxers and that had never caused any problems because of his race. He was treated well by the boxing community in San Antonio but had to drive a truck and handle freight to support his family. Harvey's household included his wife, Hazel Lee, whom he met when she was at nursing school, and a growing brood that eventually included four children. He couldn't get enough fights to make a living as a boxer because of the limitations placed on him.

"It helps to have an economic deprivation which, of course, we had here," Maverick wrote. "If Sporty could box he would make more money; thus because he was Black he was being denied an equal opportunity to make a living." Maverick could attack an unconstitutional law by arguing that it denied Harvey grocery money to take care of his family.

Not much food landed on the table from Harvey's meager

boxing earnings, unless it was food he caught with his hands. Once he and some other fighters from San Antonio drove to Beeville for a four-fight card in a tent. The eight fighters were supposed to get a share of the gate, but the gate total was $11 to be divided between the fighters and a promoter. Having fought for $1.22 purses, Harvey and Tony Castillo, a San Antonio bantamweight, left the tent disgusted and hungry. They saw two turkeys wandering around and, in their most vigorous workout of the day, chased the turkeys around the tent until they each caught one to take home.

None of this would change until Harvey and other Black fighters could fight those who held championships and drew bigger gates and paydays: white fighters. Harvey now sat in court because he couldn't just wait around for that day to arrive.

There were two instances when Maverick feared Harvey's testimony would hurt his cause. Wanting to show the absurdity that Harvey couldn't fight a white man in Laredo, Texas, but could go five miles across the border to Nuevo Laredo, Mexico, to fight the same white man—which Harvey had done—Maverick asked him, "Sporty, isn't it true that you boxed a white man in Nuevo Laredo, Mexico?"

The courtroom was silent and Maverick grew more uncomfortable with Harvey's silence. They'd rehearsed this, but now Harvey appeared confused. "Naw," he finally answered. "I didn't fight no white man."

Maverick, not believing his ears, thought they'd get thrown out of court, but Harvey continued, "I boxed a Spaniard." Laughter spilled out over the courtroom.

Under cross-examination, the assistant attorney general of Texas took notice of Harvey's thick eyeglasses and Maverick panicked again, worried that the glasses would allow the state to say they were turning Sporty down because of his bad vision and not his race.

"Mr. Harvey," the assistant attorney general said, "because of those glasses, you can't see well, can you?"

"I have perfect vision," Harvey said. "I wear these eyeglasses for sport. That's why they call me Sporty." He smiled, and the courtroom laughed again.

"Sporty could play the fool," Maverick would say, "but the next minute break your heart."

The state used Harvey's subpar record as a fighter against him. Asked what his record was, Harvey said he was only "guessing" but that he'd won eighteen out of twenty-one professional fights. The state countered, saying he had only seven wins in seventeen fights and that his lack of talent was the barrier to his fighting for a championship.

Harvey was the only Black man in a courtroom filled with white men who were lawyers, judges, politicians and journalists—men practicing their crafts and making a living in the professions they chose and wanted. All were gathered because the lone Black man in their presence was fighting for the right to do what they did, a right they took for granted: the opportunity to practice his craft and make a living in the profession of his choice.

Yet here he sat listening to these officials of the state he had been born and raised in talk publicly about how bad they thought he was at his craft—so bad, they claimed, that he should be denied the opportunity to see how far he could go. He was mocked for lacking skills and techniques by the very people denying him the opportunities to hone his skills and techniques.

Just two weeks earlier, two members of Harvey's legal team, Carlos Cadena and Gus Garcia, had argued a case that would make them the first Latino attorneys to win before the US Supreme Court. The landmark *Hernandez v. Texas* ended the exclusion of Mexican Americans from jury pools based on the Fourteenth Amendment's protections for all nationalities, not just white and Black. Cadena now argued that Harvey's talent wasn't the issue, that in fact he was being denied the opportunity solely because of his race.

During the day's testimony, Judge Roberts consistently ruled with Harvey and against the state on objections about evidence. Signs pointed toward a victory. But on February 3 came heartbreaking news. Roberts ruled against Harvey and upheld the law, citing Harvey's losing record. His decision may have been swayed by electoral concerns.

A state district judge such as Roberts depended on the ballot for his position, in contrast to a federal judge appointed for life. Years later, when Roberts was a federal judge, he ran into Maverick and told him, "If I had been a federal judge when you brought the Harvey case before me, I would have held with that nigger boxer."

While Harvey was facing a major setback, Buddy Turman, nicknamed "the Golden Boy from Noonday," got a boost in his quest for boxing glory. This came in the form of a man named Bobby Joe Manziel. The boxing promoter and wealthy oilman was impressed with what he saw in the anvil-of-a-hook on the Tyler product. Small and lithe, Manziel wore a signature fedora. Underneath was an angular face with thick eyebrows, mischievous eyes and a tight smile, features that would be shared by his great-grandson, future Heisman Trophy winner Johnny Manziel.

"You come with me and you'll become the heavyweight champion of the world," Manziel told Turman the first time they met, according to Joe Garner Turman, brother and biographer of Buddy. "You can train on my farm, and I'll set up a ring and everything else you need. I'll get you the best trainer available. Listen, I know a lot of people in the boxing world. I can get you the fights you need to move you toward becoming a top contender."

Brash, aggressive and calculating, Manziel looked for the angles that would most quickly elevate him to the top of every endeavor. He had originally moved to East Texas to wildcat oil wells. It was a $400 loan from boxing legend Jack Dempsey that allowed him to strike oil on the grounds of a Black Baptist church that showered both men in riches. Settling in Tyler, Manziel would own hotels, banks, other real estate, newspapers and fighting roosters, and pilot his own plane from a runway on his farm. He was also a promoter who lost his license after accusations of fixing a professional wrestling match.

Turman signed a contract with Manziel on a chilly fall day. To bring him to the next level, Manziel hired a Black trainer, Robert "Cornbread" Smith, who trained young fighters in a gym he owned above a liquor store in south Dallas. He had fought in the 1930s and had worked the corners of world champions like Fritzie Zivic and Lew Jenkins.

Turman ended his last amateur fight with a first-round knockout and picked up right where he left off in his professional debut, on September 27, 1954, when he knocked Bobby Babcock off his feet three times en route to a unanimous decision. The referee for the fight was Manziel ally Jack Dempsey.

What Manziel couldn't bestow on Turman was patience. Just like the young boxer, Manziel was driven to reach the top rung fast. In Turman's second fight, against Max Baird, repeated left hooks knocked out the overmatched Baird in the second round and sent him to a hospital for observation. Then, in just his third professional fight, Manziel pitted Turman against Birmingham battler Oscar Pharo for the Southern Heavyweight Championship. Raising the ante, Manziel said that after Turman beat Pharo he'd try to arrange a fight against the formidable Rocky

Marciano. Turman lost to Pharo on points, and suddenly his way forward became unclear.

Though losing in Judge Roberts's court had been a crushing blow to Harvey's case, Maverick and his team felt that Roberts, consciously or not, had set up Harvey for appeal. But Maverick had yet to receive the $500 promised by the state NAACP to cover state costs. He dashed off a letter to Thurgood Marshall, executive director of the NAACP Legal Defense Fund and future US Supreme Court justice, and within seventy-two hours he had received the funds to help keep the case moving.

Harvey's appeal reached the Third Court of Civil Appeals on October 13, 1954. In the interim, on May 17, 1954, the US Supreme Court's decision in *Brown v. Board of Education* ruled that racial segregation in public schools violated the Equal Protection Clause of the Fourteenth Amendment. Against this backdrop of upheaval, Maverick asked the appeals court to consider sociological as well as legal reasons for overturning the ban on interracial prizefights.

"We have this nation holding itself up as a democracy to the colored peoples of the world," said Maverick, a gifted orator. "And yet we have this law here where a Negro man can't even have a professional fight with a white man."

On October 27 the Third Court of Appeals ruled in Harvey's favor by reversing the state district court's decision and sending it back to retrial. The court did not invalidate the 1933 law, supposedly because doing so also would have nullified the necessary parts of the law, such as requiring strict physical examinations for fighters and the licensing of fighters and managers.

The court dismissed the state's argument that mixed-race matches would lead to race riots, writing that "even if riotous conditions did result from mixed boxing exhibitions we doubt if this statute would be sustained by the Federal Supreme

Court in view of language which we find in some of its opinions." The first of those opinions it cited was *Brown v. Board of Education.*

The thrust of the court's decision called for regulations so that mixed-race bouts would no longer be prohibited. On January 19, 1955, the Texas Supreme Court sustained the appeals court's judgment, making it official: Sporty Harvey had just beaten the state of Texas.

After the decision, a jubilant Harvey said, "I'm going to really get started good in boxing now that I'm going to get my big chance."

Just minutes into a Buddy Turman fight at the Dallas Sportatorium on February 10, 1955, Turman's vicious left hook staggered Bobby Babcock and left him covering up and clinching until the bell ended the round.

This fight suddenly had new stakes. It was announced that the winner would challenge Sporty Harvey—now known far and wide as a trailblazer in the courts—in two weeks. In the few months since Turman had stumbled against the hulking Oscar Pharo, he had put on ten pounds and cut a more dangerous figure than ever. The fight with Babcock could be a stepping stone to his redemption and his biggest spotlight yet.

Just fifty-five seconds into the second round, another Turman left hook drove Babcock into the ropes as a follow-up right to his jaw knocked him out. Ringside, Turman was swarmed by a crowd of more than two hundred. Babcock lay on the mat with only his doctor and trainer and a few concerned friends. It would be fifteen minutes before he got to his feet.

During Harvey's battle with the state, Turman, who idolized Joe Louis, sparred with Black fighters and had his Black trainer in his corner, voiced his support for Harvey's case and offered to fight him if it would help. He told his guru Manziel, "Since I'm a white Texan, I'll volunteer to fight Sporty. This will force the issue with the Texas state legislature."

But Manziel, the savvy promoter and businessman, wanted Buddy to fight Harvey for a more practical reason. "He knew the fight would generate a lot of publicity for Buddy, and he would make boxing history in Texas," Joe Garner Turman recalled. "This would move Buddy along in the boxing world."

Sporty Harvey had scored a chance to follow his dream, and now he had drawn Buddy Turman, a human threshing machine.

Turman was fast, with astonishing power in both hands, and a bob and weave later admired by Rocky Marciano, the heavyweight champion of the world. Many experts saw in Turman the potential to become the future champion. Dempsey said Turman was "the best young prospect I've seen in the last twenty years." He had movie star looks, and newspapers called him Handsome Buddy Turman or Handsome Heavyweight Buddy Turman, as if these were his given name. (In stories and headlines, Harvey's name was often preceded or followed by "Negro," as in "Negro Sporty Harvey" or "Harvey, a San Antonio Negro boxer.")

The irony was that Harvey took on the state for the right to fight white boxers so that he might have a chance to contend for titles. Now the manager of a white boxer wanted to fight Harvey to expedite his star fighter's title chances. Harvey looked to be a sacrificial lamb to a white fighter, a killer in the ring whose opponents had to peel themselves off the canvas.

The week of the fight Sporty, true to his nickname and reputation, arrived in Dallas wearing a light tan coat, brown pants, pink shirt, purple tie, robin's-egg blue hat and brown suede shoes.

In less than two months after the Harvey-Turman fight, Elvis Presley would perform at the Sportatorium for the first time. But on the night of February 24, 1955, Sporty Harvey was the headliner for the first time in his career. Walking from his dressing room to the ring and the biggest spotlight of his life, he would have seen with a sweeping glance of the arena that half of the audience, if not more, were Black.

Extra security was on hand, just in case the defense made at trial by M. D. Morgan and the state for segregated boxing came true in the form of a riot.

Years later Turman would tell the *Dallas Morning News*: "Oh, sure, people were saying this or that might happen at the fight, but it didn't seem like any big deal to me. I'd sparred a lot with Black fighters. I was just thinking about trying to win. That whole thing about not allowing Blacks and whites to fight seemed stupid. But it was that way all over the South."

Some saw the chasm in talent between Turman and Harvey as so wide as to render the fight absurd. *San Antonio Express* sports editor Dick Peebles, who testified on Harvey's behalf in court, wrote that the idea that Harvey could make a good fight of it was like thinking "a horse that draws a milk wagon is going to win the Kentucky Derby." He thought Harvey's presence was merely a sign of the promoters "trying to capitalize on the novelty of a white fighting a Negro."

Attached to Turman's future as a fighter were adjectives like "promising" and "up and coming," which had never been used to describe Harvey. Fighting is what Turman did for a living. Fighting is what Harvey did when he could. Turman, with the backing of a multimillionaire manager who believed he would win the world title, had trained daily by running four miles, chopping wood and sparring twelve rounds. All the more intimidating, the immortal Jack Dempsey was said to own a piece of his burgeoning career and future.

Harvey, when he wasn't driving or handling freight, trained by running or going to a gym, the most iconic of which was the

San Fernando Street Gym at the western edge of San Antonio. There he'd work the heavy and speed bags and spar under the eye of well-regarded but relatively obscure trainer Jimmy Scarmozi. Harvey continued his workout regimen the day before the big fight. He had boxed only three times during his court fight with the state and had lost twice. At twenty-nine years of age, he weighed in at a ponderous 196 pounds, heavier than he'd ever been.

Turman salivated for an easy match. According to a story that aired the day before the fight, on WBAP-TV of Fort Worth, Turman "says he is in good condition and can take the Negro without trouble."

At the opening bell, Harvey moved toward a twenty-one-year-old, 177-pound dynamo who in two of his past three fights had sent one man to the hospital and left another unable to get up for a quarter of an hour. The first two rounds were uneventful as the two fighters felt each other out, but in the third Turman's advantage became clear as he snapped jabs, bobbing and weaving while trying to set Harvey up for a knockout punch. With less than ten seconds remaining in the round, he decked Harvey with the notorious sledgehammer of a left hook. The hit was called "thunderous" by one beat reporter.

A former opponent had said of Turman's power, "When he hits you, you get so weak you can't stand up."

At the count of eight a weakened Harvey, struggling to get up, was saved by the bell ending the round. One minute later, when the bell rang for the fourth, Harvey was rising to his feet, ready to brawl. "[Harvey] appeared confident in the face of all odds at all times," reporter Mark Batterson had marveled, "and you finally had to get around to admiring him very much for this quality." Harvey ended up against the ropes, "eyes glazed and knees sagging," as the bell gave him yet another chance.

Knowing that Turman was best when fighting long range

where he could jab and plant his feet for his power punches, especially that murderous left hook, Harvey stayed close, smothering him and pounding blows to the body. This confused the younger fighter, who was inexperienced in handling the pressure of infighting.

In the fifth round—already a dramatically longer match than many had predicted—Harvey continued carrying the fight to Turman, forcing him against the ropes, smothering him and belting him with hard body shots, fighting not as someone who didn't want to lose but who believed he could win. Turman exuded desperation. Twice in the fifth round he was nabbed for hitting after the ref called a break. Harvey dominated in the sixth, sending Turman "coasting and retreating" away from him, as described by Turman's hometown paper. Each man had to catch his breath in the seventh.

A Turman combo in the eighth signaled the end. He dug a left into Harvey's gut before driving a right cross to the head, sending him crashing hard to the mat.

"One! Two!"

In making this a fight for eight rounds, Harvey had surprised almost everybody at ringside.

"Three! Four! Five!"

He'd given the customers their money's worth, a chance to see history and a good fight.

"Six! Seven! Eight!"

Eight. This was the eighth round, and two remained. If a man is going to headline his first ten-round fight, he should finish it. That's when the Sportatorium shook. Because Sporty stood up.

Buddy Turman went on the assault, intent on ending the fight in a knockout. He left his opponents crumpled in a corner, and this showboat wasn't going to go the distance with him. Hell no, he wasn't going to let that happen. He ripped a left hook into Harvey's face that banged him to the canvas for the third time.

Then the roof might as well have come off the place: Harvey stood up again.

As the round ended, Harvey pressured Turman, hammering punches and trying to pummel his way to an upset win. Maybe the world was just using him, like others had said, but he'd show the world. He kept charging into the ninth, shocking Turman with powerful combos to the head, leaving the favored fighter drained. In the tenth round Turman flicked jabs and crosses, wanting to unload another left hook as he "tried for the kill." But it didn't happen.

The final bell rang, and Harvey was standing face to face, toe to toe with his opponent.

On a 1978 visit to San Antonio twenty-two years later, Sporty Harvey, now fifty-two, with a face lined in wrinkles but his still unmistakable smile flashing, sat down with reporter Dan Cook. He recalled segregated life in San Antonio during the 1950s, perhaps throwing in some hyperbole.

"Sitting in the back of the bus was just a pride thing, and Black people got used to so it wasn't any big deal. It wasn't, that is, unless the back of the room was crowded. The real problem, in those days, was finding downtown public toilets and getting something to eat out of a restaurant's rear back door. After I got everything changed, me and Maury Maverick Jr., I caught a city bus and plopped right in the first seat."

When Harvey returned to San Antonio over the years to visit his mother and friends, you never knew what he'd be driving. One time it was a camper. Another year it was a baby blue Cadillac.

Harvey told Cook he was going to see Maury Maverick while he was in town. "He might need me to help bust down some more color lines."

As for the fears, looking back to 1955, about what his ground-breaking boxing match between a Black man and white man would stir up, and the race riots these pugilists would ignite for practicing their craft, police had reported only one disturbance in the stands—a fight between two white men.

Harvey could look back at his big fight with pride and some lingering bitterness. After the last bell rang, Turman won a unanimous decision by wide margins on the scorecards of the referee and two judges. But the amazing fact was that Sporty Harvey was still on his feet. What had knocked him down again and again was not as powerful as what lifted him up. And what lifted him up, leaving him standing, was a strength that score-cards could never gauge.

The older Harvey believed his technical loss in the ring was payback for taking on and beating the state in court. "They got back at me and gave the decision to Buddy."

"The only thing I know is that I did my best," he told his wife after the fight. "I thought I put up a good fight."

Harvey and Turman would meet in the ring again. In a June 1955 rematch in Tyler, Turman knocked Harvey down two more times before winning on another unanimous decision. After his two fights with Turman, Harvey would fight ten more times, losing eight of them. He never fought for the Texas state title. The closest he came to the world heavyweight championship was sparring with Sonny Liston and Joe Frazier. He settled into a career working for the Jones Tire Company in Los Angeles.

As for Buddy Turman, he would later reflect on the fight that he was "delighted to have an opportunity to demonstrate my attitude toward integration. I felt, and still do, that sports is a field where each man is proven by his feats and not by his social or ethnic background."

In late summer 1955, in his tenth fight, Turman outpointed

"Red" Worley for the Texas heavyweight title. Turman also never fought for the world heavyweight title, although in November 1960 and March 1961 he fought light-heavyweight champion Archie Moore, losing both fights on unanimous decisions. The first fight, in Dallas, was close enough that Turman thought he'd won. He wasn't alone. Afterward he was visited in his dressing room by a young heavyweight who had recently won his first professional fight.

"You beat that old man," eighteen-year-old Cassius Clay said to Turman.

Turman primarily would be remembered in Texas boxing circles as Sporty Harvey's partner in history. No footage or photographs of their groundbreaking bout have surfaced.

In summer 1997 Maury Maverick called to ask a favor. I was a columnist and reporter for the *San Antonio Express-News*, thanks to Maverick bringing me to the attention of some editors. At that paper, I would become the first African American on the editorial board of any San Antonio daily, as well as the first metro columnist.

"Kiddo," Maverick said, his nickname for anyone younger than him, "do you think you could drive me to Sporty Harvey's funeral on Thursday?"

Harvey had died in Los Angeles from heart disease on June 5, 1997, at age seventy-one. His wife, Hazel, had promised his mother that when he died she'd bring him home to San Antonio.

After a long career as a civil rights attorney, including a 3–0 record arguing before the US Supreme Court, Maverick, now seventy-six, was penning a regular Sunday column for the *Express-News*.

He was one of the few white people in the predominantly Black church we entered. Hard of hearing, he turned to me throughout the service and said, "Huh? What did he say?" or "What did she say?"

Inside the funeral program, a picture of Harvey in boxing gear ran above Samuel Ellsworth Kiser's poem "The Fighter," one stanza of which ends with these lines:

My victories are small and few,
It matters not how hard I strive,
Each day the fight begins anew
But fighting keeps my hopes alive.

Not long after the trailblazing fight of 1955, Charley Eskew of the *Austin-American Statesman* had already begun to mark Harvey's legacy not as a boxer, but as a fighter. He made the case that despite his middling record overall, Harvey would be voted into a hypothetical Texas sports hall of fame "for making his greatest stand outside the ring and, as a result, bringing life again to Texas boxing."

"He took it upon himself," Francine Romero said. "There are so many people who no one hears about who challenge big things. Because of them, we can say, 'Hey, it's starting to crumble a little bit. You can see it happening.'"

Harvey v. Morgan was cited in 1958 when a federal court overturned a similar law forbidding mixed-race boxing matches in Louisiana.

"You don't know how many people it affected," Romero writes, of Harvey.

His breakthroughs joined a slew of events still brewing—such as the campaigns of 1960s Birmingham and Selma—that helped dismantle segregation and establish political and economic justice through smaller, specific and achievable remedies.

Harvey and his family were proud of what he'd done. The children wrote school reports about how their father had knocked out Jim Crow. "I think he did a great thing at that time of his life and with what was going on in this world," Lymont Harvey said, of his father. "I'm very proud of him and glad he stood up and spoke his mind and that people listened and agreed and he won. By the time the [Turman] fight started, he'd won and opened the doors for other people."

After the funeral's minister eulogized Harvey for his courage challenging a racist law, he asked if anyone wanted to say a few words. Without hesitating, Maverick rose from his seat, excusing himself as he eased past others in the pew to get to the aisle. As he approached the pulpit, some in the church recognized him and smiled or pointed toward him.

"I'm Maury Maverick Jr., and I had the honor of representing Sporty in his lawsuit against the state of Texas," he said, as people nodded in appreciation. He recounted the summer day they met, when Harvey strolled into his office with a smile and a mission. As Maverick spoke, his rumbling drawl picked up pace and volume as it rolled over a growing chorus of "Amen!" "Tell it!" and "Preach!"

"I had two college degrees," Maverick thundered. "But that Black man"—he pointed to Harvey's gray casket—"with a sixth-grade education taught me more than I taught him!"

When he finished, there was applause, more amens and shouts of "Yes, yes!" As the lawyer walked past the casket, many in the congregation were doing what Sporty Harvey did against the state of Texas and Buddy Turman.

They stood up.

From a Distance, Hold Tight to One Another

Helium is the element of drift. It is the second-lightest element in the universe. It allows balloons, released from our hands, to ascend to the sun, whose Greek god Helios inspired its name.

On Wednesday morning in San Antonio there was no sun, and if there were balloons floating through the air they wouldn't have been seen, as the city awoke to its first day of shelter-in-place in a fog. Not just a metaphorical fog induced by COVID-19 and our inability to see ahead, to make out the outlines of a day when we'd return to normalcy, but a fog thick enough to shroud the city's skyline and obscure people at a certain distance.

At a certain distance is how we now measure our lives, whether standing in line at the store, working from home or visiting the (few) places we can go; it's how we bide our time while hoping the time is soon when the distance will be narrowed. At a certain distance—social distancing—dictates our lives so our lives will be saved. That we're becoming more afraid for our lives and the lives of others is as clear as the empty streets and sidewalks of downtown.

I'm a native San Antonian who has lived in or near and worked downtown most of my life. On Wednesday, during the 8 p.m. hour, Alamo Plaza and downtown were darker and less vibrant than any time in my memory. It was no more alive at 10 a.m. Thursday.

In his brilliant memoir, *Places Left Unfinished at the Time of Creation*, John Phillip Santos describes Houston Street as a long dark avenue of ghosts. Today that's not just Houston Street but also Broadway, Commerce, Losoya, Navarro, Travis, Alamo Plaza and Travis Park.

But even the ghosts are absent. Walking through these streets Thursday, I felt like a character in a *Twilight Zone* episode—the only person or one of a scattered few who have survived the destruction of the world. The wind blew and because motorized, and human traffic was almost nonexistent, I could hear, as well as see, dry leaves scraping along the street, a Styrofoam cup tumbling down the sidewalk, plastic clinging to a parking meter and a piece of newspaper attaching itself to a tree. Most of the people I've seen are the homeless who are sheltering in place where they've been living: downtown streets.

COVID-19 reminds us that a pandemic, like any tragedy afflicting a community and a nation, magnifies existing inequities and suffering, making more visible the people we didn't see or ignored because they were at a certain distance from our view and our conscience.

Whether through homelessness or being one rent payment away from homelessness, unstable and low-paying jobs, food insecurity, a lack of health insurance or paid sick leave, or the absence of computers and Wi-Fi for children now expected to learn online, we've allowed too many people to drift from our attention, moral concern and responsibility. Among the many challenges, some unprecedented, we now face because of COVID-19 is aggressively attacking and eliminating these inequities.

COVID-19 also magnifies the infection of loneliness. There are people—many, but not all, of them older—who were recluses before the virus came, and there are others whose only sense of community was found in the churches, synagogues, mosques, and senior and community centers now closed. One of our greatest daily challenges during these times is remembering and keeping our eyes open for them, not letting them drift away, forgotten, as a prelude to their silent and unacknowledged deaths. We can't allow the necessity of being physically apart be the reason we don't stay in touch. That doesn't only include strangers and casual acquaintances but also the people we know well and love.

Thursday morning, on my way to Central Market, I drove past the Catholic Worker House, where a long line of the poor and homeless waited to be served breakfast. The line I stood in at Central Market was shorter, faster moving and serenaded by saxophonist Joe Posada. As I entered the store, Posada was playing Al Green's "Let's Stay Together." When I exited, he was halfway through Hall & Oates's "One on One."

Because we now measure time at a certain distance with the hope of flattening the COVID-19 curve, our one-on-one interactions are spaced out, online and virtual. But in, through, and beyond this unprecedented time of separation, we must stay together. We need to stay together.

We hold on tight to the strings of helium balloons when we're not ready to let them go. Let's hold on to each other so we don't drift apart.

In Her Legacy, Notes of What Awaited Selena

She's been gone longer than she was here. But in the twenty-five years since Selena Quintanilla's death at age twenty-three, her presence as a cultural and musical icon endures.

For those unaware of her phenomenon, her significance, and how deeply she was loved among Tejano music fans and the Mexican American community, it became quickly evident on March 31, 1995, that this was more than the premature passing of a popular entertainer. Hours after the Grammy Award–winning singer was shot in Corpus Christi by the president of her fan club, Selena's music was flowing from vehicles backed up on Broadway and Mulberry Street as people headed to a candlelight vigil at Sunken Garden Theater. Her boutique, a few blocks away on Broadway, immediately bloomed into a memorial of flowers, photos and messages.

The outpouring of emotion in scenes like this was repeated across the country for weeks. In death Selena became a revelation to people who'd never heard of her or Tejano music and knew little, if anything, about the Mexican American community. She made many Americans aware of the rich veins of culture throughout the country that had been unfamiliar to them.

Celebrated San Antonio singer Erica Gonzaba has been singing Selena's songs since she was ten. "Selena's music has transcended time. She's legendary," she said. "The impact she's had on generations of people, especially in the Latin community, is incomparable. She will always be an inspiration and an icon to so many people all over the world."

The unexpected death of a young artist or athlete inevitably leads to years of speculating about what might have been. This is no less true of Selena. While we'll never know how far her extraordinary gifts as a singer, dancer and performer would have carried her, we have an idea. Her death came months before the release of the album *Dreaming*, which she hoped would bring her crossover success.

It did, posthumously. There's no reason to doubt, given the arc of her career, her talent and the album's quality, that she would have achieved crossover success and soared to even greater heights had her life not been taken.

It's Not the Cat's Meow

"Will you please shut up! I'm trying to work."

Immediately, I felt bad for raising my voice. I'm usually not like that. It's never the right way to react, especially to one who's been with you for nearly fourteen years.

I looked in her eyes and saw the hurt I'd caused. I scratched her behind the ear and said, "I'm sorry, but stop meowing so much."

"Meow."

I rolled my eyes and sighed.

I have two cats, Sinatra and Raskolnikov, the latter being the one I yelled at, although Sinatra has also been the recipient of my shortened fuse. Now that I'm working from home, I'm seeing a lot more of them—and I never appreciated how much they meow.

It was not my intention to be a cat owner or, to put it more accurately, to be owned by cats. Like everyone on both sides of my family, I prefer dogs. For the first three years of my life my best friend was a dog, Sandy, that my great-grandfather gave to my mother.

My father had an especially paternalistic relationship with his dogs. About fifteen years ago we were in my grandmother's backyard with one of them, a chocolate Doberman, and my father called out, "Son!"

"Yes," I said.

"Oh, I wasn't talking to you. I was calling for Rambo."

That's when I learned he also referred to his other two dogs as his sons, which, if you're his two-legged son, can mess you up if you think about it too much. I didn't. At least I don't think I have (although I'm writing about this fifteen years later).

I became owned by cats in 2006 when a cat who belonged to my mother's neighbor gave birth to a large litter in my mother's bathtub. I offered to take two with the goal of giving them away. I gently put a pair of three-month-old female kittens in my backseat and drove to my house.

One thing that stood out were their large paws. Normal cats have eighteen toes, five on each of their front paws and four on each of their back paws. Abnormal cats, like mine, have at least six toes on each of their front paws and at least one extra on their rear paws, and are called polydactyl. Ernest Hemingway's cats were polydactyl. That Ernest Hemingway's cats and Cary Clack's cats were polydactyl is the only way my name will ever be used in the same sentence as his, so I've taken care of that ambition.

While Hemingway defined rugged masculinity, I didn't think owning two female kittens would do anything to enhance mine. A man walking two cats by leash in a park doesn't draw the ladies compared to walking a Siberian husky or a golden retriever. A pickup line that has never worked is, "Hey, girl, you know what they say about a man whose cats have six toes?"

I decided to give my two female kittens strong masculine names that evoked toughness and power. The tannish-white one with the blue eyes became Sinatra, and the gray striped one became Raskolnikov, after the killer in Fyodor Dostoevsky's novel *Crime and Punishment*. It's Rasko for short, but everyone assumes I'm saying Rascal. There's also a "toe" in Dostoevsky's name. Being that they're indoor cats, I don't know how tough they are, but I've yet to have curtains or sofas that didn't succumb to their claws.

I've repeatedly mentioned that they were both female kittens. My bad. In 2007 Rasko gave birth to a black kitten and a white kitten. Turns out Sinatra is a male I should have named Randy. Dude, it was your sister! My cats are six-toed incestuous freaks, but I got them both fixed soon after.

The black kitten died, and I named the white one Oops, as in "Oops, I didn't know your father/uncle wasn't female." I found a home for Oops but never got rid of his mother/aunt and father/uncle. Sinatra and Raskolnikov have been with me through moves, job changes, relationships and, now, what we're all going through.

All their lives, they've lived under the shelter-in-place and stay-at-home policy I've enforced. Now I'm in their world. One way I'll adjust is to stop telling cats to not meow.

The Last Moments with a Beloved Friend

"Damn fly."

I was sitting in my car Wednesday afternoon in the Dodd Animal Hospital parking lot. On the passenger seat, in a blue pet carrier, was my tannish-white cat, Sinatra.

A fly darted in and out, circling the carrier, resting on a vent, then circling the carrier again. "Damn fly," I repeated, swatting it away, annoyed and resenting what the fly might sense.

In the carrier, Sinatra pushed his head against the netting and meowed weakly. I scratched his head through the netting and stopped, but when he meowed again I continued scratching.

Two Sundays ago I wrote about my two cats, Sinatra and his sister, Raskolnikov (Rasko), who were born in summer 2006 and whom I've had since they were three months old. I preferred dogs, and I gave the cats their names not so much to illustrate their toughness but to give myself an appearance of toughness.

Both were polydactyl, meaning they had extra toes on their paws. I couldn't understand why the drawers in my kitchen would be open when I came home from work, until the day I walked in and saw Sinatra on the counter easily opening one with his big white paw.

I'd assumed both cats were female until Rasko gave birth to a pair of kittens. As I noted two weeks ago, Sinatra and Rasko have been with me through moves, job changes and relationships.

A few days ago, Sinatra stopped eating, lost weight, grew quieter, began acting strange—like standing in one spot and not moving—and started sleeping in places he never had before. He gave off a terrible odor, leading me to suspect kidney problems. I'd pick him up to hold him and rub his head. I used to only feel fur, but now I felt his frame.

On Wednesday he was curled up in a paper bag under the kitchen sink and didn't offer his usual resistance when I put him in the carrier to take him to the veterinarian. Rasko watched from the bedroom. I walked out of the house with Sinatra, thinking he might not be back.

Because of COVID-19, customers and their pets wait in the animal hospital parking lot while employees bring the paperwork to fill out before taking in the pets to be examined.

At one point Sinatra went into such a deep sleep I had to shake the carrier to rouse him and make sure he was still alive. He began meowing, stopping only when I unzipped the carrier to scratch behind his ears. A couple of times he tried to get out, but I gently pushed him back in.

While waiting in my car, I scrolled through Twitter and saw that *New York Times* Pulitzer–winning editorial writer Brent Staples had posted a Frank Sinatra song, "Nice and Easy." That seemed appropriate, so I played it. As Sinatra lay down in his carrier, I played his namesake's "Luck Be a Lady," "There Used to Be a Ballpark," "Very Good Year" and "My Way." I took a picture of him.

Seeing that the sun was in Sinatra's face, I moved the carrier to the backseat and sat with him. My cloth mask was no defense against my cat's terrible odor. The fly was gone, but a bee flew in. I grabbed a small can of Axe body fragrance I keep in the car and sprayed the scent out at the bee. That didn't seem to faze the insect, but it made the car smell better.

After a technician took Sinatra in to be examined, I walked around the parking lot for more than a half hour, until the veterinarian called to say Sinatra had kidney failure and that at his advanced age, he wasn't going to get better. He said he'd hospitalize Sinatra and do what he could, if that's what I wanted.

I thanked him for his honesty and gave him permission to put Sinatra to sleep. He said I could be with Sinatra during the process. I declined.

I've gone to wake up one of my grandmothers only to learn she'd crossed over in her sleep; I've held my other grandmother's hand as she passed; I told my grandfather to let go four hours before he did; I've been in the presence of friends when they drew their last breath; and I've brushed the cheek of a child minutes after she'd lost her battle with cancer. Yet for some reason being with my cat as he died was too much for me.

When I got home and reached into the backseat to get Sinatra's carrier, another fly flew in.

Damn fly.

Recent Protesters Are Exact Opposite of Rosa Parks

In December 1955, when Rosa Parks refused to give up her seat on a Montgomery bus, the driver told her he could have her arrested. Still sitting, Parks answered, "You may do that."

He did, setting in motion the Montgomery bus boycott, a campaign led by Martin Luther King Jr. in which African Americans in that city distanced themselves from public transportation for a year, choosing the inconvenience of walking and carpooling until they won their case to be treated equally and with dignity.

By standing up to Jim Crow, Parks, King and the other boycotters put their lives at risk but endangered no one else. That's not what's happening today, across the country, in protests of stay-at-home orders and the closing of all but essential businesses in the wake of COVID-19.

Huddled and unmasked, spittle flying out of their mouths as they chant and shout about the tyranny imposed on them by governors and public health experts such as Dr. Anthony Fauci, whose firing they demand, the protesters' decision to violate stay-at-home orders not only endangers their lives but those of their families and strangers. These are the people one of President Donald Trump's economic advisers, Stephen Moore, compares to Rosa Parks.

"I call these people the modern-day Rosa Parks," he said. "They are protesting against injustice and a loss of liberties."

I can hear Parks's voice saying, "You may not do that."

Parks and everyone participating in the bus boycott and subsequent campaigns of the civil rights movement were protesting injustices a majority imposed on minorities, ones that kept them from pursuing life, liberty and the pursuit of happiness. The bunched-together and unmasked folks who are marching against social distancing aren't protesting injustices against a few but disruptions imposed on everyone—disruptions imposed so that we all might live and not succumb to a virus that, in less than five months, has killed nearly as many Americans as died in the Vietnam War.

No one in my or anyone else's socially distanced circles is enjoying this unprecedented disruption of American life—not being able to go out, not seeing and hugging the people we're used to seeing and hugging. Everyone wants businesses to reopen, people to return to work and economic devastation avoided. But we are staying home, doing what public health experts advise and listening to the wisest, more knowledgeable and most compassionate of our elected officials, whatever their party.

Polls consistently show that Americans, in a remarkable display of patience, good judgment and concern for each other, support stay-at-home measures and oppose any re-openings that may cause greater infections or deaths

"They have the right to protest and the right to freedom of speech, but not the right to take the right to live from others," said one of my closest friends from childhood, whose wife is a nursing administrator at a Laredo hospital. "They can play Russian roulette with their lives, but not anyone else's. This thing is so contagious that they're exposing those who choose to be safe."

Many of those protesters will be infected with COVID-19, and when they get sick they won't be saved by the medical cures promoted by the odious Alex Jones, one of the leaders of the rally in Austin and a man who called the murder of children at Sandy Hook a hoax. Nor should the infected protesters expect relief from hydroxychloroquine, the antimalarial drug hawked by Trump that has shown to be deadly when administered to COVID-19 patients.

Those who may save them, and will work around the clock to try, are the health care workers who won't care how the protesters got sick, only that they are sick and it's their responsibility to heal them, even if it costs them their own lives.

Another close friend of mine is married to a doctor who works in Seguin. She told me how life is for the spouses of health care workers. "We are stripping them down in the garage, sending them straight to shower. We know we will get it, matter of time," she said. "I've been prepping since January. We are talking about combining households. What else can we do? We took an oath." They've had to explain to their ten-year-old son that Mommy and Daddy aren't sleeping in different bedrooms because they're fighting but because they're trying to stay well. My friend then asked me to check on her mother if they got sick.

Speaking in 1995, Parks said, "I'd like people to say I'm a person who always wanted to be free and wanted it not only for myself."

In this time of COVID-19 we should all want to be healthy and want good health for everyone.

You may do that.

Strangers Unite in Tragedy
to Offer Comfort

Last weekend on Saturday afternoon, while I was driving west on Southwest Military in the far-right lane, I glanced over and saw a motorcyclist two lanes away quickly look to his right, as if he wanted to change lanes. But he couldn't because a truck was in that lane.

As the truck passed and obscured the motorcycle, I heard crashing and thudding noises, and I saw debris, including parts of the motorcycle, flying as the bulk of the vehicle slid down the street before being stopped by a curb. I assumed the truck had hit the motorcycle.

Like many others, I pulled into a parking lot, got out and ran to the accident. The motorcyclist lay conscious in the street, saying nothing, slowly rolling as people tended to him. He reminded me of a boxer who, having been knocked down, is stunned but needs a few seconds to clear his head and find his legs before standing up to fight. I was surprised at how well he looked, considering what he'd just endured. I thought he would get up. Police and EMS arrived, and he was put in an ambulance.

After the accident bystanders pulled out their cameras and began recording. I posted on Facebook that I didn't understand why people who have no connection to anyone involved feel the need to record such a traumatic event.

That evening a friend texted me about the accident. I was in the process of responding, of saying that the motorcyclist appeared to be the only one hurt, though not as badly as I had expected. Before I could finish, the news came on, announcing that the motorcyclist had died at the scene.

I realize what happened: Traffic had come to a sudden halt in the motorcyclist's lane. He saw that and tried to switch lanes, but he never had a chance. It wasn't his fault or the truck driver's fault.

Having complained earlier about gawkers recording the scene, I went back to Facebook to write about what moved me and made me marvel—the people who had rushed to try to help this man who was a stranger to them. They didn't know his name, who he supported for president, what god, if any, he worshipped. They didn't know how different he may have been from them in ways that aren't important. They rushed to his aid because he was similar to them in the only way that matters: He was a human being who needed help.

I watched as men and women got on their knees to help him, talk to him, tell him everything would be all right. The driver of the truck took off his shirt, placing it under the man's head. A woman held an umbrella over him to protect him from the afternoon sun. Another woman at a bus stop extended her hand toward him and prayed out loud. (Something I want made clear: I did none of those things. I simply watched.)

I closed my post by writing: "I don't know who the motorcyclist was, but if I could tell his family one thing, tonight, it's that he did not die alone. He died among strangers, but he was with strangers who were doing all they could to comfort and help him. I believe he knew that. I want to believe he knew that. And I want his family to know that."

I thought that was it. I wasn't expecting the response that followed. Only posts about my job changes and my father's death received greater responses as people—more strangers—expressed sympathy for the motorcyclist and offered condolences to his family, who they didn't know. There came a point when the motorcyclist's family and friends began sharing the post. As his family began writing on my page and identifying themselves, some beautiful interactions began; my Facebook friends extended their condolences, and family members responded with gratitude.

His name was Michael Guerra. He was a thirty-year-old private contractor and the father of four children. He was greatly loved by them and the rest of his family and friends, and that's why he was trying to rise up from the street.

Michael's brother, Jacob Guerra, wrote, "My brother always said he never wanted to die alone...it means the world to me that he did not die alone."

His name was Michael Guerra, and he died among friends.

Not Possible to Write Too Much about Race

Easter weekend of 1999, in Jasper, is when I first tried to redeem the soul of white America.

That's not how I thought about it then. If I had, I'd have known it wasn't original, that when the Southern Christian Leadership Conference was founded by Martin Luther King Jr. and other ministers, it was with the goal to "redeem the soul of America."

I simply wanted to give Jasper a chance to not be defined by the most notorious race crime since the civil rights movement. In 1998 a Black man named James Byrd Jr. was beaten by three white supremacists who then chained him to the back of a pickup and dragged him for three miles along a blacktop road, a gruesome journey that tore off his head and right arm.

I chose Easter weekend to visit Jasper because it was between trials and I thought I'd get a more accurate feel for the East Texas town. I left thinking it was a town with problems and a history, but it shouldn't be defined by its most heinous act.

Next came Tulia in 2003. The tiny Panhandle town was infamous because forty-six people—thirty-nine of them Black—were sentenced to prison even though there was no evidence to back up a white rogue undercover agent who claimed he made drug buys from the defendants. I left thinking a community shouldn't be labeled racist because of one bad law enforcement officer.

I took my Redeem White America tour to Mississippi in 2004 for a nine-day driving trip because I thought it was too easy to scapegoat the state. I left thinking that its well-earned reputation for racial violence didn't minimize the same problems in other states.

The first time I wrote about race was in the third grade when we had some free time in class one afternoon. I wrote a one-page essay titled "Black People Are People Too." It was 1968, and I have no idea what prompted it or what I wrote. What compels an eight-year-old to write about race? What compels his fifty-nine-year-old self to write about race?

When I began writing a column for the *San Antonio Express-News* in 1994, I made a conscious decision to avoid race for as long as possible. I didn't want to be pigeonholed as a Black columnist, with whatever limitations that implied. That lasted through four columns. My ten-year-old nephew was wrestling with why his being a Black male scared white people. So I wrote "Life's Lessons on Being Black," a primer on what he should expect as he got older.

In my first go-round at the *Express-News*, I wrote more than 2,300 columns for the paper. The great majority weren't about race, although I did write about race more than the other columnists. I also wrote more about child abuse, nonviolence and Halle Berry than the other columnists. But no one ever accused me of writing too much about child abuse, nonviolence or Halle Berry.

Yet any column on race elicited complaints from some white readers that I "wrote too much about race" or "only about race." Though I wrote about race to inform and not to inflame, to build bridges and not walls, I was always ready for the slurs that filled my emails and voicemail. I now realize I wasted too much time defending myself.

Away from the newspaper, thinking about those trips to Jasper, Tulia and Mississippi, I realized I was playing defense for whites, doing my best to be honest and create necessary discomfort while making clear I don't believe that most white people are racist or more susceptible to prejudice than anyone else. I do think many casually accept that their encounters—or lack thereof—with race are the norm and nullify the experiences of those whose encounters with race aren't so infrequent or casual. As individuals and generations, we aren't responsible for our ancestors' actions, but we are obligated to understand the consequences, good and bad, of those actions. The more we can candidly discuss this, the better we shall be.

I should have written more columns about race, but I was cowered by the "you write too much about race" voices who never wanted to have a meaningful dialogue with me.

This will change. I don't like writing about race. It's exhausting and extracts psychological, mental and physical tolls. But this nation and its immense promise are worth it. The children in my life are worth it. I have new nephews growing up in a country where some will view them with baseless fear. I'll write more about race if it reduces the chances of my nephews and nieces being profiled, stalked and having a knee on their neck as they plead, "I can't breathe."

An Urgency to Complete
Juneteenth's Emancipation

Juneteenth has always been the celebration of an incomplete emancipation, of justice denied and a dream deferred.

It was, literally, freedom delayed. Two years, six months and eighteen days after President Abraham Lincoln's signing of the Emancipation Proclamation, Union general Gordon Granger sailed into Galveston Bay to read General Order No. 3, which freed Texas's two hundred thousand slaves.

Technically the proclamation only liberated slaves in Confederate states occupied by Union troops. But slaves took Lincoln's words as the keys to unlock their shackles and emancipated themselves. For them, whether it was January 1, 1863, or June 19, 1865, emancipation was Thanksgiving because they had at long last been delivered from bondage.

For newly freed Black Texans, General Order No. 3 was their Declaration of Independence and Juneteenth was their Fourth of July. From the beginning, Juneteenth was synonymous with family reunions. Slaves searched for those loved ones they had been separated from. Many of those families, their members sold to white families and plantations throughout the South, were never reunited.

As ex-slaves and their descendants left Texas and the South, they carried the traditions and celebration of Juneteenth across the nation. But Juneteenth is Texan; it's a time when families unite in big cities such as San Antonio, Houston and Dallas, as well as small towns such as Schulenburg, Luling and Gonzales.

Juneteenth 2020, like every American tradition this year, will be tentative and different, its participants searching how best to continue given the unique challenges of the day. Juneteenth 2020 is pulled between the social distancing and isolation demanded by COVID-19—and we are seeing more and more infections—and the social justice and togetherness inspired by the brutal killing of George Floyd.

The pandemic may be responsible for fewer reunions this year, but the protests arising from Floyd's death have created unprecedented opportunities for families to discuss and plan how they can respond to this historic moment. The overflowing joy delivered to slaves by news of their emancipation spilled over into more than 150 years of Juneteenths, celebrations of good times with eating and drinking, music and dancing, baseball and dominoes, and the repeating and bequeathing of family lore.

But the news of emancipation delivered to the slaves wasn't accompanied by any materials that would help them on their way. There was no compensation for the nearly 250 years of suffering, toil, dehumanizing and barbaric treatment, rape, broken families and death that came with building so much of the economic foundation of the United States of America.

Generations of working someone else's land from can't-see-in-the-morning until can't-see-at-night didn't earn the newly freed slaves a penny they could use toward buying land. Their former masters would be compensated for losing the commodity—the bodies and labor of Black men, women and children—but former slaves didn't even get forty acres and a mule to help them make the transition to freedom.

Little thought was given to how to begin to repair the damage slavery had inflicted on generations of Black people. But significant thought and action was given to how to replicate slavery's brutality and oppression and inflict it on future generations of Black people through Black codes, Jim Crow, the convict lease system, lynching, "white primaries," separate but unequal everything, redlining and voter suppression.

Every Juneteenth has been a celebration earned for freedom denied and delayed, earned by former slaves whose existence as property made a mockery of the promise and aspirations of the Constitution; earned by the slave's descendants, given nothing in constitutional rights that they didn't have to demand, struggle and die for.

Juneteenth 2020 finds us in a historic moment when there appears to be the will, energy and moral urgency to complete an unfinished emancipation by reckoning with our nation's past to correct the injustices still infecting us. This Juneteenth should be celebrated in joy but also with the fierce urgency of purpose.

How can we best use this moment, this movement and the spirit of George Floyd to finally prove Sam Cooke right—that "A Change Is Gonna Come"?

The Ways Black People
Must Discuss Race

I'm four years old. At morning's first light I hear a tapping on
the bedroom window. I peek through the blinds and see a man
wearing a white cowboy hat, a badge on his blue long-sleeve shirt
and a gun in a holster around his light tan slacks.

It's my father, and it's part of our morning ritual. He worked
the overnight shift as a Bexar County sheriff's deputy and for
some reason he didn't have a house key. Not wanting to wake my
grandmother and uncle, he tapped on the window as the signal
for me to wake my mother to open the door.

My father loved law enforcement. His career included being
the first Black investigator in the sheriff's office and a Drug Enforcement Agency agent.

The first anger I saw in him was when I told him a policeman
stopped me as I walked to high school one morning and asked if
he could look inside my brown lunch bag because there had been
a robbery on New Braunfels Avenue. I told him no. Fortunately
he didn't press the issue. My father was torn between pride that
I'd stood up for my rights, anger at the officer for stopping me
and fear that my refusal could have endangered my life.

So he had "the talk" with me that Black parents must have
with their children about interacting with police. White parents may have a talk with their children about being cooperative
with the police, but for Black parents the talk is a life-and-death
plea, because cooperation isn't always enough, and the wrong,

misunderstood move or a wallet mistaken for a gun could lead to injury or death.

Among the inequities in the United States is that of discourse on race, with the parameters of discussion set by the majority who assume that experiences not shared by them involving race are imagined or exaggerated. Conversations like "the talk" aren't a rite of passage for white families. Neither are conversations about the first time being called the "n-word" or explaining that word to a child.

In the days following the 1992 acquittal of the officers who beat Rodney King, which was caught on tape, I'd break into tears during the day. One morning while I was working out at the Barbara Jordan Center, I told that to Bill Blair, the center's executive director. Bill, a six-foot-six Air Force veteran and basketball star at Providence College who played with the Boston Celtics, said, "Man, the same thing's happening to me. I'll be driving, think about Rodney and start bawling."

We talked about why we were hurting, about race and our diminishing faith in our country to do right. That was a conversation being held by Black men and women around the country, but I doubt if it was a staple of discussion among white people.

It is the substance of those conversations, of pain more often swallowed than spoken, that Blacks have tried to share with whites. Not for pity, but in the hope that from this knowledge will spring acceptance of responsibility. Listening and acting on what you've heard can be profound, even redemptive, when it corrects an errant course. But you must hear and not assume.

"Black Lives Matter" is divisive if you want it to be. Responding with "All Lives Matter" misses the point. It's as if this were 1862 and an organization of runaway Black slaves calling themselves "Black Emancipation Matters" provoked people into saying "You Black slaves are racist! All Emancipation Matters!" Yeah, but the Black slaves aren't emancipated.

There is a heavy weariness, generation after generation, from trying to explain a problem to people who can help alleviate it. To not be heard and to repeat it again and again is like pushing a boulder up a mountain, only to have it repeatedly roll back on you. The crushing weight of George Floyd's death on this nation is the accumulated weight of generations of these boulders.

But something extraordinary is happening. Seeing Floyd's pleas ignored on video has made this nation seem to want to listen to the living, for now, at least. The hands lifting those boulders and rolling them, coast to coast, across America aren't just Black but white, brown, red and yellow. I can't help but feel the widening peaceful protests lifting me out of despair and rekindling embers of hope.

I don't want to be disappointed by the protests stopping with nothing to show but sore feet and scattered boulders. Out in the streets they're singing the aspirational "We Shall Overcome" as they did at the March on Washington in 1963. I want us to finally get beyond the overcoming and to celebrate with another song from that day, "How I Got Over." I want George Floyd to be the reason we finally got over, and I want Mahalia Jackson holding George as she sings.

This Generation's Emmett Till Moment

The saddest and most enduring whistle in the history of the United States was pushed through the lips of a fourteen-year-old boy from up north who was unschooled in the ways of the South and didn't know how deadly it could be.

Years after those lips had been broken and silenced, the whistle from the Delta would be heard on dark lonely roads and in the nightmares of African American children and adults. The whistle would be a sibilant call to a slowly mobilizing young movement, and it would be heard in Montgomery, Birmingham, Selma and across the nation.

Rosa Parks would hear it and remain seated on a bus. In Louisville a thirteen-year-old who would change his name to Muhammad Ali, shocked after seeing a picture of the boy's corpse, derailed a diesel engine from the railroad tracks.

On August 24, 1955, a Chicago teenager named Emmett Till, visiting relatives in Money, Mississippi, went into Bryant's Grocery and Meat and may have whistled at Carolyn Bryant, who also claimed he grabbed her around the waist and used profanity.

On the night of August 28, her husband, Roy Bryant, and brother-in-law, J. W. Milam, kidnapped, beat and tortured Till for hours before shooting him and dumping his body in the Tallahatchie River with a seventy-five-pound cotton gin fan tied around his neck with barbed wire. Bryant and Milam were acquitted but later confessed to the murder in interviews they were paid for. A few years ago Carolyn Bryant confessed to lying about Till grabbing her.

The boy's lynching was a transformative event in what would become the civil rights movement, one to which the killing of George Floyd and the protests it inspired have been compared. It's the visuals of both deaths that heightened their horror, captured the barbaric injustice and magnified their impact on the country. For Floyd, it was watching his death over eight minutes and forty-six seconds. For Till, it was the photo.

Emmett Till's mother, Mamie Till-Mobley, wanted the world to see what "they" had done to her son, so she opened the casket for mourners and for *Jet* magazine to photograph. The famously gruesome picture in the Black newsweekly showed what was a fourteen-year-old boy in a casket, but he had been beaten so horribly that he looked like a monster. It is a picture seared into the minds of African Americans. Told to give up her seat on a Montgomery bus, Rosa Parks said she thought of Till and remained seated.

But the Emmett Till generation of African Americans, his peers who became the vanguard of the civil rights movement, were traumatized by his murder. Ali said, "I realized that this could just as easily been a story about me or my brother." In *Walking with the Wind: A Memoir of the Movement*, civil rights leader and US representative John Lewis wrote that Till's murder left him "shaken to the core."

In 2011, on the fiftieth anniversary of the integrated bus rides that challenged segregated bus terminals, freedom riders gathered in Money, Mississippi, to pay homage to Till. One of them, Joyce Ladner, said, "Nothing frightened me more and others of my generation than when Emmett Till was killed. I was twelve years old at the time and remember seeing the picture of his bloated body in *Jet* magazine. Everyone I knew in SNCC [the

Student Nonviolent Coordinating Committee] was galvanized by it. We're the Emmett Till generation."

Before Till, racial violence against African Americans in the South was covered exclusively by the Black press. The trial of Bryant and Milam was the first such racial crime to attract the national white press. The impact of Till's death on the civil rights movement and his generation is undeniable, which makes it even more remarkable to say it doesn't come close to the immediate impact of George Floyd's death. The key word is "immediate."

After the successful Montgomery bus boycott, the civil rights movement lost some energy before building momentum through the lunch counter sit-ins in 1960, the freedom rides in 1961, the Birmingham campaign in 1963, Mississippi Freedom Summer in 1964 and the Selma campaign in 1965, leading to the Civil Rights Act of 1964 and the Voting Rights Act of 1965.

We don't know how long the George Floyd movement will last or what the full range of its impact will be. But never in our history have protests arisen so quickly, been sustained for this long and so quickly shifted the mindset and culture of the nation and even the world.

Emmett Till's whistle was a haunting clarion call to one generation. George Floyd's last breaths are inspiring a new generation.

An Overdue Retirement of Racially Stereotyped Brands

In one of my old notebooks is an idea for a sketch I never wrote, about the nighttime airing of racial grievances in the kitchen pantry between Aunt Jemima, Uncle Ben and Rastus, the Black chef on the Cream of Wheat box. In the conversations I imagined, they'd complain about being used as mascots to sell food and make money for others. Their smiling masks of accommodation would fall as they lit into white people and said the things that Black folk, in the era they represented, would say behind the safety of closed doors.

I didn't imagine conversations between the Quaker Oats man, Little Debbie and Betty Crocker because they weren't being used to stereotype a group of people. I never included Mrs. Butterworth in those conversations because, despite the coloring of Mrs. Butterworth's syrup, I assumed she was white.

But whether she was white, Black or passing, Mrs. Butterworth will soon be joining Aunt Jemima, Uncle Ben and Rastus in retirement. Racially stereotyped brands, which have endured more than a hundred years of complaints, are crumbling after three weeks of cultural ground shifting caused by the killing of George Floyd.

Floyd's death, the mass protests it has sparked and the demands for specific policies to address the nation's wide-ranging inequities appear far more important than the images of fictional characters on food packaging. But this is about more than pancakes and rice.

Images are chosen for reasons, among them to uplift and affirm, or dehumanize and demoralize. Many of the racist and stereotypical images of African Americans are rooted in the aftermath of Reconstruction, that brief post–Civil War period when African Americans, many of them former slaves, expanded the nation's democracy by their participation as voters and officeholders, and by establishing free education for Black as well as white children. In *Stony the Road: Reconstruction, White Supremacy, and the Rise of Jim Crow*, Henry Louis Gates Jr. writes of post-Reconstruction that "it was in this period that white supremacist ideology, especially as it was transmuted into powerful new forms of media, poisoned the American imagination in ways that have long outlasted the circumstances of its origin."

These images, meant to allay white fears about former slaves, portrayed Black people as dumb, inarticulate, lazy, happy-go-lucky and grateful for their lot in life. Aunt Jemima was a minstrel show depiction of a "mammy" from a slave plantation. Uncle Ben was the kind, genial old Black man always there to "yes, sir" and "yes, ma'am" to white people.

Rastus? Well, an ad from the early twentieth century featured Rastus holding a sign reading "Maybe Cream of Wheat ain't got no vitamins. I don't know what them things is. If theys bugs they ain't none in Cream of Wheat but she's sho' good to eat and cheap. Costs bout 1 cent fo' a great dish. Rastus." No racism there.

Images like these are meant to demean and to instill inferiority.

The first time I remember feeling embarrassed about being Black—and I'm a light-skinned brother—was in third or fourth grade while reading, along with my classmates, *The Story of Little Black Sambo*. I still feel uncomfortable thinking about it—Sambo being chased by tigers until they turned into butter and his mother used the butter to make pancakes. What the hell is it about pancakes and racist images?

These images are so insidious that around the same time I was feeling uncomfortable about Little Black Sambo, I had a Frito Bandito eraser on my pencil and knew every lyric of his Frito Lay corn chips jingle, which was to the tune of the beautiful Mexican song "Cielito Lindo." It wasn't until I was an adult that I realized how racist the character was and how it may have made some of my Mexican American classmates feel the way Little Black Sambo made me feel. I'm embarrassed that whenever I hear "Cielito Lindo," to this day, for a couple of seconds I think of the commercial.

Retiring images such as Aunt Jemima, Uncle Ben, Rastus and the Land O'Lakes Native American woman is important, but it's easy lifting for these corporations. They're removing problems they're responsible for. What more will they do, and what took them so long?

Johnson & Johnson announced that Band-Aids will now be made in dark skin tones to recognize Blacks and Latinos. It took George Floyd getting killed for them to do this?

What Is Heritage if Not Truth to History?

A few years ago I attended a meeting of the San Antonio chapter of the Sons of Confederate Veterans, an organization I am eligible to belong to (though I don't) through an ancestor's service to the Confederacy, an ancestor who would later be killed by Wild Bill Hickok.

I was the only one at the meeting who would also be eligible to join the Sons of Slaves Who Would Remain Slaves Had the Confederates Won, if such an organization existed. Despite this, everyone was wonderful, and, at meeting's end, a very nice woman approached me and said, almost apologetically, "For these guys, it's about heritage."

She was speaking not just about the local chapter but of all the Confederacy's devotees. I told her I understood. How could I not when "heritage," more than any other word, is used to defend the Confederacy, deny the Civil War was fought over slavery and justify Confederate monuments?

These monuments are now coming down for the same reason they went up. They represent the degradation of Black lives. They glorify the defense of an institution in which the value of Black bodies wasn't in their shared humanity with whites but in their labor and what they could be sold for on the auction block.

In recent speeches, President Donald Trump has said bringing down Confederate monuments is an assault on "our heritage." Some see their heritage in a lost cause on a battlefield between 1860 and 1865.

Others see their heritage in a bill of sale dated September 1, 1837. Written out by Nathaniel Hunt Greer, it reads, in part, "have this day bargained, sold and delivered unto Philip Coe a certain Negro girl by the name of Louisa for the sum of eight hundred dollars, the payment of which is hereby acknowledged and the right and title of said Negro." Philip Haddox Coe was my great-great-great-grandfather. That "certain Negro girl by the name of Louisa" was my great-great-great-grandmother. This was a heritage that was "bargained" and "delivered." For $800 my white great-great-great-grandfather purchased "the right and title" to own and rape my Black great-great-great-grandmother. She would give birth to three of his children in Gonzales. The middle child was Dan, my great-great-grandfather.

In 1852 Coe was shot while playing poker in a saloon. Before he died eight days later, he wrote out his will, portioning out to his wife and twelve children his estate, which included stock, racehorses and slaves. To his daughter Rachel he bequeathed twenty-one-month-old Dan, her half-brother.

In defense of the Confederacy, the word "heritage" is romanticized. But its literal definition is property that is or may be inherited. Even if the property you inherit is your little brother. Dan was fourteen when the Civil War ended, and I've long wondered about the work he had to do for his sister and at what age he started.

One of Coe's white sons was also named Phil Coe, and his claim to fame is that in 1871, in Abilene, Kansas, he became the last known man killed in a gunfight by Hickok. There once was a wax museum in Grand Prairie that depicted Hickok shooting Coe. When I visited it as a kid, my grandfather pointed and said, "That was your great-great-uncle."

The information thrilled me. "Really! Wild Bill Hickok was my uncle?"

"No," my grandfather said. "The man getting shot is your uncle."

What Is Heritage if Not Truth to History?

My grandfather was dark-skinned, but I didn't think about how that white man could be my great-great-uncle and his uncle. Family history and the horrible implications would be filled in later. To put it simply: Phil Coe, a white man, fought for the Confederacy so that his Black half-brother, Dan, could remain the property of his sister.

Two years ago, through the lens of my family's history, I wrote a piece for the *Texas Observer* about a plaque, since removed, that had hung in the Texas Capitol since 1959. Placed there by the Children of the Confederacy, it pledged to "study and teach the truths of history (one of the most important of which is that the war between the states was not a rebellion, nor was its underlying cause to sustain slavery)."

This was a lie. Sustaining slavery was the reason for the Civil War. Yet in 2020 defenders of the Confederacy continue to deny what the creators of the Confederacy admitted in 1861 and 1862: slavery was the reason they were seceding. In his farewell speech to the US Senate, Jefferson Davis, future president of the Confederacy, said:

> Had the Declaration announced that the negroes were free and equal, how was the Prince to be arraigned for stirring up insurrection among them? And how was this to be enumerated among the high crimes which caused the colonies to sever their connection with the mother country? When our Constitution was formed, the same idea was rendered more palpable, for there we find provision made for that very class of persons as property; they were not put upon the footing of equality with white men—not even upon that of paupers and convicts; but, so far as representation was concerned, were discriminated against as a lower caste, only to be represented in the numerical proportion of three fifths.

In his "cornerstone speech," Alexander Stephens, the Confederacy's vice president, said: "Our new government is founded upon exactly the opposite idea; its foundations are laid, its cornerstone rests, upon the great truth that the negro is not equal to the white man; that slavery subordination to the superior race is his natural and normal condition. This, our new government, is the first, in the history of the world, based upon this great physical, philosophical, and moral truth."

Declarations of secession by states that made up the Confederacy specifically mentioned slavery. The Texas declaration read,

> She was received as a commonwealth, holding, maintaining and protecting the institution known as negro slavery— the servitude of the African to the white race within her limits—a relation that had existed from the first settlement of her wilderness by the white race, and which her people intended should exist in all future time. Her institutions and geographical position established the strongest ties between her and other slave-holding States of the confederacy.

Isn't being true to history part of respecting heritage? Shouldn't Confederate defenders who speak so often and passionately about heritage believe the words of Davis, Stephens and the men who wrote the declarations of secession? These are men whose heritage they celebrate and who told us in real time of their belief in white supremacy and Black inferiority, and that the preservation of slavery was why they were seceding from the Union.

The denial of slavery as the primary reason for secession and the Civil War will be more difficult in this new reckoning of history, a period in which a statue of Robert E. Lee is coming down in Richmond, Virginia; military bases named after Confederate generals, including Fort Hood in Killeen, may change their names; and NASCAR has banned Confederate flags.

Most of the Confederate monuments didn't spring up until decades after the Civil War. As a Southern Poverty Law Center report in 2016 showed, there was an accelerated rise in these monuments during two periods in history—in the early 1900s when states were enacting Jim Crow laws against Black people, and in the mid-twentieth century during the civil rights movement.

At one time nearly two thousand Confederate monuments stood across the United States, including one of a Confederate soldier in Travis Park erected in 1900 and removed in 2017. These were monuments to men who took up arms against the United States. In what other conflict would enemy combatants against our government, be they American or foreign, be honored with statues?

We're repeatedly told that removing these statues is an erasure of history, but the truth is they were raised to distort history and perpetuate myths. We're living in a time when more Americans—specifically, white Americans—seem open to learning more of their nation's history and the experiences unique to some of their fellow citizens.

At the heart of that history is slavery, which in generations of school textbooks was briefly described as a bad thing done to Black people. But a war was fought, the bad thing ended and everyone lived happily and equally ever after.

Slavery was an institution that lasted nearly 250 years in the United States. It was critical to the founding, governing and economic development of our nation and the legacy it bequeaths to future generations. Historically, throughout the world, slavery wasn't driven by racism, but it lasted so long in our country that eventually racism was used to justify it.

Emancipation and the Thirteenth Amendment ended slavery

but not racism. In her essay "The Slavebody and the Blackbody," Toni Morrison writes,

> In this racism, the slavebody disappears but the blackbody remains and is morphed into a synonym for poor people, a synonym for criminalism and a flash point for public policy. For there is no discourse in economics, in education, in housing, in religion, in health care, in entertainment, in the criminal justice system, in welfare, in labor policy— in almost any of the national debates that continue to baffle us—in which the blackbody is not the elephant in the room; the ghost in the machine; the subject, if not the topic, of the negotiations.

The Civil War wasn't simply a national metaphor of brother fighting against brother. In my family, it was brother fighting to keep brother enslaved. Phil took up arms to keep Dan in chains.

Most of the men fighting for the Confederacy didn't own slaves, and many were poor. But had they prevailed, all slaves would have remained slaves. The Confederate monuments commemorating them are symbols of slavery and the racism justifying slavery. That doesn't mean that people passionate about honoring their ancestors who do not want to see the monuments come down are racists or bad people. I've interacted with enough to know that some are, but many are not.

It hasn't crossed their minds that when they talk about heritage and put "Sons" and "Daughters" and "Children" in the names of pro-Confederacy organizations, they're not thinking about the heritage of those sons, daughters and children of the Confederacy who were Black and enslaved. Through bloodlines, I'm a son of the Confederacy and a son of slavery, but it's my white heritage they have in mind, not my Black heritage. They want to celebrate my great-great-uncle for fighting in the Civil War, but they don't want to consider the consequences for my great-great-grandfather had the Confederates been victorious. My great-great-grandfather who, along with his two siblings, were conceived in violence because their father owned the right and title to the body of their mother.

Where is the statue that honors the heritage of my great-great-great-grandmother, "a certain Negro girl named Louisa"?

The Goodness inside Elf Louise

As a child, Louise Locker found magic in the flight of birds, the picking of four-leaf clovers, the smell of freshly mowed grass and the twinkling of stars as her mother told stories about the constellations.

Her mother, Anne Locker, taught her to see magic in everything, whether it was Christmas, which they'd prepare for by making homemade decorations, or people. When she was seven and in the grocery store with her mother, Louise would sneak away to wander down the aisles and say hello to everyone. People smiled, waved back and talked with her.

"Can you imagine if everybody knew the potential for goodness inside of them and they acted upon it, how different the world would be?" she'd tell her mother.

That faith in strangers became the foundation for the Elf Louise Christmas Project, which she created to deliver Christmas gifts to children who otherwise wouldn't receive any. It was a faith fulfilled through people who found the goodness within themselves to make it possible for 1.5 million San Antonio children to receive gifts for fifty years.

That sense of magic and faith in people Locker had at seven is stronger now that she's seventy and eager to pursue "new and soulful callings." So the woman whose name is synonymous with Christmas in San Antonio is stepping away from the nationally known organization that bears her name. In a letter sent Friday afternoon, July 17, 2020, to the Elf Louise board of directors, volunteers and supporters, Locker announced her retirement.

A breast cancer survivor, she wants to be clear that her health is not the reason for her retirement. She's in good health, and it's the good health of the Elf Louise Christmas Project, with its five thousand volunteers, that makes this the right time. "This project is in such good hands," she said. "So many people have made it their own. I'm excited by the next important thing I need to be doing. There's other things I need to do. Some I know. Some I don't."

A licensed therapist, Locker said her counseling has taken on deeper importance and urgency these days. Besides enjoying being a grandmother, she's writing a memoir and working on other projects, all inspired by looking for the good in people, because "everybody's got this potential."

The origins of Elf Louise are San Antonio lore. A few days before Christmas 1969 Locker, who was a Trinity University student at the time, was inspired by watching late-night talk show host Johnny Carson read children's letters to Santa. She went to the post office and asked to see letters to Santa there and read through hundreds before finding this one:

Dear Santa,

I know the only reason you've never visited me before is because we've never written. Won't you please visit us? We've never had a Christmas tree. Please bring us a tree, a doll, some toy cars for my brothers and bring mom a bible and please don't get lost.

Anna

Virginia O'Hanlon, who inspired the famous "Yes, Virginia, There Is a Santa Claus" newspaper editorial in 1897, was a child needing reassurance of Santa's existence. Anna was a child needing to reassure Santa of her existence. Locker chose Anna's letter and twelve others representing sixty-five children and two hundred requests for presents. She and her mother gathered items from around their house to give, and she secured help from friends and strangers she approached in Earl Abel's restaurant.

Media personality and Ticket 760 sports talk host Chris Duel has been friends with Locker since working on the Elf Louise Radiothon on 1200 WOAI in the mid-1990s. "I remember being struck by her infectious positive spirit and the way she lights up a room when she walks in," Duel said. "She represents the best each of us can be."

In the early years Locker tried to be anonymous. A newspaper reporter dubbed her "Elf Louise." She's now one of the city's most iconic figures, used to adults telling her she came to their houses when they were children.

In 2018 I drove her to Port San Antonio where volunteers came to collect the toys they would later deliver. She wanted to hear stories without anyone knowing who she was. But while she was talking to members of Guardians of the Children, a motorcycle club protecting victims of child abuse, a passerby shouted out her name.

"You're Elf Louise?" the biker she was talking to said. "The Elf Louise?"

When Locker smiled and nodded, all of the bikers wanted their pictures taken with her. It was like that all morning.

For more than fifty years she's used the magic of Christmas to remind us of our capacity to do good. Christmas isn't going anywhere, and neither is Elf Louise. She'll be using other forms of magic to discover, in her words, "Whose heart is open? Whose heart is touched?"

Is This Moment When We Bend the Arc?

"The great majority of Americans are uneasy with injustice but unwilling to pay a significant price to eradicate it," Martin Luther King Jr. wrote in his last book, *Where Do We Go from Here: Chaos or Community?*

We are in a moment that may be evolving into a movement, an inflection point in our nation's history that may be historic. In the time of an unprecedented pandemic that has taken the lives of more than a hundred thousand Americans in four months, an unprecedented wave of marches over the death of one man is spreading across the nation. We have been delivered here by the death of George Floyd, pinned under the knee of a Minneapolis police officer now charged with murder. But why George Floyd? Why now?

For generations African Americans have protested unfair and brutal treatment by law enforcement and the criminal justice system. The list of names of unarmed Black men, women and children killed by police and vigilantes is long. Floyd isn't the first Black man whose unjust death in the custody of police was captured on video, so why has he captured the sustained outrage of millions of people around the world?

One reason may be that his death didn't happen in the flash of a gunshot but over nine deliberate minutes after he'd begged for his life. Even after Floyd was no longer responsive and another officer said he couldn't find a pulse, Officer Derek Chauvin, cool, casual and seemingly unconcerned, continued kneeling on him.

The philosopher Hannah Arendt coined the phrase the "banality of evil" in writing about Nazi war criminal Adolf Eichmann, whom she didn't find monstrous but ordinary and "terrifyingly normal." For African Americans, racism isn't always the monstrous face of a Klansman or Bull Connor sicking dogs on Black marchers in Birmingham, Alabama. It's more often the cool, casual and unconcerned demeanor of a Derek Chauvin unable to acknowledge the damage being done by his knee to the neck.

In *Where Do We Go from Here?*, King also wrote: "Whites, it must frankly be said, are not putting in a similar mass effort to reeducate themselves out of their racial ignorance. It is an aspect of their sense of superiority that the white people of America believe they have so little to learn."

Slavery is the original sin of the United States, but redemption begins only with acknowledging the racism that justified the "peculiar institution" and infected all American institutions to this day. For millions of Americans, racism isn't a fictional crutch excusing failures but a real chokehold on opportunities.

For whatever reasons, the death of George Floyd has moved many white Americans into acknowledging the burden and despair African Americans carry and, importantly, understanding that using one's experiences as the reference point to judge others' experiences isn't a pathway to understanding. Never has the death of one person stirred the conscience of this nation and mobilized so many into daily, nonviolent, multiracial and multigenerational protests.

But if this inflection point is to rise and not dip, if we are to have community and not chaos, the protests must be transformed into policies correcting the inequities of institutional racism. This could range from bail reform to address the inequities of cash bail, to closing our ongoing digital divide, to requiring warnings before police officers shoot and reporting any time officers brandish their weapons. The policies are almost endless because our long-standing inequalities are so entrenched and pervasive.

If there's truth to the saying that the arc of the moral universe is long but bends toward justice, in this moment the arc is in our hands to bend in the direction we choose.

A Man as Saintly as Humanly Possible

On the night of April 4, 1968, John Lewis was in Indianapolis, working on Senator Robert F. Kennedy's presidential campaign, when Martin Luther King Jr. was assassinated in Memphis.

Lewis listened as Kennedy, standing atop a flatbed truck, broke the news of King's murder to a predominantly Black audience. It was a remarkable and moving extemporaneous speech that sent the crowd home in stunned and peaceful silence as other cities erupted in violence.

"I was thinking," Lewis told me in a 2008 interview, "maybe Dr. King was gone, but we still had Bobby Kennedy." Kennedy was assassinated two months after King.

Lewis had said something similar in articles I'd read. Over the years, whenever a veteran of the civil rights movement passed away—Coretta Scott King, Fred Shuttlesworth, Dorothy Cotton, Joseph Lowery—Lewis's comment would come to mind, and I'd think, "We still have John Lewis." We also had, and still do, the likes of Andrew Young, Diane Nash and Bob Moses.

On the afternoon of July 17, 2020, after reading that another civil rights movement giant, C. T. Vivian, had died that day, I thought, again, "We still have John Lewis." Until we didn't, when Lewis died later that night.

He was eighty, a remarkable age for a man so often photographed beaten, bruised, bandaged and brought into custody.

Find another person whose abuse at the hands of mobs and the billy clubs of police is as prolifically documented on film.

Find another American whose wounds and public suffering from Nashville, Tennessee; Birmingham, Alabama; Rock Hill, South Carolina; and Selma, Alabama mirror the datelines of a movement struggling to correct a nation's sins. His redemptive suffering was so often on display because his belief in the ideals this nation professed was stronger than his fear of losing his life trying to make the nation live by them.

Reflecting on King, his mentor, and Kennedy, his hope for the nation, Lewis said, "Something died in us in 1968 with the deaths of these two young men. We'll never get over it. If they'd lived, this country would be much further down the road toward what Dr. King called the Beloved Community and toward a truly interracial democracy." And yet we're farther down the road because Lewis lived to model for us the behavior needed to create the Beloved Community and interracial democracy.

Before that 2008 interview, I'd met Lewis twice. The second time was at the 2001 San Antonio Martin Luther King Jr. March when I introduced him as the keynote speaker. The first time was in August 1984 when four other interns and I from the Martin Luther King Jr. Center for Nonviolent Social Change gathered at his home with Lewis and his wife, Lillian, a woman as gracious and inspiring as her husband.

At the time Lewis was an Atlanta city councilman, two years from being elected to Congress. I knew about him, but I didn't know of him. I don't recall much about that night's conversation, but I do remember leaving his house believing he was unlike anyone I'd met.

I've been in the presence, and have known well, people who radiate goodness and live on a higher spiritual plane. Lewis is the only person I've encountered with whom I felt I was in the presence of a saint. For years I've privately referred to him as a saint. I would hesitate to publicly call him that but for hearing historian Jon Meacham, who has a book on Lewis coming out in October, also use the "s" word.

Lewis wasn't charismatic or mellifluous, although he was a riveting and moving orator. His power was in his being, his moral presence, and the grace and love he exuded. To call him a saint or saintly isn't to hail him as perfect and deny his flaws (all saints were flawed), but it's to recognize his uncommon decency and his extraordinary capacity for forgiveness and forbearance.

Lewis practiced humanity better than most of us. He embodied King's definition of nonviolence as love in action, a love for humanity so strong that it refused to cooperate with any form of hatred, violence or indignity that scarred lives and souls and separated people from justice. To honor Lewis is to continue his march toward bridging the gap between this nation's aspirations of what it can be and what it is.

What Lewis said of King can be said of him: "He taught us how to love, he taught us nonviolence. He liberated a nation and is one of the founding fathers of the new America. He started us on the journey toward reconciliation. We're still on that journey."

Unease on Both Sides

It was 11 p.m. I was getting ready for bed when there was a hard knock on my door. Family and neighbors know never to knock like that. Peeking out the bedroom window, I saw a San Antonio police officer on my porch and two units on the side of the street.

I opened the door, leaving it open as I stepped outside; I wondered if that was aggressive. A bespectacled officer on the porch was joined by another one. Both were white, and from the time I opened the door and we saw each other, I felt as if the three of us shared a wariness greater than the typical unease when police question a citizen; we shared an unspoken acknowledgment of the history of such encounters, our present moment in history and whether we could trust each other not to contribute to that history. At least, that's what I was feeling.

The officer wearing glasses was genial and said they were looking for a sixteen-year-old runaway. He gave her name and described her. I told them I didn't know her. All true, but I felt guilty as I told them this, felt that I must sound, to them, like someone who wasn't telling the truth. I wasn't terribly nervous, but I was also surprised at how nervous I felt.

"Is there anyone else in there?" asked the other officer, who was a little more intense but polite. Both were looking over my shoulder into my house.

"No, sir," I said.

He gave the name of another woman, asking if I knew her. It

was the grandmother of the teen, and my address was supposed to be where she lived. I told them I didn't know her either.

"They probably got the address wrong," the officer with glasses said, as the other one went to his car to check. Both were wearing masks and social distancing, and I realized I didn't have my mask on.

I started patting my pockets. It wasn't a quick move but one that, as I made it, I knew was a mistake. The officer on the porch didn't flinch, and I told him I'd left my mask in the house.

He nodded and repeated, "Yeah, they probably got the wrong address."

His easygoing and non-accusatory manner put me at ease, so much so that I sat on my porch rail with my right leg stretched out, my back against the house. I wasn't so much at ease, though, as to not give him a brief history of the house, a history that wasn't necessary and which he wasn't interested in. I felt compelled to let him know no one they were looking for had lived there.

The other officer came back and said something to him.

"Yeah, they butchered the address," the bespectacled officer said. "It's way on the other side. We apologize to you, sir."

"Not your fault," I said. "Glad this worked out okay."

"Can I have your name to show that we talked to you?" he asked, pulling out a notebook.

I gave him my name.

"Oh," he said, writing it down. "Well, Mr. Clack, again, sorry for the inconvenience."

They went to their vehicles. As the bespectacled officer drove away, he again apologized. I told them to be safe.

I immediately began thinking of scenarios where their coming to the wrong address, my house, could have gone wrong, how the slightest movement or misunderstanding could have produced a different outcome. What if I'd taken Ambien and when the officer knocked I'd stumbled to the door foggy-headed and confused? Had I been driving, I wouldn't have been so careless as to reach for my pockets. I would have placed my hands over the steering wheel.

Last year when I was driving home one night, I pulled into my driveway and a car suddenly appeared behind me with red and blue lights flashing. I put my keys and cell phone on the passenger seat so I could get out of the car empty-handed. I wasn't sure if I was supposed to exit my car at my house, but I did.

It was a Department of Public Safety officer. He had followed me for a few blocks, and he said I had a brake light out. He shone his flashlight into my car and then onto my house when I told him I lived there. He was cordial but, I later learned, my brake lights were fine.

The officers at my door were professional, polite and respectful. Still, I wish I didn't have to reevaluate my actions after every encounter with the police so I don't make mistakes the next time.

I hope the officers found the sixteen-year-old runaway and she's working things out with her grandmother.

The American President Who Stood Two Feet Tall

In the 1962 *Twilight Zone* episode "Four O'Clock," a self-absorbed, obsessive and harshly critical man, living in his apartment, sees the world as a grand conspiracy involving all kinds of subversives and murderers. He plans to expose and punish all of the world's evil people. The source and accuracy of his moral certitude, and his right to cast judgment and retribution on anyone, is never established. It also happens that these evil people include just about everyone in the world except him.

In the episode's beginning Rod Serling, the *Twilight Zone*'s creator and narrator, says, "That's Oliver Crangle, a dealer in petulance and poison." He proceeds to talk about Crangle's "metamorphosis from a twisted fanatic, poisoned by the gangrene of hate, to the status of an avenging angel, upright and omniscient, dedicated and fearsome."

Crangle is a man of no empathy who's always threatening and hectoring. He calls and writes employers of these evil people, people he doesn't know, demanding that they be fired. He calls on law enforcement to arrest them. He lacks the ability for self-reflection. He's a man who gazes into the mirror and sees his innocence but gazes out his window to see the guilt of millions. For Crangle, the fault isn't in the stars or with him but with everyone else. The beams in his eyes don't keep him from seeing the countless motes in the eyes of his fellow human beings.

He contacts the FBI to tell them that at 4 p.m. the world's

evil people will be marked and easily identifiable for arrest because he will shrink them to two feet tall. Out of his mind with anticipation, when the hour arrives he attempts to look out the window to rejoice but struggles to find it. He himself has been shrunk to two feet tall.

For four years Oliver Crangle has been president of the United States, seeing conspirators seeking to undermine him everywhere and viewing all who don't support him and say not-so-nice things about him as evil people who are liars deserving to be investigated, locked up and not allowed to vote by mail.

No one in this land of 330 million Americans so lustfully enjoys the daily and incessant routine of mocking, insulting, threatening and expressing contempt for fellow Americans as President Donald Trump, who never treats tyrants such as Vladimir Putin, Kim Jong Un, Recep Erdoğan and Rodrigo Duterte with anything other than fawning respect. No American has used so many words to make so many Americans feel two feet tall.

That I'd be critical of Trump and not vote for him isn't a surprise. My politics are left of center, pragmatic, not ideological. Of course I oppose policies like separating families at the border, attempting to gut the Affordable Care Act and depriving millions of Americans of health insurance, including those with preexisting conditions. But my objections to the man are based more on his character, sheer absence of decency and inability to respect anyone not kissing up—be they prisoners of war, Gold Star parents, Black athletes, Black female reporters, female reporters of any ethnicity, John Lewis, health care workers fighting on the front lines of a battle with COVID-19 (which he abdicated), the US Postal Service . . .

He became the leading proponent of the racist birther conspiracy that Barack Obama wasn't born in this country, and he has tried to replicate that with California senator Kamala Harris.

He will connect any looting to Black Lives Matter even when there's no connection.

I believe he's a bad man, and that has nothing to do with his party. He was the same man when he was a Democrat. It's telling that his most consistently incisive critics have been conservatives such as George Will, Jennifer Rubin, Bill Kristol, Steve Schmidt, David Frum and Mona Charen.

The breakout star of last week's Democratic National Convention was thirteen-year-old Brayden Harrington, a stutterer who was helped by Democratic presidential nominee Joe Biden, himself a stutterer. Courageously, Brayden spoke to the nation Thursday night.

For me, the defining image of the 2016 campaign was Trump's mocking of a disabled *New York Times* reporter, an act of cruelty he played for laughs in front of an audience. Trump likes to portray himself as tough and strong, but mocking the vulnerable isn't tough. Treating people with respect doesn't have an ideological bent. Decency isn't partisan.

When we lift others up with our words, we grow in stature. When we attempt to cut them down with words, we diminish ourselves.

That's why there are windows this president will never see out of.

Black Athletes Again Call for Justice

In 1968 Martin Luther King Jr. and Muhammad Ali were the two most famous Black men in America—and two of the most despised people in the country.

King's nonviolent protests for civil rights had grown wearisome to people, especially since he had expanded his focus to include poverty and the Vietnam War. Ali's refusal to be inducted into the US Army to fight in the Vietnam War cost him his heavyweight championship belt and the peak years of his livelihood while earning him the most intense hatred ever experienced by an American athlete, a hatred that was deepened by his being a Black Muslim.

Today King's birthday is a national holiday and Ali is arguably the most revered athlete in history. At the time of his death in 2016, he was as beloved as anyone in the nation. Visionaries and prophets aren't always appreciated in their times. Sometimes it's not until they're dead, silent, and less threatening that they become popular, easy to embrace, and hailed as heroes deserving of emulation. Until someone emulates them.

On Wednesday afternoon, moved by the close-range shooting of a Black man seven times in the back by a police officer in Kenosha, Wisconsin, the Milwaukee Bucks refused to take the court for their NBA playoff game against the Orlando Magic. The Bucks' surprise strike on August 26, 2020, inspired two days unlike any seen in American sports as more teams in the NBA, Major League Baseball, WNBA, and National Hockey

League voted not to play or had their games postponed by their leagues. Players on several National Football League teams, now in training camp, voted not to practice.

We are in an era of unprecedented social and political consciousness among athletes, especially Black athletes who no longer will "just shut up and dribble." Their awareness of the power they possess through celebrity, wealth, the profits they generate and the platform they have emboldens them to speak out against injustices and racism in the United States, to talk candidly and painfully about their experiences as Black men and women in a nation that they love but that, as Los Angeles Clippers head coach Doc Rivers powerfully said, "doesn't love us back."

Rivers was just one of at least four prominent sports figures, including former NBA stars Robert Horry and Chris Webber and New York Mets first baseman Dominic Smith, who publicly got emotional last week speaking about their experiences.

The Bucks' action came on the fourth anniversary of San Francisco 49ers quarterback Colin Kaepernick kneeling for the first time during the national anthem to protest the killings of Black people by police. Kaepernick and his supporters repeatedly explained that he wasn't protesting the military, the flag or all police officers, but his critics insisted that's what he was doing.

How arrogant are you that when someone tells you why they're protesting, you tell them they're wrong? And it's arrogant to tell athletes that they shouldn't protest but should be grateful for their lifestyles. Never mind the heaviness you feel over Ahmaud, Breonna, George and Jacob, go out there and entertain us.

Presidential son-in-law Jared Kushner, a man born and married into wealth, gave snarky voice to the "just shut up and dribble chorus," saying, "Look, I think that the NBA players are very fortunate that they have the financial position where they're able to take a night off from work without having to have the consequences to themselves financially."

America has never been comfortable with Black (or white) athletes nonviolently protesting the nation's racism or challenging the status quo, whether it was Ali, Bill Russell, Curt Flood, Tommie Smith and John Carlos, WNBA players or Kaepernick. Then again, America has never been comfortable with any nonviolent protests that force it to acknowledge and correct wrongs. In 2016 the *Washington Post* reviewed polling data from the civil rights era and found that 57 percent of Americans believed demonstrations such as the lunch counter sit-ins and the freedom rides would hurt Blacks' cause for civil rights. In the days leading up to the March on Washington, where King delivered his "I Have a Dream" speech, 60 percent of Americans thought it was a bad idea.

Many people who say they admire King would admire him much less were he alive and doing his thing today, making them uncomfortable with his demonstrations and forcing them to think about things they'd rather not.

King isn't alive to do his thing, and neither is Ali. But we are amid a generation of young athletes who want to change their nation for the better. They're not doing it through rioting, vandalism or crossing state lines with an AR-15 to kill protesters. They're doing it through nonviolence.

For those who disagree, what would you have them do? Or do you want them to do nothing but play your games?

Clock of Justice Still out of Sync

When we were children, my grandmother regaled us with ghost stories. Not the ones made up merely to scare and entertain but "real" ghost stories, ones experienced and retold by her family and friends in Gonzales.

One of our favorites was about why, for decades, the four faces of the courthouse clock seemed to always be broken. It was, my grandmother told us, because of a curse put on them by a man hung for a crime he insisted he did not commit. While waiting for his hanging day, the man stared at the north face of the clock from his cell window in the Gonzales County jail. Focusing all his fear and anger on the clock, watching it count down his life to its final days and hours, he vowed that the proof of his innocence would be that after his death, the clock would never again keep accurate time. He was hung, and the clock was often broken.

In my grandmother's telling, the man never had a name or ethnicity, nor was it said what crime he'd been accused of. But I always assumed he was Black.

Years later, as an adult, I was reading Ed Syers's *Ghost Stories of Texas* when one of his tales gave me the thrill of recognition; it was the one my grandmother had told. Syers filled in some of the details. The man's name was Albert Howard, and on March 18, 1921, he became the last man hanged in the old Gonzales County jail. Syers talked to someone from the Gonzales Chamber of Commerce who confirmed that for years the clocks were out of sync despite repeatedly being fixed. Syers said that as he was leaving Gonzales, he circled the courthouse and saw that the clock faces displayed four different times.

A few years ago I did some research and learned that Howard was a young Black man who'd been accused of sexually assaulting an elderly white woman. One of the things that fascinates me about his story is how, in its telling and retelling, passed down through generations, his ethnicity is never mentioned and he stops being Black. Yet when telling the story of a man feeling so wronged that his only recourse is to put a curse on the courthouse, it's important to note that he was a young Black man accused of sexually assaulting a white woman. In Texas. In 1921. It may explain a lot.

It's as if the whitewashing would spare people from making the connection between Black men and nooses and keep them from knowing that the long history of Black men protesting their innocence before being hanged is as American as Jim Crow, Black codes, and white vigilantes on horseback and in cars.

If Howard was killed for something he didn't do, then the second-worst thing that happened to him is being stripped and denied his Black identity, which may have been what led to his being falsely accused, convicted and executed. That would transform him from a local tale to one of the countless anonymous ghosts who have drifted across America's haunted landscape of racial injustice for centuries.

Breonna Taylor will never be one of those anonymous figures using signs beyond the grave to prove the injustice of her death. She's become one of those tragic iconic posthumous figures produced too often by Black America, people who became icons by death and through the marches and protests demanding justice for their killings.

Breonna became the first person other than Oprah to be on the cover of *O* magazine, and a painting of her is on the new issue of *Vanity Fair*. The city of Louisville is paying her family

$12 million and promising significant police reforms, and on August 12 radio stations across the country played her favorite song, "Everything," by Mary J. Blige.

Breonna Taylor is everywhere—except in the indictment charges brought by the grand jury considering her death. One officer was charged with firing shots into apartments, which could have wounded people. No one was charged for the shots fired into Breonna Taylor's apartment that killed her. She's been removed from the narrative of her death, a death that made this a story but one there is no accountability for.

The night she was shot, Breonna lay on her apartment floor for several minutes before she was given medical care. Six months later, the one officer indicted was charged for endangering the lives of Breonna's neighbors. The only charges in the case had nothing to do with Breonna Taylor.

It's almost as if her Black life didn't matter. Justice's clock is still out of sync.

Yearning to Breathe Free
of Trump's Politics

There are historical moments that are breathtaking, moments that make us hold our breath in suspense or wonder, that steal our breath with their beauty or make us gasp in horror.

We are living not only in a breathtaking time but in a time defined by the ability to take or denial of taking a breath.

Famously inscribed on the Statue of Liberty are Emma Lazarus's words, "Give me your tired, your poor, your huddled masses yearning to breathe free." In this moment we are tired, exhausted even. The inequities endured by our poor have widened and become more visible. Our masses are not so huddled (nor should they be) because of social distancing. At no time in our nation's history have so many of us yearned to breathe free.

To breathe free of a deadly virus passing in the air. To breathe free of chokeholds, to breathe without a knee on the back of our necks blocking off passages of air. To breathe free of the smoke from wildfires.

We are now several months into the year in which the historic convergences of COVID-19 and George Floyd's death have reminded us that public health and social justice are part of the same social contract and moral obligation binding us to care for one another and treat each other with dignity.

These two inflection points in our history, especially COVID-19, have revealed that many of us are willing to protect not only ourselves but each other. We've stayed away from those we love so we may touch them again. We've stopped going to places we cherish so we can return to them safely. We've refrained from doing some of the things we enjoy until we can do them without the consequences of anyone getting sick.

And we've worn our masks. However uncomfortable they may be, they've never felt like government restraints on our freedom or as heavy as the chains that shackled slaves. We wear them because if wearing them is the least we can do to stop the spread of a deadly virus, it will be the most many of us ever do to save the lives of others. We wear them because it's the humane, patriotic and practical thing to do. We do this, and make all the other sacrifices, because of our yearning to breathe free and return to some sense of normalcy.

So the least of our worries should be whether the president of the United States will leave the office if he's voted out by the American people. Every four years, the nation holds its collective breath to see who will be elected president. Most voters are anxious to see if the candidate they voted for won. This year, with less than seven weeks before the election, many of us are holding our breath because for the first time in our history, we aren't certain that if the incumbent loses, he will leave.

Throughout the summer, President Donald Trump, in tweets and speeches, has assaulted the integrity of this November's election, repeatedly calling it rigged before a single vote had been cast. It's a waste of breath to try to tell some Trump supporters it's not normal, appropriate, factual or healthy for democracy for an American president to undermine an American presidential election with absurdities such as "The only way we're going to lose this election is if the election is rigged."

Respecting the outcome of an election and abiding by the Constitution's peaceful transfer of power isn't a partisan scam the radical left came up with to get Trump. Both Democrats and Republicans have done a good job obeying the rules.

Maybe Trump wouldn't be frightened of losing to Democratic nominee Joe Biden, and maybe we'd all be breathing easier and not having to wear masks, if he'd voiced to the American people what he did to the *Washington Post*'s Bob Woodward about the threat of COVID-19. Instead he underplayed the danger of the pandemic, ignored it and refused to model safe behavior, such as wearing a mask and not holding massive, largely unmasked rallies.

We live in troubling and uncertain times, but because we yearn to breathe free, most of us will continue doing what's right—including the simple lifesaving act of wearing a mask.

We do it because we want, as it says in the preamble to the Constitution, "to insure domestic tranquility, provide for the common defense."

Headed to the Polls with History to Guide Me

On Tuesday morning, the first day of early voting, I walked to my polling place. I was by myself but not alone.

This wasn't a march, and there was no bridge to cross, no state trooper's club to fear, but I heard the voice, in the wind, of John Lewis encouraging all to make "good trouble" and "necessary trouble." Walking past Buffalo Soldier Park, I heard the smooth rumble of the Rev. James "Shack Daddy" Orange's baritone as he sang "Ain't Gonna Let Nobody Turn Me Around."

Orange was a young field staffer for the Southern Christian Leadership Conference on the morning of February 18, 1965, when he was arrested in Perry County, Alabama, on charges of contributing to the delinquency of minors by encouraging them to participate in voting drives. His arrest was a catalyst for a series of events culminating with the passage of the 1965 Voting Rights Act.

On the night of Orange's arrest, afraid he'd be lynched, four hundred people marched to the jail, where their plan was to sing a freedom song for him. They were attacked by state troopers who shot twenty-six-year-old Jimmie Lee Jackson, a veteran, as he defended his mother and grandfather.

Jackson's death eight days later led to plans for a march from Selma to Montgomery. The first attempt was Bloody Sunday, when state troopers beat and gassed activists, including Lewis and Orange, preventing them from crossing the Edmund Pettus

Bridge. Later that month Martin Luther King Jr. would lead the march from Selma to Montgomery, which would lead to the voting rights legislation being signed in August.

As I continued walking, I heard in the distance the baritone of King exhorting, "Walk together, children, and don't you get weary. There's a great camp meeting in the promised land!" I heard Fannie Lou Hamer say she was sick and tired of being sick and tired before she began singing "This Little Light of Mine."

Walking through Pittman-Sullivan Park, I stopped at the Little Free Library in the community garden and thought of the literacy tests once used to prevent Black people from voting in Texas and throughout the South. One of the books in the little library was a Berenstain Bears story, *Play a Fair Game*, which made me think of the voter suppression efforts being used today. On the back of the book is the question, "Will Brother and Sister choose to win at all costs, too, or will they show how peacemakers are the true winners?" I took the book.

Walking past the baseball field in Pittman-Sullivan, where Negro League games were once played, I imagined my walking stick to be a baseball bat and took a hard swing, driving a Satchel Paige fastball over the fence, across Nevada Street, over where a water tower once stood, and across Dakota Street and into Saint Mary's Catholic Cemetery, where it landed with such force that it woke the dead.

As I approached the Davis-Scott Family YMCA, I was disappointed that there were no lines, but when I walked in I learned it wasn't a voting site. My bad. Walking home, I passed Saint Mary's Catholic Cemetery, where I saw a yellow softball on the other side of the locked gate. Once home, I drove to the Claude Black Community Center, where I saw a long line looping around the parking lot. In line ahead of me was my cousin, raised on the East Side but now living on the far North Side.

"I always come back here to vote with my people," she said.

We looked around and smiled. People were talking, joking, laughing, catching up, sermonizing, wisdom-sharing, and offering food, water and good cheer.

It would be three hours before we'd vote, but it didn't matter. Voting is the most sacred of our civic duties, the greatest weapon in the arsenal of democracy. Black folks turn long voting lines into Juneteenth family reunions. My cousin and I talked about family, loved ones who'd passed on but whose presence we feel every day. Closer to the door, I heard King ask, "How long? Not long." I shook hands with the Rev. James Reeb and hugged Fannie Lou.

Walking in, I patted the backs of Michael Schwerner, James Chaney and Andrew Goodman. Standing with me at the ballot box were Jimmie Lee Jackson and Viola Liuzzo. But then I thought about the children who never had a chance to vote.

Surrounding me were Carole Robertson, Addie Mae Collins, Cynthia Wesley and Denise McNair, four little girls from a Birmingham church. Next to them was Trayvon Martin and Tamir Rice.

I never vote alone.

The Greatest San Antonio
Singer You Never Knew

Doris Belvin wanted more people to know about her cousins. The man who died on an Arkansas highway in 1960. The one who was one of the greatest singer-songwriters to come not just out of the East Side but all of San Antonio. The performer who Etta James thought would be bigger than Sam Cooke and Nat King Cole. The singer who Marvin Gaye tried to emulate.

"Not because he was my cousin," she once told me, "but because he was such a great singer and songwriter. He deserves to be recognized."

Belvin was a popular retired teacher and counselor who worked in the San Antonio Independent School District for forty-two years, many of them at Lanier High School. She died on September 27, 2020, at age eighty-one.

She was right. Her cousin Jesse Belvin was one of the greatest singer-songwriters most people will never know about. He deserves to be recognized and for people to know that a song they love or are familiar with may be one of his.

Belvin was born in San Antonio in 1932 and lived on Paso Hondo Street on the East Side until his family moved to Los Angeles when he was five. He began singing in church before gravitating toward Los Angeles's R&B and doo-wop scene.

He became a prolific songwriter, cowriting one of the classic songs of the rock and roll era—"Earth Angel" by the Penguins, as well as "Goodnight My Love," which he recorded himself and for years was the closing theme for Dick Clark's *American Bandstand*. That was the biggest of his hits, which included "Girl of My Dreams" and "Guess Who," written by his wife and manager, JoAnn.

We'll never know all the songs Belvin wrote because he'd often forgo writing credits in exchange for a few hundred dollars. He also used pseudonyms for some of his songs.

But to truly appreciate him is to listen to the magnificent instrument that was his voice. His cousin Doris said she could hear shades of Nat King Cole and Billy Eckstine, and so do I. But Belvin possessed a range neither of those two legends did.

The incomparable Marvin Gaye told an interviewer: "When I saw Sam Cooke and Jesse Belvin, I'd try to avoid my friends and family for days. I didn't want to talk or be talked to 'cause I was busy practicing and memorizing everything I heard those singers do."

The great Etta James and Belvin grew up in the same Los Angeles neighborhood, where, she writes in her autobiography *Rage to Survive*, he was a legend. She called him "the golden boy" and was unsparing in her praise for his voice. "Even now I consider him the greatest singer of my generation—rhythm and blues, rock and roll, crooner—you name it," she wrote. "He was going to be bigger than Sam Cooke, bigger than Nat King Cole. He was heading in that direction."

He never got there. On February 6, 1960, just hours after a concert in Little Rock, the twenty-seven-year-old Belvin, his twenty-five-year-old wife and another man were killed in an automobile accident on US 67, a few miles outside Hope, Arkansas. The Belvins, who were buried in Los Angeles, left behind two young sons.

"What if?" is always attached to the unfinished legacies of

artists, athletes and political leaders who die young, and Doris Belvin often wondered what if her cousin had lived longer and had written and recorded more songs. Surely he'd be a household name and his gifts universally appreciated and recognized.

Let's listen to the songs he did write and record, and appreciate and recognize that based on talent alone, "Guess Who" is one of the greatest singers of his or any generation.

It's Jesse Belvin, the kid from San Antonio's East Side.

In Race for Equality, More
Finish Lines to Cross

Whether a race is a sprint or a marathon, runners are told to "run through the tape"—to not ease up until they break the tape at the finish line, signaling the race's end.

On August 6, 1965, President Lyndon Johnson, thinking a tape had been broken, told Martin Luther King Jr. to ease up, because they'd crossed a finish line together. On that historic day Johnson signed the Voting Rights Act, which King and countless others had marched and demonstrated for. Many had been beaten; some had died.

Passage of the bill was among the major achievements of both men's careers, and the one they were most closely aligned in.

In his speech in Statuary Hall of the US Capitol, Johnson said,

> The vote is the most powerful instrument ever devised by man for breaking down injustice and destroying the terrible walls which imprison men because they are different from other men. Today what is perhaps the last of the legal barriers is tumbling. There will be many actions and many difficulties before the rights woven into law are also woven into the fabric of our nation. But the struggle for equality must now move toward a different battlefield.

From there, Johnson invited guests to the President's Room, where he signed the act and distributed the pens he used. As he gave one to King, he told him his work was done and protest was no longer needed.

Perhaps a finish line was crossed with the act's passage, but Johnson also knew, as he acknowledged in his speech, that there were more battlefields, their finish lines not in sight, in the fight for equality. King's work wasn't done, and the protests did not stop.

We are two days away from an election in which the astonishing early vote is a legacy of the Voting Rights Act and the barriers removed with its passage. But the passion fueling this massive turnout can't lessen if the desired changes in policies and values are going to be achieved. King knew in 1965 what we should know in 2020: that we keep bursting through tapes until we win the prizes we run for or can't run for anymore.

Assuming the policies and the uniquely repellent behavior of President Donald Trump are sending people to the polls, voting him out of office is simply the beginning. If the demonstrations and marches can be described as mass resistance to his policies, there'd be nothing wrong with acts of "mass insistence" by supporters of Joe Biden and Kamala Harris if their administration, though like-minded and far more open and friendlier, isn't moving fast enough on its promises. Speaking out, even marching against those in power, is an antidote against complacency for the governed as well as those who govern.

The extraordinary pain, bewilderment and historic moments of 2020 have also reminded some and awakened many to their civic responsibilities and the power they possess when those responsibilities are exercised. More of us see with greater clarity that rights we've taken for granted can be taken away, rights that still elude too many.

These are responsibilities that go beyond voting. That which pains and disturbs us on November 3, whoever is elected president, will pain and disturb us on December 3, January 3 and February 3. Those issues we want corrected will continue needing to be corrected if, come Wednesday morning, we think we've done all we're supposed to do. However high the exhilaration or deep the depression after crossing this election's finish line, we'll still have the concerns that drove us to the polls.

One of those issues is that of voting itself and the repeated attempts by Trump and Republican state officials, such as Governor Greg Abbott, to make it more difficult. Last week, looking at voter suppression efforts across the country, conservative writer David French tweeted, "It is deeply disturbing that—virtually everywhere—the concerted litigation strategy of the GOP is to make sure that fewer votes count. The strategy goes far, far beyond any legitimate concern and fraud."

Johnson, so right in his advocacy and signing of the Voting Rights Act, was wrong in assuming it precluded the need for more work for voting rights. As it is with other injustices and inequities, more work, protesting, marching and strategizing are needed before we cross the finish lines ahead.

With Hope after Ruins of Past Four Years

Four years ago today, Donald Trump was elected president of the United States. Eight days later, on November 16, my father died. Before the month was over, I was telling people that the worst of those two events was Trump's election.

This wasn't because of any difficulties between my father and me, of me not loving him or ever doubting his love for me. Dad was seventy-seven and had been sick for several months, and while his death was unexpected, it was imminent.

Dad's death brought me grief. Trump's election delivered me to despair.

Family and friends felt and continue to feel the pain of Dad's death. Death and the passing of loved ones is a tragic but natural part of the normal cycle.

But that pain would be nothing compared to the millions of people who'd suffer under a Trump presidency. There was nothing natural about electing an abnormally awful human being whose insatiable need to denigrate and humiliate anyone was matched by his perpetual whining of those who'd been "very unfair" to him.

Then came four years of Trump not caring enough about the job of presidency to study and work; four years of daily lies and boasting; four years of bullying; four years of insulting, belittling any human being who wasn't a tyrant: widows of slain soldiers, Gold Star parents, front-line workers fighting COVID-19, entire states, Black athletes, Muslims, Mexican Americans, prisoners of war, deceased prisoners of war, US servicemen and women killed in duty, women, women journalists, Black women journalists, and Black, Puerto Rican and Muslim congresswomen. Four years of his emboldening white nationalist groups and his refusal to condemn any of their acts of violence just as he's cowardly refused to confront Vladimir Putin over bounties on American soldiers and his other schemes to hurt the United States.

Who needs foreign interference to damage American institutions when the American president has been doing it for four years, including now, as he lies about an election he lost and makes the most dangerous and disgusting attempt to undermine trust in our democracy.

If there's but one issue Trump should be expelled from the White House for it's his lying, incompetence and disregard about COVID-19 and its wreckage of millions of lives in this country. Treating COVID-19 as if it were part of a conspiracy against his reelection, he claimed that no one would be talking about COVID-19 on November 4. On November 4 the United States hit the hundred thousand daily mark in new cases. On November 5 it rose to 120,000. Trump will do nothing as he pouts and incites violence over the election.

During the Nazi occupation of France, writer Albert Camus edited an underground newspaper, *Combat*. When Paris was liberated in 1944, the future winner of the Nobel Prize in Literature for novels like *The Stranger* and *The Plague* wrote four essays addressing an imaginary German friend and explaining that he wasn't opposed to Germans but to Nazism. In the first letter he wrote about what France had been through but looked forward to what it could become:

> I belong to a nation which for the past four years has begun
> to relive the course of her entire history and which is calmly
> and surely preparing out of the ruins to make another

history and to take her chance in a game where she holds no trumps. This country is worthy of the difficult and demanding love that is mine. And I believe she is decidedly worth fighting for since she is worthy of a higher love. And I say that your nation, on the other hand, has received from its sons only the love it deserved, which was blind. A nation is not justified by such love. That will be your undoing. And you who were already conquered in your greatest victories, what will you be in the approaching defeat?

The United States will soon have no Trumps in power to loot, debase, tarnish and diminish it. But 70 million voters looked at Trump's behavior over the past four years and said they wanted four more years. He will leave. His legacy won't.

No country or leader deserves blind, uncritical love. Those wishing to give it to them should ask themselves why. Over the past four years, whether horrified by family separations at the border, the killings of George Floyd and Breonna Taylor, or the growing threat of white nationalist violence, well-meaning people have said, "This is not who we are as a nation."

It is. And many of us have known that for centuries. Yet we love this country. As Camus felt for France, we feel about the United States, that it's worthy of the difficult and demanding love that is ours. Though we are bruised and disappointed, it's with hope that we prepare out of the ruins of the last four years to make another history. A better history.

When Gunfire Is Routine, so Is the Response

I have a routine when I hear gunshots in my neighborhood, which is often enough for me to have a routine. I immediately check the time, replay the gunfire in my head to count the shots, listen for the screeching tires of an accelerating car, wait for the sounds of sirens, and then—usually the next day, because gunfire tends to be nocturnal—look for news of a shooting. For me, gunfire is such a nighttime thing that I'm more startled when I hear it during the day.

In my youth and early adulthood, sitting at night on my grandmother's or mother's porch and seeing a car slowly coming down the street—too slowly—I'd casually step back into the porch's shadows. I never wanted to appear to panic in case there was no threat. Nothing ever came or was fired from those slow-moving cars, but maybe it was because I was hidden in the porch shadows.

I lived in my Denver Heights neighborhood during the first half of my life and moved back three years ago. It's a rapidly gentrifying neighborhood, but as in other neighborhoods throughout the city, gentrification hasn't muzzled the gunfire. Sometimes it's not gunfire but an engine backfiring or a firework or two. You can usually tell the difference by the crispness of the gunshot.

Last Sunday night, a little after 10, I was walking up and

down the sidewalk, taking more of a stroll for reflection than a fast-paced jaunt for exercise. It was quiet except for conversations rising above my neighbor's privacy fence across the street.

Pop-pop-pop-pop-pop (pause) pop. It came from the south and sounded less than a block away, sounded so close that it rattled me into forgetting to check the time, especially when I heard a vehicle racing down the street from the south. Conversations from across the street paused or were drowned out by the sound of the approaching vehicle.

I remembered that I was carrying a walking stick, which isn't really a walking stick but a hobbyhorse minus the horse's head, which I've had since I was three years old. I'm sixty. I have "letting go" issues. But no one racing away from or toward a shooting would think that the man, walking at night, was holding a hobbyhorse stick in his hand.

For the first time in my life, on hearing gunshots, I ran. Dignity was a consideration as I ran up my driveway, hobbyhorse stick in hand. I later imagined someone looking down at me and saying, "Oh, my God, what happened to him? Wait, is he holding a hobbyhorse stick?"

But avoiding getting shot was a greater consideration. I hid behind the car. Of course, hiding behind a car, at night, holding what may or may not be a beheaded hobbyhorse, certainly doesn't look suspicious.

An SUV sped by, conversations from across the street continued, and I went in my house. I didn't see any news about a shooting.

A lot of times these drive-by shootings—which are usually young people targeting other, specific young people—don't hit anyone. Too often, they do, and each time I hear gunfire, I wonder, Who was on the other side of those shots? Whose bodies did the bullets tear through? There have been times when I've heard gunfire in the night, only to learn a few hours later that someone had been killed. The last time was during the summer when a couple of teenagers were killed while sitting in a car.

As I wrote this column, it began to have a familiarity. I went into the *San Antonio Express-News* archives and found an op-ed I'd submitted to the paper, which ran May 7, 1994. This is how it began: "The first thing you do when you hear the gunshot in the night is see what time it is, in case anyone needs to know. On this night, the last one in April, it's 11:20. The second thing you do is listen for more shots. Within seconds one more rings out. Then you wait for the sound of police sirens rushing to the site of the shooting."

The op-ed ended with these lines: "You think about your three-year-old niece who lives in one of the most dangerous housing developments in San Antonio. You make plans to see her tomorrow."

That niece is now thirty. Last year, her then ten-year-old daughter, my great-niece, was spending the night when gunfire exploded down the street.

"Uncle Cary!" she asked, scared but calm. "Are we going to die?"

"No, baby," I said, embracing her. "It's just people acting crazy."

People, please stop acting crazy.

Which Christmas Star Is She?

Decembers remind him of green wagons, silver bells and stars. It was December 1997 when he walked into a hospital room on Santa Rosa Hospital's eighth floor, the floor for children with cancer, leukemia and AIDS.

A four-year-old girl was there, the youngest sister among siblings he knew from the West Side. He was curious about the limp in her gait. Like their mother, she was often sick.

That December he received a call that the mother had died from AIDS, which also afflicted the four-year-old. He hung up and went to the hospital, across the street from his apartment. Walking into the child's room, he found her swallowed in her bed, a hospital gown draped across her skeletal frame. Her already short hair had been shaved because of lice, and her face was smeared with white cream because of a rash. All her teeth were capped with silver, like miniature silver bells.

She was crying. Three nurses were treating her and trying to cheer her up. He stayed for a while and returned that night. He kept returning, two or three times a day or night. He wasn't sure why except that the child was dying and hated being alone. There were family issues, and usually her only visitors were the nurses and him. People assumed he was her father.

In those first days she wasn't allowed to eat solid food. "But I'm hungry!" she'd cry.

The decision was reversed to allow solid food. Why deny the pleasure of food to a dying child? She craved mashed potatoes, so he brought her homemade ones. Taking a spoonful, she smelled it, took a small bite and was satisfied. That was the first time he saw her silver smile.

On his visits they watched *Lion King*, *Little Mermaid* and *Toy Story* so often that she anticipated the dialogue.

At the end of the eighth floor was the hospice room for children. When a child died, the nurses closed the hospital room doors so no one would see the body being rolled away. Looking at the laughing child watching cartoons, he wondered when she'd be in the "Butterfly Room."

One Sunday afternoon that first December, he looked out of the window of her room facing Milam Park and watched a silver balloon drift past the window over the large Christmas tree in the park and ascend like a disappearing star.

On Christmas Eve he stopped by the hospital to see her before going to a Christmas party. She was restless and cried when he tried to leave.

She didn't like being alone, so the nurses made a makeshift bed out of an old green-framed wagon and kept her with them behind their station. She had a little cassette player she listened to children's music on.

During the day he pulled her down the corridor until he had to leave or she fell asleep. If she was connected to her IV, maneuvering the wagon was trickier. Up and down the floor they rolled, talking or listening to music from her radio. Often, when he looked behind to see if she was getting sleepy, she was looking at him and sometimes broke into her silver smile.

Around 8 p.m. the nurses put her in the wagon and he pulled her around the floor, hoping she'd fall asleep. Christmas morning, at 3 a.m., she did.

She wasn't supposed to turn five. In May 1998 her fifth birthday was celebrated at the children's home where she now lived. In December she was back in the hospital. Again, he stopped by on Christmas Eve before going out. Again, she was restless, and so he pulled her wagon until she fell asleep in the early hours of Christmas Day.

The last time he saw her was December 1999, at a Christmas party. It had been several months. He picked her up; they hugged and spoke, and after a few seconds he put her down. She followed him, smiling her silver smile, but he had to leave and told someone to get her.

His last memory of her was the way she followed him with that limp in her gait.

Her last memory of him was his walking away from her.

She kept living, and through the years he received pictures and updates. Her life became one of extraordinary hardship and struggle.

When he learned that she had died on her twenty-fifth birthday, he pulled from his notebook pictures of her smiling the night she tasted mashed potatoes and on her fifth birthday.

On December nights, he scans the sky, wondering which star is she.

The Light That Still Beams
on Maury's Kids

If you knew Maury Maverick Jr., it's impossible to drive down Broadway, past Brackenridge Park, and not imagine him on his morning walk—nature's child and freedom's apostle striding to the drumbeat in his head, on the lookout for stray dogs in need of care, and thinking about life's underdogs and the marginalized who needed a voice to amplify theirs. Maybe his voice.

As a state legislator, attorney and *San Antonio Express-News* columnist, Maury's life was about using his voice for those in the shadows of the Constitution's sunlit promises. He was one of American liberalism's preeminent and unapologetic advocates.

Civil liberties had no greater defender. Injustice and ignorance had no fiercer adversary.

Fearless is how poet Naomi Shihab Nye describes him. "Unafraid of what others might say of him or think about him. He was a true advocate for others (Palestinians, for example) because he did not fear blowback."

Jan Jarboe Russell, a journalist and former *Express-News* columnist who knew him as well as anyone, wrote, "There was no greater patriot in America than Maverick. He loved this country so much that it hurt."

He didn't love the South Texas heat. When Naomi suggested he summer someplace cooler, he said, "Oh, I couldn't do that. It's too much of a minor ego trip to be a Maverick in San Antonio."

Maury's great-grandfather, Samuel Augustus Maverick, was

a signer of the Texas Declaration of Independence and a wealthy landowner. He didn't brand his longhorns, so when one strayed from the herd it was called a "maverick." His father, Maury Maverick Sr., was a two-term New Deal congressman and San Antonio mayor.

Today would have been Maury's hundredth birthday. He and his wife, Julia, who died last year, had no children of their own. But because of the paternal interest he took in younger people, there are many of "Maury's children," including the Vietnam War–era conscientious objectors he defended pro bono, Jan, Naomi, former *Express-News* writer Bob Richter and myself.

Maury took credit for "discovering" me, and he was right. I was either unemployed or a community organizer—little difference in pay—the first time I met him in a typewriter shop in the late 1980s or early 1990s. I introduced myself, and the first thing he said to me, in that gruff voice, was, "Black people need another Malcolm X!"

I was down with that, though I thought it an unusual greeting. Learning that I wanted to be a journalist, he took some of my few published pieces to Bob Richter at the *Express-News* editorial board. One thing led to another, which eventually led to a career. Maury remained a source of encouragement, dispenser of books, and fount of advice and phone calls pretending to be Frederick Douglass, Sam Houston or G. J. Sutton.

One of Maury's most famous legal cases was that of I. H. "Sporty" Harvey, a Black boxer from San Antonio. Together, in 1954, they overturned the Texas law prohibiting professional boxing matches between white and Black fighters.

In 1997 Maury phoned me. "Kiddo," he said, "do you think you could drive me to Sporty Harvey's funeral on Thursday?"

He was one of the few white people in Bethel United Methodist Church. Hard of hearing, he'd turn to me and ask, loudly, "Huh? What did he say?"

When the minister asked if anyone wanted to say a few words, Maury rose, stumbling past others in the pew to get to the aisle. I slumped in my seat.

Once he was in the pulpit, the church became his. Within seconds, his rumbling drawl was rolling over a growing chorus of "Amen!" "Tell it!" "Preach!"

"I had two college degrees," Maury thundered. "But that Black man," he said, and pointed to Harvey's gray casket, "with a sixth-grade education taught me more than I taught him!"

By the time he finished half the church was standing, and I was sitting up, proud and smiling, like, "Yeah, I'm the one who drove him here."

In January 2003, knowing he was about to be hospitalized for major surgery, I wrote a birthday column about him. He couldn't believe the positive reaction. "Kiddo, you're not pulling a sick old man's leg, are you?" he said.

On January 28 he died at eighty-two.

"I miss the sound of Maury's voice," said photographer Michael Nye, Naomi's husband and another of "Maury's children." "I miss his wit and teasing. A voice that floated with seriousness and sudden humor."

A few years later, at Julia Maverick's request, Jan, Naomi, Bob and I spent a couple of Sundays cleaning out Maury's office, a little stand-alone in his backyard. The dusty books, correspondence, photos, files and political memorabilia made it akin to being immersed, for several glorious hours, in a museum of family, San Antonio, Texas and US history.

We were like children going through our late father's things and marveling anew at the life he led. It bonded us closer to Maury and to each other.

Happy birthday, kiddo!

Trump Lit the Matches,
and the Nation Burned

> When you teach a man to hate and fear his brother, when
> you teach that he is a lesser man because of his color or his
> beliefs or the policies he pursues, when you teach that those
> who differ from you threaten your freedom or your job or your
> family, then you also learn to confront others not as fellow
> citizens but as enemies, to be met not with cooperation but
> with conquest; to be subjugated and mastered.
> —Robert F. Kennedy, "On the Mindless Menace of
> Violence," April 5, 1968

> Statistically impossible to have lost the 2020 Election. Big
> protest in DC on January 6th. Be there, will be wild!
> —Donald J. Trump, Twitter, December 20, 2020

This was the match that was one too many, the match lit by President Donald Trump last Wednesday, the one he couldn't put out. The match that ignited a conflagration so spectacular and frightening that it riveted Americans and the world to television screens in a way they'd not been for almost twenty years. That was 9/11, when men from other countries, fueled by a fanatical hatred of the United States, flew planes into buildings.

On Wednesday, American men and women, fueled by a fanatical devotion to the president of the United States, threw themselves into the US Capitol to terrorize Congress. They were there because Trump, the country's premier merchant of lies and rhetorical violence, told them to fight for him and help him steal an election that he lost by more than 7 million votes. They were there because some of the dishonorable members of Congress, led by Senator Ted Cruz, indulged their and Trump's delusions.

"We're going to walk down, and I'll be there with you," Trump told his supporters shortly before they advanced on the Capitol. "You'll never take back our country with weakness. You have to show strength, and you have to be strong."

Because he's a liar and a weak man, he didn't walk with them, sending them off to fight his battle. I know that my Black life doesn't matter to Donald Trump, but I don't understand why so many of his supporters don't know that their white lives don't matter to Donald Trump. Having lit his match, he retreated behind the White House gates while his supporters crashed the gates surrounding the Capitol, stormed the building, vandalized and looted offices, and forced Congress into lockdown.

After the images we've seen of the mob, does anyone doubt they would have harmed any member of Congress they'd gotten their hands on?

It's well and good for people who have until now enabled Trump to suddenly demand his resignation or impeachment for inciting his supporters. But for years Trump has repeatedly and recklessly tossed matches into kindlings of grievances, resentment and racism. Now they're learning he's a verbal arsonist?

Where were they when he lit a match in Birmingham, Alabama, in November 2015? That's when a Black activist yelled, "Black lives matter!," and from the stage Trump shouted, "Get him the hell out of here! Get him out of here! Throw him out!" What about the match he struck in February 2016? That's when he said of a protester, "I'd like to punch him in the face.... We're not allowed to punch back anymore. I love the old days. You know what they used to do to guys like that when they were in a place like this? They'd be carried out on a stretcher, folks." Or the matches in 2019 when he attacked Black and Muslim congresswomen, telling them to go back to the "crime-infested places from which they came"?

The Department of Homeland Security reports that white supremacist extremists are the deadliest domestic terror threat to the United States. Since 2018 white supremacists have conducted more lethal attacks in the country than any other domestic extremist movement. Despite this, Trump consistently downplayed that threat, just as he's consistently downplayed any violence committed by anyone aligned with him politically. Given his history of inflammatory language, it shouldn't have required his inciting an insurrection two weeks from leaving office for people to understand the danger he was sowing.

No matter the caliber of the guns they carried or number of flags they waved, those in Wednesday's mob weren't patriots but insurrectionists attempting to overthrow an election at the behest of a demagogue.

The patriots are those of us, across party and ideological lines, who vote, honor the results, don't want to harm anyone and, on our best days, look out for one another.

We the people will need more of those best days of looking out for one another because, I fear, Trump's matches have lit trains of powder that have yet to explode.

Trump Insurrection Steeped in American Racism

Imagine awakening from a five-year coma on January 6 and the first thing you see on TV is a yelling mob stampeding past barricades and police to break into the US Capitol.

The mob runs amok through the hallways, chases and attacks police—one of whom, you hear, has been killed—breaks windows, barrels through doors, smears human waste on walls, and ransacks and loots offices while looking for members of Congress and the vice president, who some are chanting should be hung.

Having just awakened with no idea of what's going on—"Who is Mike Pence? Who is AOC?" you wonder—is your initial reaction revulsion and fear that an angry mob has taken over and desecrated the "People's House," or do you wait to see who these people are and whether their politics align with yours before you decide whether to condemn or justify their actions?

Shouldn't revulsion and fear, independent of political allegiance, be the natural reaction of any human being? Look at all the videos of the mob storming the Capitol, including those shot by the insurrectionists. Look, especially, at the one where the mob is fighting with Metropolitan Police officers in a doorway, dragging one down the steps. Chants of "USA! USA!" erupt, and one man can be heard yelling "Get that mother [expletive] out of there! Drag him!" as the officer is punched, kicked and hit with objects, including poles bearing American flags.

Imagine being a Black man in the 1890s, 1920s, 1930s—pick a

decade—sitting in a jail cell, accused of a crime you've not been convicted of and/or one you've been falsely accused of. Imagine sitting—or, by now, standing—in that cell and hearing and seeing that crowd coming for you.

Imagine you're Henry Smith in Paris, Texas, in 1893 or Jesse Washington in Waco in 1916 and thousands have gathered to maim and burn you. Or imagine you're a Mexican American like Antonio Rodríguez, seized from a jail cell in Rocksprings in 1910 before being doused with oil and set afire. Or that you're Elias Villarreal Zarate, taken from jail in Weslaco in 1922 to be hung.

Lynchings were often advertised in newspapers. Thousands of people, including parents bringing children, would travel with picnic baskets to enjoy the spectacle of a human being—usually a Black man—dying a horrible death. Often body parts would be distributed as souvenirs and commemorative postcards printed. Look at any of the hundreds of lynching photographs that exist, and take in the smiles and demented joy on the faces in the crowd, including children, as they pose with human remains.

You don't need to go back decades to imagine the terror felt by people certain they'd die at the hands of a mob. Less than two weeks ago men and women in the US Capitol hid for their lives as a mob of their fellow citizens, fueled by a lie that a presidential election had been stolen, looked for them. After all the images we've seen and all we've heard of the mob, including the beating of policemen, is there doubt what they would have done had they gotten their hands on lawmakers, including the vice president, for the man for whom they ignited an insurrection?

The United States is no stranger to mob violence, particularly when inflamed by election results brought about by African Americans' participation. Consider the Opelousas massacre of 1868, the Colfax massacre of 1873 and the Wilmington insurrection of 1898.

We are not a nation unfamiliar with political violence. On

Monday we celebrate the birthday of Martin Luther King Jr., who was a victim of political violence.

But it cannot be appreciated enough how narrowly, on January 6, members of Congress avoided being assassinated, some lynched in public, to the glee of a mob. And it cannot be overstated, leading up to and beyond Inauguration Day, the threat we face from domestic extremists. Those extremists must be condemned and stopped, and those who encourage and justify them renounced.

Comparing King to the Founding Fathers, his biographer Taylor Branch has written: "Nonviolence is an orphan among democratic ideas. It has neatly vanished from public discourse even though the most basic element of free government—the vote—has no other meaning. Every ballot is a piece of nonviolence, signifying hard-won consent to raise politics above firepower and bloody conquest."

This week, in honoring King and the nonviolence of voting, as well as the Founding Fathers and the peaceful transition of power, we stand together and against those seeking bloody conquest. We must.

A Shameful Ending to a Shameful Presidency

A nation that has survived the Civil War, the assassinations of presidents, a history of racist lynch mobs, the bombing of federal courthouses, the 9/11 attacks, and the morally bankrupt and disastrous one-term presidency of Donald Trump is a nation with no more innocence to lose.

But on Wednesday, as we watched a mob of Trump supporters overpower Capitol Hill police, storm the Capitol, indulge in violence and vandalism, and temporarily stop the certification of Electoral College votes for president, we were reminded of our capacity to be shocked and outraged by something we'd never before seen—American citizens assaulting the cradle of democracy, inspired by the baseless claims of a president who lost a fair election.

These were American citizens waving scores of American flags, but they weren't patriots pledging allegiance to the United States of America and the democratic values the flag represents. They had become domestic terrorists, pledging allegiance to Trump, whose allegiance is to only his own insatiable self-interest.

This was not a nonviolent protest nor an act of civil disobedience to dramatize an injustice they'd be willing to go to jail for. This was not respectful dissent worthy of American political tradition. The rioters assaulted police officers, broke windows, paraded on the House floor and stood at the Senate dais shouting, "Trump won that election!" They marauded through the offices of House members and sent elected officials scurrying for their lives while stopping them from doing the work they were elected to do.

What we witnessed is the inevitable nadir of the presidency of a man who, beginning in the 2016 campaign, encouraged violence in his speeches and texts. Pick your metaphor—"striking matches," "pouring kerosene on fire," "lighting a train of powder"—it all applies to Trump's penchant for inflammatory language and his refusal to ever meaningfully condemn any act of violence committed by any group that supported him. To those who stormed the Capitol, he said, "We love you."

Wednesday's insurrection may have been the lowest, most shameful moment for an American president. But what about those who have looked the other way, kept quiet and enabled him as he acted on his delusional and authoritarian impulses?

Little wonder what happened Wednesday was as predictable as a Trump lie. Trump, never committing to a peaceful transfer of power, has for two months lied about having the election stolen from him.

The insurrectionists were in Washington, DC, because Trump invited them to come fight for his attempt to stage a coup. And they've been encouraged by more than a hundred House Republicans and a dozen Senate Republicans, led by Texas's US senator Ted Cruz, who said they would not certify the election results in a stunning abandonment of democracy. Cruz must also be held accountable for his ignoble and divisive brand of politics. He will forever own his supporting role in this moment. After the assault on the Capitol, he took to Twitter denouncing the violence, telling rioters to stop.

Cruz had four years to tell Trump to stop his violent rhetoric. He didn't. Cruz had two months to tell Trump to stop trying to steal an election. He didn't. Cruz could have refuted baseless claims of voter fraud. He didn't. He could have shown conscience. He didn't. Instead the junior senator from Texas fanned the flames and played with fire in a cynical attempt to court the kind of Trump supporters who have assaulted the People's House, trampled our democracy and cheered him on as he advocated Trump's lies.

Trump watched the assault on the Capitol on television before taping a video telling his supporters to go home, all while continuing to lie about winning the election.

So much sound and fury, for nothing. Joe Biden will be the next president. He won the election. But the violence of today will haunt. It is the most shameful ending to a shameful presidency.

Cherish Our Living Links to the Past

They made their way through the world by sky, road and rail, segregated travelers denied access by their nation to broader and more traditional routes. The Tuskegee Airmen flew overseas to defend countrymen and -women who wouldn't defend them here at home; the Negro League players rode in cars and buses, from town to town, to play games where only the ball was white; and Pullman porters served white passengers in railroad sleeping cars where Black people weren't allowed.

Nearly a thousand pilots were trained in the program, and they became legends, losing just twenty-five planes on 1,500 escort missions. Tuskegee Airmen refers not only to the pilots but to the support group of mechanics, instructors, nurses, cooks and so on.

"They did things for their country that their country didn't want them to do," said Rick Sinkfield, president of the San Antonio Chapter of Tuskegee Airmen. "They were there to prove that they could do the job, that it has nothing to do with race or color. If you're going to bring it, bring it strong. And they did."

The Negro League was formed in 1920 because Major League Baseball had placed a barrier that wouldn't be hurdled until Jackie Robinson made the leap in Ebbets Field in 1947. Until then scores of Black professional baseball players had the light of their talent hidden under the bushel of racism, Black diamonds lost in the rough of ignorance and injustice.

But if they were unknown to most of white America, they

were heroes to Black America—mythic figures whose exploits became part of Black folklore. Was Satchel Paige's fastball not detectable to the human eye? Was Cool Papa Bell truly so fast he could turn the lights out and be in bed before the room got dark? Was it true that he once batted a ball and was hit by the line drive as he rounded first base? It's said that Josh Gibson hit a ball out of Forbes Field in Pittsburgh that disappeared; the next day, during a game in Philadelphia, a ball mysteriously dropped from the sky into an outfielder's glove, causing an umpire to point at Gibson and say, "You're out! Yesterday in Pittsburgh."

For Black fans, Negro League ballgames weren't simply athletic contests but social affairs and communal gatherings they wore their best clothes to. Weekend games drew five thousand to ten thousand fans. Players took the field after grueling journeys, covering thousands of miles along dusty and solitary back roads fueled by the Dutch lunches they carried with them—boxes of bread, lunch meat, ham, tomatoes and sandwich spread—or Mason jars of crackers and sardines.

Pullman porters became the job of Black men because after George Pullman introduced his railroad sleeping cars after the Civil War, he figured ex-slaves would be the best porters—they'd work long hours for low pay and knew how to please white people.

In the early years of the twentieth century, the Pullman Company was the largest employer of Black men in the country. The porters were often humiliated, called "boy" or "George" or worse, but their salaries helped create a Black middle class. Because of their constant travel, they also served as reporters, carrying news about political and cultural happenings from one part of the country to another.

Recently there was an hourlong hundred-vehicle procession on San Antonio's northwest side honoring the hundredth birthday of retired Air Force senior master sergeant James Bynum, a Tuskegee Airman. In the same section of the newspaper as

San Antonio Express-News reporter Vincent T. Davis's column about the celebration was an article on the death of another Tuskegee Airman, Ted Lumpkins Jr. of Los Angeles, who was also one hundred. Bynum and Eugene Derricotte are San Antonio's only surviving Tuskegee Airmen.* There are only a handful still living across the country.

Rare is the African American who hasn't known someone who flew as a Tuskegee Airman, rode the buses in the Negro Leagues or worked the rails as a Pullman porter. Although women were part of the Tuskegee Airmen support group and three women played in the Negro League, these were jobs exclusively associated with Black men.

Many of us knew people who represented each of those jobs. John "Mule" Miles was a Tuskegee Airman and a Negro League player. They were our neighbors, church members and family. But the time is coming, very soon, when there will no longer be living Black men who were Tuskegee Airmen, Negro League players or Pullman porters.

"They're a link to the past," Sinkfield said of the Tuskegee Airmen, which also can be said of the baseball players and porters. "They sent forth a legacy of what we should be about. What they did was timeless."

---

* Since this piece was first published, San Antonio's last surviving Tuskegee Airmen passed away: James Bynum in 2022 and Eugene Derricotte in 2023.

Slavery of the Past Looms
over the Present

The Emancipation Proclamation was signed 157 years before George Floyd's killing amplified voices for racial justice. This passage of time is not so great. The last of the former enslaved died in the early 1970s. This means that more than 100 million Americans living today, one-third of the population, were alive at the same time as men and women freed by Abraham Lincoln's signature. Children of former enslaved people are still living. Last July the *Washington Post* profiled Daniel Smith, the eighty-eight-year-old son of one of them.

In the United States, African Americans own about one-tenth the wealth of white Americans. Black households with a college degree have less wealth than white households without a college degree. The wealth inequity between whites and Blacks is as directly a descendant of slavery as is Daniel Smith.

Structural or systemic inequity and racism mean they were designed and institutionalized. For most of this nation's history it was the intent, through government policies, that African Americans not acquire generational wealth.

Slavery was an institution in which Black lives didn't matter even as Black bodies were valued for the profits from their sale and the labor extracted from them that enriched their owners and the nation, North as well as South. Their lives mattered so little that during the three most critical periods in US history—the creation of the Constitution, Reconstruction after the Civil

War and recovery from the Great Depression—the freedom, safety and opportunities for Black people were bargained away in compromises.

In his "To Fulfill These Rights" speech at Howard University in June 1965, President Lyndon B. Johnson spoke of this entrenched inequality. Noting that the battle for true equality between Blacks and whites was losing ground, Johnson said, "We are not completely sure why this is. We know the causes are complex and subtle. But we do know the two broad basic reasons."

The first reason, he said, was the "inherited, gateless poverty" in which Blacks and whites were trapped. "But there is a second cause," he added, "much more difficult to explain. It is the devastating heritage of long years of slavery, and a century of oppression, hatred and injustice."

What's curious is that after expressing uncertainty about why equality between whites and Blacks wasn't narrowing, Johnson accurately explains the root of the inequality in the heritage of slavery.

George Floyd's death shocked many white Americans into an awareness there was much they didn't know about the daily and historical treatment of African Americans, and it awakened an unprecedented willingness to listen, read and learn more about the history of Black people in this country—history that is American history.

To understand where we are today is to know slavery's centrality to the legal and economic development of the United States. At the time of the American Revolution there were about half a million enslaved people in the thirteen colonies, or 20 percent of the population. To justify the brutality of chattel slavery, racist theories took root establishing Black people as inferior to white people and closer related to beasts.

The word "slavery" doesn't appear in the Constitution, yet its passage wouldn't have been possible without two compromises that extended its life and empowered slaveholding states in the South. With Northern states wanting to abolish the slave trade and Southern states wanting to keep it, the compromise was that the Constitution prevented Congress from stopping the slave trade until 1808, allowing it to continue for at least twenty years.

For the House of Representatives, slave states could count a member of its enslaved population as three-fifths of a person. This three-fifths compromise gave those states disproportionate representation and power over free states. This led to another compromise. In the debate about whether the president should be elected by Congress or direct vote of the people, it was decided that the people would vote for delegates to an Electoral College, which would elect the president.

The number of delegates a state could have in the Electoral College would be determined by the number of representatives it had in the House, again giving slave states an advantage over free states and giving the South disproportionate power in Congress, which it would exercise into the twenty-first century.

This power, exercised through slavery, was converted into wealth. By 1861 the 4 million enslaved in the United States were worth $3.5 billion, more than all other businesses combined. The most valuable financial asset in the nation was human beings who were brutalized for their uncompensated labor. A civil war would be fought to free them. But how free would they truly be?

Inequality Can Only Be
Reversed with Intent

It's not difficult to compromise when you don't have much skin in the game. It's especially easy when Party A makes a deal with Party B so that Party C suffers most from the compromise.

Slavery has long and frequently been called America's original sin. Sinners are supposed to show repentance, first by refraining from committing the sin, and then by acknowledging, apologizing and atoning to correct some of the harm done.

Instead of discontinuing the institution of slavery, America's Founding Fathers allowed the nation to continue sinning with constitutional compromises that continued the slave trade, counting the enslaved as three-fifths of a person, which gave slave-owning (Southern) states disproportionate power in representation; and a fugitive slave clause requiring the return of escaped enslaved people to their owners.

Thus began a century-transcending tradition of political bargaining between white politicians, North and South, Republicans and Democrats in which what was compromised was the freedom and citizenship of Black people. From their importation until integration, a people used as property to create a nation's generational wealth were denied opportunities to acquire the property and means by which they could create generational wealth for their families. American slavery was a multibillion-dollar barbaric enterprise, worth more than the combined wealth of the rest of the nation's businesses.

On April 11, 1865, two days after Confederate general Robert E. Lee surrendered to Union general Ulysses S. Grant to end the Civil War, John Wilkes Booth listened to President Abraham Lincoln speak about giving Black freedmen the vote. Booth told a co-conspirator, "That means [n-word] citizenship." Three days later, he shot Lincoln, who died the following day.

The North won the war. But the Black men, women and children whose uncompensated labor was worth $3.5 billion to the nation received not a dime with which to begin new lives.

Reconstruction was America trying to address its inequities and its first attempt at a multiracial democracy. Public schools for Black and white students were opened throughout the South; Black men were elected to local and federal offices; federal troops were placed in the South to protect Black people; civil rights legislation was enacted; and new constitutional amendments abolished slavery, established birthright citizenship and allowed all men to vote regardless of race, color or previous condition of servitude.

But Reconstruction was aborted in the Compromise of 1877, which removed federal troops from the South. Political and economic gains made by African Americans were wiped away by Jim Crow laws and an escalation of racist violence.

Having been compromised out of the Constitution in the eighteenth century and out of Reconstruction in the nineteenth century, African Americans would be compromised out of the full benefits of the New Deal in the twentieth century. Because of the power of southern Democrats, arising from the compromises made in 1787, the only way President Franklin D. Roosevelt could push his programs through Congress was to allow the Dixiecrats to exclude farmworkers and domestic servants (Black people) from the Social Security Act and minimum wage legislation. The nation's postwar housing policy was also designed to deny African Americans the same opportunities afforded to white people to build wealth through home equity. That's another column for another day.

The point of these past two columns is that inequality in the United States was created with intent—and it must be reversed with intent.

The civil rights movement brought this nation a long way into being more intentional in narrowing inequality, and the killing of George Floyd opened eyes and minds to the distance we still must travel.

Only with the signing of the Voting Rights Act of 1965 did the United States become a multiracial democracy. There are millions of Americans who are older.

The ex-president of the United States and his enablers in Congress lied about the results of last November's election and tried to invalidate the ballots of millions of Black citizens in four states whose votes decided the election—Black voters exercising the citizenship that frightened and enraged Booth to the point of assassinating Lincoln.

Last week that twice-impeached ex-president was put on trial in the Senate for inciting a mob to attack the US Capitol, a mob that would have assassinated his vice president, the speaker of the House and any elected official they got their hands on, a mob that did what the Confederate Army couldn't do—brought a Confederate flag into the Capitol.

The House managers presenting the case against the ex-president with devastating clarity and moral indignation included men and women who were Jewish, Latino, Asian American and African American. They were uncompromising in their defense of democratic values and civic virtues.

The Founding Fathers may not have imagined all of them as citizens. But it's easy to imagine that they would be pleased that these citizens didn't compromise in their defense of the Constitution and the democracy we still try to perfect.

May This Winter Storm
Thaw Our Conscience

Late Valentine's Day drifts of snow, like feelings you don't see coming, began floating across the dark, then landing and sticking to the ground. By morning the snow, sugary and wedding-cake white, was glistening in sunlight. Photos of the rare sight, especially of the children enjoying it, were shared across social media and will be part of family albums for decades. But as the day progressed, the novelty of San Antonio's most significant snowfall since 1985 began to wear off as people began to feel just how cold it was...indoors...with decreasing power.

By noon Monday many of us were, for the first time, becoming familiar with the name and responsibilities of the Electric Reliability Council of Texas, or ERCOT, realizing that it and elected leaders had failed in preparing for a winter storm we all knew was coming. We tried to understand if rolling blackouts or outages were causing the electricity to go out more frequently and for longer periods of time.

I stopped counting the outages in my neighborhood by the time they reached twenty, a number higher than the temperature. Following ERCOT's updates, I reflected that "outage" and "outrage" were separated by one letter. I was tempted to run outside to shout out my revelation but was afraid I'd slip on the ice and snow.

Speaking of slipping, I'd read that sprinkling cat litter on ice gives you traction, which is true. What I hadn't read was that in a couple of days, when the cat litter had become mud-like, it would be easier to slip on than the ice.

By nightfall, with water having long ago stopped and electricity coming on less, I was using my phone's flashlight and its Wi-Fi hot spot. I could see my breath in white puffs. I was curious if there was a pattern to which neighborhoods and sides of town were having problems, and went on Facebook to ask if people had or hadn't experienced outages and on what side of town they lived.

I received nearly four hundred responses, and it was clear there was no rhyme or reason to where there were outages and where there weren't. Low- and middle-income neighborhoods had no outages, and high-priced neighborhoods had some of the worst. The difference, of course, is that some San Antonians had resources to ease the problem while others had none. Like the pandemic, the winter storm equalized who could be hit yet magnified who could better respond.

Monday night's last spurt of power lasted twenty seconds, the time it took for Usain Bolt to run two hundred meters. By Tuesday morning in my house, I could see my breath in white puffs, and a pan of water was crusting to ice. I emptied the refrigerator and placed the contents on the counter, where it was colder. By Thursday afternoon I had full power and water.

This wasn't an ordeal but an experience. Throughout the week, I kept saying to myself, "People live like this. People shouldn't live like this." But they do, every day, in this city. Not just the homeless, but also those who live in deteriorating housing where cold air pours through holes in the ceiling, walls or floors.

Family and friends from out of town called, texted and emailed to check on me. I'm fortunate. I had people who cared enough to check on me, but also, I told them, unlike many, including in my neighborhood, I had options and resources.

Last week many of us were greatly inconvenienced by the

weather and poor leadership. But we weren't in pain. What we went through for hours and days, our sisters and brothers endure for weeks, months, years. There's a difference between knowing that discomfort will soon end and doubting, as tens of thousands do each day, that their suffering will ever stop.

In his short story "Gooseberries," Anton Chekhov writes about awareness of another's hardships:

> The happy man only feels at ease because the unhappy bear their burdens in silence, and without that silence happiness would be impossible.... There ought to be behind the door of every happy, contented man someone standing with a hammer continually reminding him with a tap that there are unhappy people; that however happy he may be, life will show him her laws sooner or later, trouble will come for him—disease, poverty, losses, and no one will see or hear, just as now he neither sees nor hears others.

A friend in Houston told me that the sense of urgency we felt to get heat, water and comfort for ourselves and families should now translate into a heightened sense of urgency to help all in need. Like Chekhov, she was saying the winter storm should be the hammer tapping our conscience and reminding us of those still trapped and suffering in storms, bearing their burdens in silence.

Pop Only Says What Nation
Needs to Hear

On the week Jackie Robinson Day was celebrated throughout Major League Baseball, the greatest coach in NBA history spoke out for voting rights and against the violent overthrow of the government while a US senator who'd enabled the insurrectionists went on the attack against the national pastime.

On Monday San Antonio Spurs head coach Gregg Popovich, speaking about the fatal police shooting of unarmed twenty-year-old Daunte Wright, said, "It just makes you sick to your stomach."

Over the course of the pandemic, Pop's beard and hair have whitened and his locks now flow down to his shoulders. If his look of an Old Testament prophet is newly acquired, his penchant for prophetic denunciations of racism and injustice is not.

In 2006 I met former Spurs play-by-play announcer Jay Howard, and we got to talking about Pop. "People think that because he's an Air Force veteran he's some kind of hard-core conservative, but he's not," he said.

That became clear during the Donald Trump presidency. But I've always seen Pop's criticisms as extending beyond Trump and into a larger, structural critique of historic inequality, and as a challenge to the nation to live up to its values and treat each other well.

On Spurs Media Day in 2017, he said:

Obviously, race is the elephant in the room and we all understand that. Unless it is talked about constantly, it's not going to get better. "Oh, they're talking about that again. They pulled the race card again. Why do we have to talk about that?" Well, because it's uncomfortable. There has to be an uncomfortable element in the discourse for anything to change, whether it's the LGBT movement or women's suffrage, race—it doesn't matter. People have to be made to feel uncomfortable, and especially white people, because we're comfortable. We still have no clue what being born white means. And if you read some of the recent literature, you realize there really is no such thing as whiteness. We kind of made it up. That's not my original thought, but it's true.

In speaking out against Trump's lie about the election being stolen, and the January 6 insurrection and restrictive voting legislation fueled by that lie, Pop challenged NBA owners—including Spurs ownership—on why they donate to candidates advancing the lie.

"One has to question why one would give money to people who participated in that sort of lie, whether it's people in Texas or any other place," he said. "How did they enjoy January 6? How do we enjoy the rise of the extremism we are seeing? And to have politicians who divert attention, or out-and-out lie about it, seems to me to be unbelievably dangerous. We are talking about our country, our democracy."

Pop's outspokenness has turned off those who decry the intersection of sports and politics. These are the same people who got upset when Colin Kaepernick took a knee or Megan Rapinoe made a stand. Many of those upset with mixing sports and politics celebrated on Thursday, the seventy-fourth anniversary of Robinson breaking Major League Baseball's color bar. As if Brooklyn Dodgers owner Branch Rickey wasn't political in signing Robinson. As if Robinson's breakthrough didn't have political repercussions beyond sports. As if Robinson wasn't the most politically outspoken athlete before Muhammad Ali.

As if where to award a professional sports franchise and where to build a stadium aren't political decisions.

Major League Baseball moved this summer's All-Star Game out of Atlanta because of Georgia's new law making voting more cumbersome, legislation denounced by scores of corporations, including Coca-Cola.

Republican senator Ted Cruz of Texas and co-insurrectionist senator Josh Hawley of Missouri, along with Senator Mike Lee of Utah, proposed legislation that would punish Major League Baseball by stripping it of its antitrust exemption. Pretty rich, as this has been long advocated by liberals, unions and the Major League Baseball Players Association before free agency. (Google "Curt Flood and Marvin Miller.")

"This past month, we have seen the rise of the woke corporation. We have seen the rise of big business enforcing a woke standard," said Cruz, who's not woke to how lame it is to use "woke."

Let's break this down: Atlanta got the All-Star Game because the Braves play in Atlanta. The Braves moved from Milwaukee and began playing in Atlanta in 1966. Braves legend Hank Aaron, a Mobile, Alabama, native, didn't want to return to the Deep South. The move was facilitated by a decision prohibiting segregated seating and facilities at sporting events in Atlanta—a very political decision supported by corporations such as Coca-Cola. The Braves' arrival in Atlanta led to the NFL, NBA and NHL following MLB south.

Cruz and Hawley can play games with lies and stir more violence. But Prophet Pop, righteously indignant, will keep reading, pushing and asking questions needing to be answered: "How did they enjoy January 6? How do we enjoy the rise of the extremism we are seeing?"

Still Exalting Valleys
and Making Low Hills and Mountains

There are twenty-eight of us. Twenty-eight Black children looking in the direction of a photographer. We're standing on my
grandparents' patio in their East Side neighborhood near the
Freeman Coliseum.

It's a party for my third birthday. A few years ago I came
across the issue of the newspaper it appeared in, the *San Antonio Register*, which was the oldest Black newspaper in the city.
What struck me was the date of that edition, August 16, 1963,
which I looked at through the lens of history knowing that in
less than two weeks we would be immortalized.

Not us specifically, but on August 28 at the March on Washington, Martin Luther King Jr. would deliver his "I Have a
Dream" speech and talk about little Black boys and Black girls
joining hands with little white boys and white girls as sisters
and brothers. We were among the millions of other anonymous
children he imagined as inheritors of a "Beloved Community."
In our small hands would be placed the promise and responsibility of living out a democracy untethered by the restraints of
injustice and inequality.

Standing on a patio in Texas, we were unaware that on the
roads before us were long-standing barriers built to detour our
dreams and ambitions, to delay and, if possible, deny.

We were also unaware that a great wind was gathering
strength, in the form of the civil rights movement, to blow

away those barriers before we saw and were deterred by them. We couldn't have known we'd be part of the first generation of Negro, Black, African American children not to run into those legal barriers to public accommodations and the voting booth.

In less than a year would come passage of the Civil Rights Act of 1964, followed the next year by the Voting Rights Act of 1965. We would be the beneficiaries of legislation that would afford us rights denied our parents. By the time we started going to the downtown Majestic Theatre, we wouldn't have to enter through the back alley to sit in the balcony as they did. We walked through the front door like our white peers—who, by law, would be our peers.

Looking at the birthday photo, I wondered what became of those children. We may have never been as secure and protected as we were on my grandparents' patio that long-ago August afternoon. But we had to leave the patio to enter the world they helped shape. We had to leave the patio to engage the world so we would profit and suffer from our encounters with it and try to live well enough and long enough to make some difference.

Did we, I wondered? Did we embrace the future King imagined, the future he and others died for and our families toiled for? What did we do to make it easier for the generations that came after us? Did we exalt the valleys, make low the hills and mountains, make rough places plain and crooked places straight?

How many of those children, still living, could I find and interview?

I signed a contract with Trinity University Press to write *Dreaming US: Where Did We Go from There?* The subtitle referred to King's last book, published in 1967, *Where Do We Go from Here: Chaos or Community?*

I did interviews and started writing, and there came a point when I stopped. Beyond thinking about it and writing notes, I pretty much abandoned it. I no longer knew where to go with the story because the embrace of Donald Trump by white supremacists and neo-Nazis, and he of them, made it clear that the story was ongoing and that chaos may yet be the answer to King's question. I didn't want to write a book of despair.

Then George Floyd was killed, and out of that horror rose a multiracial, multigenerational movement that was perhaps the largest social movement in history. It revived my hope that community—the Beloved Community—is still possible.

I don't know when, if ever, I'll get back to *Dreaming US*. It certainly won't be before the end of the year. But the uncertainty of whether chaos or community is our destination no longer blocks me from continuing. The conclusion of any story can never be assumed. Like the fight for justice, most stories are ongoing. The conclusion, like justice and rights fought for and won, can never be taken for granted.

The children from that birthday party photo are now at least sixty years old. We're older than our parents and grandparents were in 1963, yet it blows my mind that in 2021 the right to vote is under attack, the Voting Rights Act is in danger of being eviscerated and our democracy is threatened.

The caption under the photo called me "the young celebrant." But there are some things, it's clear, we celebrated too early.

With a Guilty Verdict, the Moral Arc Slowly Bends

It would rise into the hundreds of millions, maybe even a billion, the number of people who saw a man die on the street.

Only one other time in history has the murder of a man on an American street—on any nation's street—been watched by so many and so stopped the world: the assassination of President John F. Kennedy in 1963. Within a week, George Floyd had become one of the most famous names in the world. His death, like Kennedy's, was one of the most infamous and consequential.

Tuesday, when it was announced that the jury had reached a verdict in Derek Chauvin's trial, millions gathered around televisions and radios, in public and private. Upon the announcement that the former Minneapolis police officer had been found guilty on all three counts, including the most serious charge of second-degree murder, people cheered, cried and hugged in joy. I felt nothing.

I'm emotional. It doesn't take much movement on the sadness-to-joy scale, in either direction, for me to choke up and shed a track of tears. On the night of May 25 I watched Floyd die, and it unplugged new tears from old wells of memory and history. I've taken the transcript of that fatal encounter, removed the words of Chauvin and the other officers, and cried as I read the painfully poetic soliloquy of a man who knew he was dying.

But I listened to the verdict and felt neither happiness nor sadness. When the jury began deliberations Monday, we collectively tensed because we weren't certain a jury would see a truth, a crime, that was self-evident. We knew that if it weren't for a cell phone recording, the verdict in 2021 would have been the same as it would have been in 1921. All that I felt was relief that this nation didn't break.

The United States has been bent and fractured by race, world wars, depressions and recessions, terrorist attacks from abroad and, more frequently, terrorist attacks from within. The Civil War was the one time we broke, and we're still fighting that battle, including white nationalist terrorist attacks dating back to Reconstruction.

Had the jury not confirmed the murder we saw, had it not concluded that a Black life mattered even when taken by a police officer, the country could have broken irreparably. Broken not only in what would have been the immediate visceral response to a different verdict but in destroying the belief that a historically inequitable justice system could be changed and was worth working for.

I have faith in this nation, in its ideals and aspirations, its capacity to correct itself and to change and grow for the better, albeit at a maddening slow pace. I have faith that we can grow into the best example of a multiracial democracy that appreciates each of its parts while denigrating none. But my faith isn't as strong as those who had no doubt that the jury would arrive at a just verdict. I know history well enough to know that too many times people have waited at the station for that just verdict only to never see it arrive.

The case of Floyd, his murder and this verdict, has a different feel. It continues to be a moment that is evolving into a historic inflection point. Never has the death of a single individual stirred the nation into mobilizing into so large of a nonviolent, multiracial and multigenerational movement. Not JFK. Not Martin Luther King Jr. Nobody.

In her brilliant and metaphor-rich book *Caste: The Origins of our Discontents*, Isabel Wilkerson compared America and its unaddressed systemic racism to an old house. "The owner of an old house knows that whatever you are ignoring will never go away," she writes. "Whatever is lurking will fester whether you choose to look or not. Ignorance is no protection from the consequence of inaction. Whatever you are wishing away will gnaw at you until you gather the courage to face what you would rather not see."

George Floyd is the neighbor we saw get killed in the front yard of our old house. We couldn't call the police because a policeman killed him. His murder struck a chord and helped many find the courage to look, for the first time, in the basements and attics of their old house, to learn histories they didn't know and talk to neighbors they'd not spoken to before. It's the only way to understand someone else's struggles, affirm their humanity and fix the things that must be repaired.

Last week's verdict strengthened the railing of hope we lean on to keep from falling.

It's Voter Suppression in Texas, not Ballot Security

The best thing about Senate Bill 7—the attack on voting access in the Texas senate—is that it doesn't criminalize giving someone water to drink. Texas Republicans may want some voters to stand in long lines for unconscionable periods of time for no good reason, but, hey, unlike Georgia Republicans, they don't want them to go thirsty.

Call it voter suppression with compassion (or hydration) if you want, but make sure to call it voter suppression because the goal is to reduce the number of people who vote or register to vote—or, to be even more blunt, to discourage people who probably aren't inclined to vote for these Republican legislators.

As SB 7 moves forward, passed in the Senate along partisan lines early Thursday, we know this drill. On March 25 Georgia governor Brian Kemp signed a package of restrictive voting bills into law less than two hours after it was passed by the state's general assembly. The new Georgia law reduces the time people can request an absentee ballot and limits where drop boxes can be placed and when they can be used.

The partisan dynamics are painfully obvious. There were no problems with drop boxes or more time requesting absentee ballots before Joe Biden beat Donald Trump in the November presidential election in Georgia. There were no problems before January 5 when two Democrats, the Rev. Raphael Warnock and Jon Ossoff, won the state's US Senate races.

More than 1.3 million Georgians voted by mail in last year's elections; from henceforth, they must have a voter ID to cast a ballot. Most ominously, the elected secretary of state will be replaced as chair of Georgia's election board by an appointee of the legislature. There was no problem with Republican Brad Raffensperger chairing the state election board until he resisted Trump's begging and bullying to overturn Georgia's election results.

This new arrangement makes it possible for the partisan chair of the state election board to meddle with the election results, say, in Fulton County, whose Democratic and African American base propelled Biden, Warnock and Ossoff to their wins. And, of course, the new law makes it illegal for outside groups to offer water or food to voters standing in line. This wasn't an issue until Democrats won.

Georgia officials best brace themselves in 2022 for a massive civil disobedience campaign in which thousands of "outsiders" risk going to jail for handing out food and water to people sweltering in long lines to vote.

People will swelter in Texas too. Senate Bill 7 heads to the house, having been approved along partisan lines. The bill limits early voting hours, ends drive-through voting, prevents local elections officials from encouraging qualified voters to fill out applications to vote by mail and raises the risk of voter intimidation by allowing partisan poll watchers to record voters receiving help with their ballots.

State senator Bryan Hughes, R-Tyler, said the legislation is an effort to strike a balance between "maintaining fair and honest elections with the opportunity to exercise one's right to vote." But SB 7 is unnecessary because in 2020, in Texas and across the nation, we not only had "fair and honest elections" but the most secure elections in history. Voting fraud is virtually nonexistent in the United States, leading critics of these voting suppression measures to call them "solutions in search of problems."

Let's not forget, Republicans fared very well in Texas's last election with record turnout and no measurable voter fraud (the Big Lie). Is the issue that races are—gasp!—becoming competitive as Texas's population grows, demographics change and more Democrats vote? Is the fear that one day Texas will go purple or blue as has Georgia?

Voting shouldn't be a Hunger Games competition or a test of endurance and strength like the twelve labors of Hercules. Politicians discouraging citizens from exercising their right to vote instead of encouraging their participation are a threat to democracy, especially when they are claiming to protect it.

To Sanitize 1619 Is to Deny America's History

There must doubtless be an unhappy influence on the manners of our people produced by the existence of slavery among us. The whole commerce between master and slave is a perpetual exercise of the most boisterous passions, the most unremitting despotism on the one part, and degrading submissions on the other. Our children see this, and learn to imitate it; for man is an imitative animal.

    —Thomas Jefferson, *Notes on the State of Virginia*

I think that issue that we all are concerned about—racial discrimination—it was our original sin. We've been working for two hundred-and-some-odd years to get past it....We're still working on it, and I just simply don't think that's part of the core underpinning of what American civic education ought to be about.

    —Senate minority leader Mitch McConnell

History is a book of sequences and consequences. Chapter builds upon chapter, one event leading to another, until a story is more fully told and its lessons—it is hoped—better understood.

Thomas Jefferson, brilliant and immortal, was torn by the benefits his nation derived from its public sin and the pleasure he received from his own. In a draft of the Declaration of Independence, he excoriated King George III over the African slave trade even though, as he wrote, the enslaved he owned tended to his Monticello plantation. One of the greatest of our Founding Fathers was also the father of six of the children of one of his enslaved women, Sally Hemings. In *Notes on the State of Virginia*, it was Jefferson's fear of the consequences and legacy of slavery that compelled him to write, "I tremble for my country when I reflect that God is just: that his justice cannot sleep for ever."

Slavery in America is traced to the arrival, in 1619, in Jamestown, Virginia, of an English ship carrying more than twenty kidnapped Africans. In 2019 the *New York Times* marked the four hundredth anniversary with publication of a special section, the 1619 Project. Guided by *Times* reporter Nikole Hannah-Jones, who won a Pulitzer Prize in commentary for her lead essay, the collection of essays, poetry and pictures spotlights how slavery shaped the United States' history and economic development—and how its legacy continues to haunt us.

The 1619 Project has spawned a curriculum of readings schools can use as supplemental resources, much to the objections of Republicans in state legislatures and Congress who have attacked the idea of more education about slavery as Marxist, unpatriotic and a form of critical race theory. The latter has become a catch-all phrase to denounce teaching any less than a sanitized version of American history.

On Tuesday the Texas House passed HB 3979, which limits what can be taught when it comes to race. Its author, Representative Steve Toth, R-The Woodlands, said his bill was about "teaching racial harmony by telling the truth that we are all equal, both in God's eyes and our founding documents." In God's eyes, yes, which is why Jefferson trembled. But the Constitution, among other things, allowed the slave trade and required the return of escaped enslaved people to their owners.

Senator Mitch McConnell doesn't consider 1619 a significant date. "I think this is about American history and the most important dates in American history. And in my view—and I think most Americans think—dates like 1776, the Declaration of

Independence, 1787, the Constitution, 1861 to 1865, the Civil War, are sort of the basic tenets of American history," McConnell said last week at the University of Louisville.

Without 1619, the Constitution is a different document and the balance of power changes. Without 1619, there's no Civil War. Without 1619, there's no reason for Juneteenth.

Texas-born and -raised historian Annette Gordon-Reed won a Pulitzer Prize for *The Hemingses of Monticello: An American Family*. In her superb new book, *On Juneteenth*, she writes, "As painful as it may be, recognizing—though not dwelling on—tragedy and the role it plays in our individual lives, and in the life of a state or nation is, I think, a sign of maturity."

McConnell says we've been working for more than two hundred years to get past our original sin and that we're still working at it. We're not past it because we still flinch at what made Jefferson tremble: the consequences of 1619.

Marvin Gaye's Genius Timeless

It wasn't only the music of Marvin Gaye that was synonymous with romance. It was also his name. I can't say with certainty that no other musician has been name-checked and had more songs written about him across a wider genre of music than Gaye. But I'm confident there's no other singer whose name has been more frequently invoked as a prelude to making love.

The Whispers, on "In the Mood," sing: "We'll dance to sweet music / How about some Marvin Gaye? / Feel like some sexual healing." In "Rock Wit'cha," Bobby Brown suggests: "How bout a little music now / Let's hear some Marvin Gaye." Spandau Ballet, in "True," talk about "Listening to Marvin all night long." Most explicitly, in the song "Marvin Gaye," singers Charlie Puth and Meghan Trainor use his name as a verb for, well, you know: "Let's Marvin Gaye and get it on."

For Marvin Gaye to be the Avatar of Romance isn't a stretch for a singer who during the 1960s was Motown's leading man of love songs and who during the 1970s and 1980s wrote and recorded more erotic songs. But May 21 marks the fiftieth anniversary of the release of the album that elevated Gaye as an artist and established him as a genius. *What's Going On* was a suite of nine impeccably crafted songs, each flowing into the next, guided by Gaye's humane vision and remarkably expressive and elastic voice.

The album was an artist's soulful and prophetic response to the strife and turmoil of his times—a thoughtful and melodic commentary on racism, the Vietnam War, poverty, the environment, drug addiction and spiritual longing. The title song, "What's Going On," has been called a musical question, but it's not a question. It's a demand to be heard, an insistence to listen and learn. Gaye isn't a seeker looking for answers. Having borne witness to suffering, to the wreckage left in the wake of war, indifference and hate, Gaye is the prophet saying, "Talk to me, so you can see. What's going on . . . I'll tell you what's going on."

His fellow genius and Motown legend Smokey Robinson called it the greatest album ever. He's not alone. Last year in a ranking of the five hundred greatest albums of all time, *Rolling Stone* magazine ranked *What's Going On* no. 1.

It was an album rising from Gaye's concerns about what was happening in the country and from conversations with his brother about his experience serving in Vietnam. But it was also an album that grew out of his depression over the death of Tammi Terrell, whom he'd teamed with for memorable duets. In 1967 Terrell collapsed in his arms on stage and was diagnosed with a brain tumor. She died in 1970.

Motown founder Berry Gordy Jr. thought the album would flop. When the single "What's Going On" was released in February 1971 and became an immediate hit, Gordy gave Gaye one month to create the rest of the album.

As Curtis Mayfield and Nina Simone had done before him, Gaye infused Black music with a social conscience, showing that soul music wasn't only music to dance and make love to but could be a music that made you think and inspired you to act. Wedding jazz elements to a funk groove with layered multi-tracks of his voice gave the impression of a chorus of Marvin Gayes. Threading through each song is Gaye's anguished plea for love, understanding and peace. Not only was it Gaye's most political album, it was his most spiritual.

Because Gaye had complete artistic control over the album, he paved the way for other Motown artists, such as Stevie Wonder, to be given the same creative license. The album inspired more socially conscious music among Black artists, most notably with Kenneth Gamble and Leon Huff's Philly Sound.

Great art is timeless. The social ills Gaye addressed remain. Given only one artist I could listen to, it would be Marvin Gaye. Limited to only one album, it would be *What's Going On*.

His relevance is as undeniable as his talent. Every day I see the news, and it "make me wanna holler and throw up both my hands."

Remember These Other
Massacres of Blacks, Too

By this date in 1921 the thick black smoke from arsonists on the ground and in the sky that hovered over Tulsa's Greenwood district had cleared, revealing the smoldering ruins of a Black community destroyed by hate. Today the history of the Tulsa race massacre, which took place May 31–June 1 that year, is seen in stunning clarity, its centennial surrounded by unprecedented media coverage—including a spate of documentaries, books and newspaper, magazine and online articles.

But Tulsa wasn't an aberration, an atrocity never seen before or since. Greenwood wasn't the only Black community in the United States to be attacked by white supremacists. Still shrouded and buried deep in our history are other datelines of racist mob violence.

It was a violence rooted in the institution of slavery. John Locke, the seventeenth-century English political philosopher, wrote that when a man enslaves another man, he has entered a state of war with him. After emancipation and the Civil War, Black people sought to raise families, own land, build businesses, create safe and self-sustaining communities and live in freedom and peace. But Jim Crow, Black codes and white mobs, especially in the South, continued to wage war on them.

During Reconstruction, on Easter Sunday in 1873 in Colfax, Louisiana, armed Black men who'd gathered to defend a courthouse surrendered to a white paramilitary group known as the

White League. Upon surrender, as many as 150 of the Black men were killed, some after being held prisoner for several hours. In 1898 Wilmington, North Carolina, was a city with a Black majority, Black elected officials who served as part of a multiracial government and a prosperous Black middle class. On November 10 white supremacists declared a "White Declaration of Independence," overthrew the local government and murdered sixty to three hundred Black residents. David Zucchino, author of *Wilmington's Lie: The Murderous Coup of 1898 and the Rise of White Supremacy*, calls it America's first and only armed overthrow of a legally elected government.

In Slocum in East Texas, whites in July 1910 went on a rampage against Black residents, shooting them down, torching their homes and running them out of town. No one knows how many were killed. It could be in the dozens. It could be one hundred to two hundred. As is often the case in these massacres, bodies were buried in mass graves or thrown into rivers. The year 1919 was so bloody with racial violence across the United States that it was called the Red Summer. That July in Longview, white people burned down homes and business of Black residents, killing one. In September in Elaine, Arkansas, a white mob attacked Black farmers attempting to unionize, killing up to two hundred Black residents.

Before Tulsa's centennial, the 1923 murders of 150 Black people in Rosewood, Florida, may have been the better known of the massacres because of John Singleton's 1997 film *Rosewood*.

There were other massacres, along with more than a century of domestic terrorism—lynchings, Black citizens being run out of towns and Black citizens having their land confiscated. Animating all these attacks were white supremacy and the desire to suppress the rights and ambitions of Black citizens. Beyond terrorizing Blacks, these were assaults on democracy, a decades-long campaign of pillage and plunder that, paired with the use of laws, limited the opportunities of African Americans to fully participate in the political system and create generational wealth.

This isn't Black history that should be taught and known. This is American history that should be taught and known. The only reason for not wanting to learn all your nation's history, the ugly as well as the glorious, is that you don't want to feel uncomfortable or be held accountable. Our intelligence agencies warn that white nationalist groups are the greatest threat to the nation. In 1921 white supremacy destroyed Black Tulsa. In 2021 white supremacy threatens to destroy the United States. This time, as violence escalates and democracy is dismantled, Black people won't be the only ones who suffer.

Whatever discomfort we feel learning unpleasant facts about our history pales to the pain we'll feel in refusing to learn from that history.

Leave Fears about the Colonoscopy Behind

For reasons that don't satisfy me, the editors and powers that be of this otherwise great newspaper won't allow this column to be accompanied by photos from my recent colonoscopy. Among their objections offered, all of which I find insufficient, are that publishing eight color photos of my colon would be "disgusting," "gross," "sick" and "inexcusable self-indulgence." All these things were said without anyone taking up my offer to look at the photos before they declined.

Colonoscopies have an image problem.

"Wait, you're going to put a camera on a long, flexible tubular instrument and insert it WHERE and to do WHAT? While I'm alive? Isn't that an autopsy thing?"

The optics are poor, but the preventive power of a colonoscopy is priceless. It is painless, and those images captured by the camera can save your life, should you have colorectal cancer and it's caught in time. Those images can add years spent with loved ones and, if you had more imaginative editors and powers that be, provide you with pictures of your colon worthy of being published in a newspaper.

I had my first colonoscopy in November 2010, a few months after I turned fifty. It turned out well. I only had one polyp and was told to have a second colonoscopy in five years. I didn't. My personal physician kept on me about it, but I always found a reason not to do it. Not because I was afraid. Having already gone through one, I knew it was painless and essential. But I'm a procrastinator by nature and—when it comes to getting something checked out by a doctor—by gender.

Finally, after blood tests from my physical this year revealed a marker for colon cancer, my doctor had enough and was nononsense about what I had to do.

Everyone will tell you that the worst thing about a colonoscopy is the prepping the day before and the gallon of liquid solution you must drink to clean yourself out. This time I took the pills, and while you still must drink ninety-six ounces of water, it's not a gallon.

Last Monday I went in for the procedure at the San Antonio Gastroenterology Endoscopy Center where, it turns out, the prepping area had a great soundtrack playing, although it was strange undressing and slipping into a hospital gown as Smokey Robinson sang "Ooo Baby, Baby." I had the same team as the first time—Dr. Ernesto Guerra, a nurse named Mary and an anesthesiologist named Chris.

I don't have many fears beyond clowns, rats, unwashed hands, ghosts named Maggie, the flying monkeys from *The Wizard of Oz*, and hooking up with a Kardashian and thinking I've found true love. But one of those fears is the anesthesia not working before the doctor starts working. I was worrying about that when I heard the words "wake up." It was over. Soon Dr. Guerra came over and told me, "It was a beautiful procedure."

All was good. No polyps. I looked at the eight photos and thought, "These are beautiful. I've got a photogenic colon." Which you, dear reader, would see for yourself were it not for jealous editors and powers that be.

Kidding aside, the American Cancer Society says that colorectal cancer is the third-most common cancer diagnosed in both men and women in the United States and, combining both men and women, the second-deadliest cancer in the country. African

Americans are twenty times more likely to get colorectal cancer and about 40 percent more likely to die from it than other groups. Also, men of color are less likely to have their cancer detected in time because of a reluctance to get tested.

Brothers and sisters, whatever your ethnicity, get your colonoscopies. There is absolutely no pain. The only pain you're leaving behind (pun intended) is the mourning of loved ones who you left too soon because you didn't get tested. Don't be afraid of what you shouldn't fear. Do fear that which you can prevent.

I'm sorry you can't see photos of my beautiful colon. But the Christmas cards I'm sending out this year will be special.

Don't Just Use MLK's Thirty-Five Words as Protective Shield

On August 28, 1963, in Washington, DC, Martin Luther King Jr. took to the podium and said, "I have a dream that my four little children will one day live in a nation where they will not be judged by the color of their skin but by the content of their character."

That was his entire speech—thirty-five words. Before that day, it would seem, King had never written or said anything else. After that day he would never write or say another word.

You can look it up. Or you could if you're able to find the books used by people such as Senator Josh Hawley and House minority leader Kevin McCarthy, which, apparently, teach that from 1955 to 1968 King gave only that one speech. In that one oration of thirty-five words, he gave lifetime cover to people to avoid discussing the difficult issues that King spent—and gave—his life addressing. The same people who, were he alive, would be lambasting him as a communist, troublemaker and un-American as their parents and grandparents did when he walked the earth.

Last month on the Senate floor, Hawley used those thirty-five words to attack critical race theory. But he has yet to find any of King's passages on nonviolence to criticize the violent insurrectionists he encouraged in January. Last week McCarthy said, "Critical race theory goes against everything Martin Luther King Jr. taught us—to not judge others by the color of their skin."

How long are we going to do this, people? (In my mind, I hear King in a speech—not "I Have a Dream"—saying, "How long? Not long!")

Before 2021 none of the loudest critics of critical race theory—most of whom are white—had ever used the words "critical," "race" and "theory" in the same day, much less strung them together. It's not just most white people who had never said those words before 2021; most Black people had never said the words either. I've been around a few Black folks in my life, have spent hours in the pews of Black churches and in the chairs of Black barbershops. As of 10:51 a.m. on July 15, 2021, I had yet to be in or hear any conversation about critical race theory.

Forgive me for being skeptical that McCarthy has learned anything from King beyond what he thinks he knows about the thirty-five words from "I Have a Dream."

King's daughter Bernice King responded to McCarthy with a tweet: "Rep. McCarthy, I encourage you to study my father's teachings and words well beyond the last lines of 'I Have a Dream.' This nation has yet to firmly commit to the intensive, multifaceted work of eradicating racism against Black people. You should help with that."

She also encouraged him to read King's last book, *Where Do We Go from Here: Chaos or Community?* in which King writes passages like: "The persistence of racism in depth and the dawning awareness that Negro demands will necessitate structural changes in society have generated a new phase of white resistance in North and South." This isn't the cuddly and comfy Tickle-Me-Martin doll who speaks thirty-five words and is loved by all. This is the challenging, prophetic King who was despised by most of his fellow Americans at the time of his assassination. A few months before his death, a Harris poll showed King had a disapproval rating of nearly 75 percent.

Going back to 1963 and the March on Washington, where

King delivered the speech everyone loves to quote: 60 percent of Americans, in the days leading up to the march, thought it was a bad idea. The likes of Hawley and McCarthy invoke critical race theory and King for the same reason: to avoid the difficult but essential conversations about race and other issues that are uncomfortable.

Don't just quote King as a protective shield—study him, all his work, to be proactive in attacking social ills and injustices.

Considering the crowd they're playing to, Hawley and McCarthy should ponder King's last two lines in *Where Do We Go from Here?*: "We still have a choice today: nonviolent coexistence or violence coannihilation. This may well be mankind's last chance to choose between chaos and community."

Yeah, That's My Dad

Last week, a woman asked me, "Are you related to Charlie Clack?"

"Which one?" I asked.

"He worked for the Sheriff's Department."

"That's my father," I said with pride.

The woman's brother had also been a Bexar County sheriff's deputy and was good friends with my father, and, she said, talked about him often.

She tiptoed around the inevitable question, "Ah, is Charlie—"

"He passed away, five years ago," I answered. "But, yeah, he's my dad."

On Mothers' Day I wrote that in the neighborhood where I grew up, there were, with two exceptions, no fathers because of divorce, death or desertion. My parents divorced when I was four or five, and Dad, after leaving the sheriff's office where he was the first Black investigator, spent most of the rest of his life living and working outside San Antonio, including when he was a DEA agent. So we didn't have a lot of memorable moments together. Dad apologized to me, more than once, for not being around during those years. It was an apology not asked for but appreciated.

But one memory that has never faded is from a morning I was in kindergarten at Carmelite Learning Center. We were playing outside when Dad came striding up the sidewalk to the gate in his sheriff's deputy uniform—khaki pants, long-sleeve light-blue shirt, tie, white Stetson hat and a holster with a gun. I can still see him opening the gate, making sure it closed, then walking toward me. I'd left home without something, and he was bringing it to me.

The playground went silent except for the "oohs" and "aahs." I think it was the first time we, as children, experienced awe. Because everyone now knew this was my daddy, it was the first time I felt pride. After he squatted to give me whatever it was I forgot and kissed me on the forehead, he left, and some of the kids followed him to the gate, watching as he got in his squad car. Others gathered around me and transferred their awe to me. If kindergarten had a bar, I wouldn't have had to buy a drink all year.

Dad told me he learned of the Beatles because I went around the house saying, "Yeah, yeah, yeah." At that same time, through Dad, I fell in love with Muhammad Ali, the first person I became aware of outside of my family. We'd spend hours, and then decades, retelling Ali stories and reliving his fights.

On the night of June 3, 2016, I called Dad in Houston to tell him Ali was dying. Dad had just been released from the hospital, was in pain and hadn't heard about Ali's condition. "Don't tell me that, son," he said, before going to bed.

A couple days later he was readmitted to the hospital, then to a rehab facility where he passed away that November. Of all the regrets of things said and not said, of visits not made or left too short because of my impatience, one is that we didn't get to talk about Ali one last time. Or talk in depth about anything.

I never lived a day doubting my father's love for me and hope he never doubted my love for him, but I didn't visit or talk to my father in the three months before he passed because I took his presence for granted.

Sons spend lifetimes in consideration of their fathers, trying to understand them and navigate the roads leading to their approval or away from their disappointment. Because fathers are often their sons' first heroes, they are also their sons' first lessons that heroes are flawed. Those lessons can quicken harsh and bitter judgments that are tempered with time, maturity and the sons becoming aware of their own imperfections and the clay their own feet are made of.

A son's consideration of his father doesn't stop when his father leaves this world, nor do unresolved issues disappear. But deeper and stronger grow the admiration and love, and the gratitude, that you were blessed with such a life as his to consider.

Charles Edward Clack Jr. Yeah, he's my dad.

History Won't Judge Texas's Voter Suppression Law Kindly

Consider, if you will, two photographs of legislation being signed in carefully staged ceremonies. The subject of both pieces of legislation is voting, a citizen's most powerful tool in the workshop of democracy. The men signing the documents are both Texans.

Fifty-six years separate the two photographs, but the distance between the intent of the two pieces of legislation is much greater. The first was a voting rights bill, the second a voting restrictions bill.

In the first photo President Lyndon B. Johnson, on August 6, 1965, signs into law the Voting Rights Act, a bill that was not only the crown jewel of the civil rights movement but also the culmination of 178 years—since the writing of the Constitution, which limited voting to propertied white males—of efforts to expand that right to vote. Too slowly, too painfully and against too much resistance, that expansion would include, chronologically, Black men (the Fifteenth Amendment), women (the Nineteenth Amendment) and all the barriers still disenfranchising Black people (the Voting Rights Act). In 1971 it would expand that right to eighteen-year-olds through the Twenty-Sixth Amendment.

The thread running through all fights to expand the vote was the understanding that elections have integrity only when the ballot box is easily and equally accessible to all eligible voters. That was the accomplishment activists such as Martin Luther

King Jr. and John Lewis, and politicians such as LBJ and Senator Everett Dirksen, R-IL, celebrated with the Voting Rights Act's signing.

In the second photo Texas governor Greg Abbott, on Tuesday, signs into law Senate Bill 1, whose purpose is to suppress the vote by making it unnecessarily restrictive in a state that already has the most restrictive voting laws in the nation—and just completed a fair and accurate election. No feature in this new law—not the bans on drive-through voting, twenty-four-hour voting and the distribution of mail-in applications; not the new ID requirements for voting by mail; not the enhanced partisan poll-watcher protections; not the new rules and possible criminal penalties for voter assistance—is in response to any problems during the 2020 primary and general elections. These are elections the Texas secretary of state called "smooth and secure."

LBJ and his bipartisan supporters, including Dirksen, the Republican minority leader, were moved to correct injustices, but Abbott and his colleagues in the Republican-led Texas legislature appear afraid they can't honestly compete for all votes. Abbott signed SB 1 in Tyler, home of the bill's main author, Republican senator Bryan Hughes. Throughout the ceremony Hughes seemed almost giddy.

To get to the Voting Rights Act in the summer of 1965, the Edmund Pettus Bridge had to be crossed in Selma, Alabama, women and men were beaten, and lives were lost. Sacrifices and suffering led to the passage and the signing of the legislation. What bridges were crossed to get to Tyler in summer 2021? How many bodies were beaten? How many lives were lost?

What sacrifices and suffering did the smiling Hughes and preening Abbott endure to make it harder for fellow Texans to vote?

The 1965 photograph preserved a moment when historic figures gathered to expand the democratic promise of the United States. The 2021 photograph captured a moment when small, unimaginative elected officials responded to the falsehood of widespread voter fraud with very real voter suppression.

Fifty-six years from now the latter won't hold up as well as the former.

Reproductive Freedom— That's Male Privilege

One afternoon when I was in the seventh grade at Our Lady of Perpetual Help, everyone in my class was given a strange and horrible paperback book. Its glossy pages had pictures neither we nor our parents had been warned about: images of dead babies.

The book was about abortion, a word I'd never heard, and while I don't remember its title or who wrote it, these many years later I still remember a picture of what looked like a trash bag full of dead babies. I question the wisdom and purpose of sharing such graphic images with twelve-year-olds, especially without their parents' consent, and I don't know if the book had the long-term effect on me that the nuns wanted.

Of all the columns, editorials and stories I've written over the years none has been about abortion. I doubt if I've even written the word "abortion" before now. More than all the other emotional and controversial topics, abortion is the most personal, with consequences that may last for years.

Because I believe the decision to have an abortion is so personal and that such a personal decision should be left to pregnant women, I'm pro-choice. But I reject the cookie-cutter caricatures of what it means to be pro-choice and pro-life.

While there are many in the pro-life movement who want to have control over the bodies of women over which they should have no control, I know many who identify as pro-life who are moved out of genuine concern for the lives of children. Their concern doesn't stop at birth but is supportive of programs that enhance the quality of children's lives.

I don't know anyone who identifies as pro-choice who is "pro-abortion." I don't know anyone who likes, looks forward to and can't wait to suggest to a girl or woman that she have an abortion. Behind every decision to have an abortion are painful considerations and looking ahead to the consequences. But it must be a choice, and it must be a choice made by the pregnant woman.

Texas's new abortion law, SB 8, banning the procedure after six weeks of pregnancy—a time span when most women don't know they're pregnant—is unspeakably intrusive and cruel on different levels. There are no exceptions for rape or incest, and there is no consideration for fetuses who will be born with an illness resulting in a short and pain-filled life. In the most personal, emotional and painful decisions individuals and families must make, the state has intervened to make it for them.

The same state that won't enact mask mandates to protect a fifteen-year-old girl in school now mandates that the same fifteen-year-old carry the child of her rapist to term. Who has a right to force that decision on one already victimized? The law allows private citizens to sue anyone—including people they don't know and have no connection to—who "aids or abets" an abortion in the state. The plaintiff would recover legal fees and $10,000 were they to win. The Texas legislature has created an incentive, a cottage industry, for neighbors to spy on neighbors and strangers to snoop on strangers.

As dark as SB 8 is, it became darker when, just before midnight Wednesday, the US Supreme Court refused to block it. Just like that—not in October at the start of a Supreme Court term or in the frenzied final days in June. While many of us slept, the court essentially rendered *Roe v. Wade*, the 1973 decision protecting a woman's right to have an abortion, invalid for women in Texas.

SB 8 and the Supreme Court remind us that some of us are privileged in not having to live by the restrictions forced on others. They also remind us that, as a society, we continue to harbor an unhealthy obsession with a woman's uterus and what she can and can't decide about her body.

Male privilege is never, for a second in our lives, having to worry about our reproductive rights being compromised or denied by legislatures and courts. Male privilege is having an unregulated reproductive organ.

9/11 Attacks Reverberate Twenty Years Later

To speak to you, the dead of September 11, I must not claim
false intimacy or summon an overheated heart glazed just
in time for a camera. I must be steady and I must be clear,
knowing all the time that I have nothing to say—no words
stronger than the steel that pressed you into itself; no
scripture older, or more elegant, than the ancient atoms you
have become.

—Toni Morrison, "The Dead of September 11"

The blueness of the sky and the beauty of the day. So many accounts of September 11, 2001, begin with the blueness and beauty of that New York City morning. It's recalled as a prelude to the approaching horror, an ordinary but lovely remembrance of a time before terrorists cleaved history into "before 9/11" and "after 9/11."

Memories of the beautiful blue of that Tuesday morning are cherished, because at 8:46 a.m. and 9:03 a.m. the sky would be the backdrop for the airplanes that brought down the twin towers of the World Trade Center. Combining the casualties—not the nineteen terrorists—from the planes that crashed into the World Trade Center, the Pentagon and a field in Shanksville, Pennsylvania, nearly three thousand people were murdered in one of the darkest days in our nation's history.

When Billy Forney III recounts his escape from the eighty-fifth floor of the north tower, he begins by saying, "It was a beautiful Tuesday morning after *Monday Night Football*. A beautiful blue sky." Forney, from Houston, was twenty-seven and had moved to New York with his wife at the beginning of the year. He worked as an assistant options trader for SMW Trading. He was at his desk at 8:46 a.m. when he heard a "horrific explosion."

"The building was swaying significantly, like a roller coaster," Forney says. He opened the door to a dark hallway.

"I remember seeing this thing and thinking it was a creature," he says. "It was smoke crawling toward me." Forney says that colleagues who'd lived through the 1993 bombing of the World Trade Center remembered the dark stairwells and wanted to wait for help, but the younger ones like himself said, "We're getting the [expletive] out!" With the help of firefighters they met on their way down the stairwell, they did get out.

Twenty years later the 9/11 Memorial and Museum sits where the towers once stood. Covering most of the museum's central wall is an homage to the blue sky. *Trying to Remember the Color of the Sky on That September Morning*, the creation of artist Spencer Finch, is made up of 2,983 individual squares of Fabriano Italian paper. The squares represent each person killed in the 9/11 attacks and the 1993 bombing, and each square is hand-painted a different shade of blue.

On the wall is an inscription whose fifteen-inch letters were forged from the steel of the twin towers. It's from Virgil's *Aeneid*: "No day shall erase you from the memory of time."

"Where Were You?"

There are tragedies that stop time for a nation or the world, that will never be erased from the memory of all who experienced them. These are the "Where were you when?" events. I was too young to remember the assassination of President John Kennedy and not old enough to comprehend the assassinations of Martin

Luther King Jr. and Bobby Kennedy. The great "Where were you when?" tragedies in my memory, before 2001, were the Challenger explosion and the murders of John Lennon, Marvin Gaye and Selena. But 9/11 surpasses all of them, not just because of the ferocity and scale of the attacks or the enormity of the death toll. It stands out because we will always remember where we were the first time we felt doubt that the survival of the United States was guaranteed.

That morning I'd been to the barber, and from there I drove to the newspaper. On the radio Tony Bruno, a national sports talk show host, was saying a second plane had flown into the World Trade Center and another had crashed into the Pentagon. He then said something I never imagined I'd hear and that, twenty years later, remains surreal: "It is now clear that America is under attack."

I'd taken only a few steps into the newsroom when Kym Fox, an assistant city editor, said, "Go home and pack. You're going to New York." At 10:40 a.m. photographer Ed Ornelas and I were in a *San Antonio Express-News* jeep headed for New York, the plan being to drive until we came across an airport that was open, which wasn't going to happen. Ed did most of the driving, allowing me, for most of the nearly two thousand miles, to collect images of a stunned nation trying to comprehend what was happening.

As Ed drove, I punched the radio buttons looking for any news about the latest developments. We were amped on adrenaline, sharing the same fears as the disembodied voices coming from the radio—fears and voices that grew more ominous as we went into our first night as a nation under attack. When New York mayor Rudy Giuliani said that the casualties "would be more than any of us can bear," we sat in silence before trying to comprehend what those numbers would be. On National Public Radio, a young mother, desperate to get home to her child, cried out what so many were feeling in those first hours after the attacks: "Will there be a tomorrow? Will there be a future for my baby?"

Hurtling down the highway, we wondered the same thing, the certainty of our nation's future not extending beyond the darkness pierced by the headlight beams. I kept clicking stations for more news, skipping any playing music. Except once. Sometime after midnight, somewhere in Tennessee, I clicked onto a station that was about halfway through "The Star-Spangled Banner." Without looking at each other or saying a word, Ed and I spontaneously began singing, our voices rising at the song's end.

We drove for thirty-one straight hours, reaching New York City around 5 p.m. on September 12. (Arriving the next day from the *Express-News* would be photographer William Luther and reporter Jeanne Russell.) From the New Jersey Turnpike we saw the large space where the twin towers had stood. Spiraling from the rubble were thick, white plumes of smoke that crossed, yes, the blue sky.

Ed went to ground zero, so he dropped me off in Union Square Park, where I sat in a shop window, called the news desk and dictated a column to reporter Vince Davis, the first of the thirteen columns I would file on consecutive days.

It was the next day, September 13, when the scope of the lives lost became palpable and, in Giuliani's words, "more than any of us can bear." That was the day flyers of missing people, all of whom were in the World Trade Center, began to cover the city. Two have stayed in my mind. The first I saw and would see most often was of Giovanna "Gennie" Gambale, a twenty-seven-year-old vice president at Cantor Fitzgerald last seen on the 105th floor.

Walking down the Avenue of the Americas, I followed a trail of flyers until I was at Saint Vincent's Hospital, an impromptu command post for media and family and friends of the missing. I felt the gravity of so many pictures of the missing. When I saw a flyer on a Univision truck of Janice J. Brown, a thirty-five-year-old accountant, holding her young son and the words, "Help her only child find his mother," I cried for the first time since the attacks.

Holding photographs of their missing loved ones, the families spoke in floors.

"What floor was he on?"

"The ninety-first. What floor was your sister on?"

"The hundred and second."

Anthony Luparello was on the 101st. His son, Anthony Jr., held a picture of him as he told me that he and his father were working in the World Trade Center in 1993 when it was bombed.

What none of us knew then was that the last person pulled alive from the rubble was rescued September 12. None of the people on the missing flyers, none of the people whose families held vigils at Saint Vincent's, had survived. They were all gone.

Place of Remembrance

Yet not all the victims are gone from the ground hallowed by their deaths. Twenty years later, at the 9/11 Memorial and Museum, a pair of acre-size recessed pools fill the area where the towers once stood. Water continuously flows downward from each wall into a bottom that can't be seen. Around the pools are bronze panels engraved with the 2,983 names of the victims from the 9/11 attacks and the 1993 attack on the World Trade Center.

The museum's exhibit center is below ground, under what would have been the twin towers. An already solemn tour through the museum becomes more so when the guide tells us that behind the *Trying to Remember the Color of the Sky on That September Morning* exhibit is a special storage repository of the New York City Medical Examiner's Office containing thousands of human remains from the attacks.

More than 1,100 victims have yet to be identified, and many never will be, because there's nothing left, some families didn't submit DNA tests or some families don't want to be notified until all the remains of their loved ones have been recovered. Other families just want to leave it in the past as best they can.

Last month I went back to New York hoping to reconnect with some of the people I met in 2001 and 2002 at the one-year anniversary. I reached out to the girlfriend of a young man who was on the ninety-sixth floor of one of the towers. She was gracious in her refusal: "I'm trying to maintain a healthy and calm mindset these days and reopening Pandora's box isn't a path I'd like to walk down."

At FDNY Engine 54, Ladder 4, Battalion 9 at 48th Street and 8th Avenue, the fifteen firefighters killed on 9/11 are memorialized on a wall. Three weeks ahead of the twentieth anniversary, it was the most visible reminder of that day.

Billy Forney III, back in Houston and CEO of Palace Social, was to give two speeches over the weekend about his experiences. His public speaking began after his daughter came across numerous inaccuracies and conspiracy theories while researching a paper on 9/11. He wants to keep the memories alive of the first responders who saved his life and the memories of all who perished.

"We should be remembering and not forgetting every year," he says.

A Chilling Threat

On the day of the 9/11 attacks members of Congress from both parties stood on the steps of the US Capitol and sang "God Bless America." That was to symbolize how the nation came together in the aftermath of the disaster. Those were fleeting moments, more so if you were Muslim, or assumed to be a Muslim, and subject to scapegoating, harassment and assault.

But the unity feels especially distant now, following January 6, when insurrectionists stormed those Capitol steps and tried to overturn an election. Twenty years ago the greatest threat to our nation's security came from afar. In 2021 our greatest terrorist attack and the greatest threat to our democracy comes from within.

The events of 9/11 made us love and cherish our country, and each other, a little bit more. As we remember the lives lost on that day and the families destroyed, let's think about all we may yet lose if we're not vigilant. Let's dedicate ourselves to protecting our democracy and each other.

Let's commit ourselves to doing better at protecting each other from harm, whether that harm comes from violence or through virus.

Attacks on Critical Race Theory Reflect Willful Ignorance

Each of us is ignorant. Every single one. However much we may know about this or that, each of us is ignorant about countless subjects and issues. To be ignorant is nothing to be ashamed of because we have the capacity and opportunity to overcome our ignorance with information and education. But to be arrogant in one's ignorance, unwilling to acknowledge or understand the ignorance, and then want to spread one's ignorance like a virus isn't simply ignorant, it's ignant.

In the United States today, there may be no group of people more comfortable and secure in their ignorance than opponents of critical race theory. They have no idea what it means, had never heard of it until 2021, and before this year had never used the words "critical," race" and "theory" in the same month, much less strung those words together in a sentence. Yet now they see critical race theory everywhere: in classrooms, under beds, lurking on street corners, ready to infect white children with guilt.

Having no idea or inclination to learn what critical race theory is, opponents such as Governor Greg Abbott, Lieutenant Governor Dan Patrick and Republicans in the Texas legislature have banned the teaching of something that has never been taught in Texas classrooms. They invoke it as an all-purpose defense against any honest and fruitful discussion of the legacy of slavery and racism in the United States. They use it to reject any exploration of American history that makes people uncomfortable because it detours from primrose lanes into a landscape with weeds, shrubs and a scorched earth.

Falsely calling something critical race theory is a deflection to avoid learning history long ignored and filling in the gaps of ignorance some Americans have about the lives and experiences of other Americans. No one invokes critical race theory more than those who are clueless of what they're talking about but weaponize it against people whose work would make them less ignorant.

The latest target of these absurd attacks is the brilliant cartoonist and graphic novelist Jerry Craft, whose upcoming speaking event in Katy was canceled after 400 parents in a school district of 88,000 students signed a petition saying Craft's books promoted critical race theory. His books were also pulled from all Katy school libraries pending further review. Those books included his graphic novels for children, *New Kid* and *Class Act*, about the experiences of Jordan Banks, a preteen African American boy, and his friends at a prestigious school in New York City. Last year *New Kid* became the first graphic novel to win the coveted Newbery Medal. "Respectful of its child audience, it explores friendship, race, class and bullying in a fresh and often humorous manner," the judges said of it.

In response to his cancellation in Katy, Craft wrote this on the American Library Association's Office of Intellectual Freedom website: "As an African American boy growing up in Washington Heights in New York City, I hardly ever saw children like me in the books assigned to me in school. Books aimed at children like me seemed to be only about history or misery. That's why it's always been important to me to portray children of color as ordinary children, and to create iconic African American characters."

The books are wise, enlightening, funny and enjoyable. Like

the best children's literature, they also appeal to adults. In *Class Act* Black adults will understand—and white adults will learn—why Jordan's friend Drew is sensitive to his classmates touching his hair or why his grandmother always tells him "You have to work twice as hard to go half as far."

Whatever critics of critical race theory imagine, it's not in the work of Craft, who is simply writing about what it's like to be a Black child. If that upsets parents, they should ask themselves what is it about the experiences and culture of Black children that frightens them.

In *Class Act* Jordan and Drew are invited to dinner at the home of Liam, their wealthy white friend. Jordan reciprocates by inviting Liam to his home for dinner. The experiences deepen the bonds between the friends as they fill the gaps of their ignorance.

Singing the Blues over Ted Cruz's Misuse of "Woke"

Last week Ted Cruz, the junior US senator from Texas and heroic protector of the nation's children from the evils of Big Bird, tweeted about "woke" Democrats. Earlier this year he tweeted about a "woke" emasculated army, "woke" CEOs and the "woke" media. It's as if upon waking each morning Cruz can't wait to "woke" someone with his promiscuous misappropriation of the word.

Cruz is among the mob that has hijacked "woke" and moved it further from its African American origins, taking its soul not unlike the way the singer Pat Boone downplayed the soulful rhythms and beats of the songs of the Black artists he covered during the 1950s.

In the explosion of the rock and roll era Boone became a star by recording versions of songs by some of the Black architects of rock, songwriters and performers such as Fats Domino, Little Richard, Big Joe Turner and Ivory Joe Hunter. They were tepid renditions of the originals but, to Boone's credit, earnest and sincere. And he treated the material and their creators with respect. He cared about the words coming out of his mouth.

The same can't be said for Cruz and all the others who think it clever and cool each time they invoke "woke" as a pejorative to discredit ideas, stances and agendas they disagree with. It's tiresome and redundant, and what's lost on them is that however clever and cool a word "woke" once was, the fact that it's now being used by Cruz means it's no longer clever and cool.

But "woke" and the idea of being awake is a part of African American culture that shouldn't be surrendered to those who don't understand or appreciate it. Even if most of us rarely use the word. To be "woke" or awake is to literally not fall asleep but also to be attentive to your surroundings, the world, injustices and suffering. The most recent incarnation of "woke" arose during Black Lives Matter protests in 2014 as encouragement to "stay woke" to police brutality. In 2017 "woke" was added to the Oxford English Dictionary and defined as being sensitive to social issues. To be awakened is to be focused on what we as individuals, communities and nations need to do to be better to ourselves and each other.

In 1938 legendary Texas bluesman Huddie "Lead Belly" Ledbetter wrote a song, "Scottsboro Boys," about nine Black teenagers in Scottsboro, Alabama, who were falsely accused in 1931 of raping two white women. In an interview Lead Belly said, "I made this little song about down there. So, I advise everybody, be a little careful when they go along through there—best stay woke, keep their eyes open."

In a 1962 *New York Times* op-ed, "If You're Woke You Dig It," novelist William Melvin Kelley wrote about the appropriation of Black idioms by beatniks. During the civil rights movement, activists took the gospel song "Woke Up This Morning with My Mind on Jesus" and changed it to "Woke Up This Morning with My Mind on Freedom." A staple of radio and even some grocery store soundtracks is the 1975 song "Wake Up Everybody" by Harold Melvin & the Blue Notes with Teddy Pendergrass singing lead. In 2008 singer-songwriter Erykah Badu released the song "Master Teacher," which repeats the line "I stay woke." (One song I'm not including in this woke/wake list is Marvin Gaye's

"Sexual Healing," which repeatedly pleads "Wake up, wake up, wake up." That's not the socially conscious "What's Going On" Marvin but the "Let's Get it On" Marvin asking for something a little more immediate.)

The words "wake up" are the first ones spoken in Spike Lee's movie *Do the Right Thing* and the last ones spoken in his *School Daze.*

Watch Night or Freedom's Eve became an African American tradition on New Year's Eve in 1862 when enslaved people stayed awake to welcome in the new year when the Emancipation Proclamation took effect.

In a 1965 speech, "Remaining Awake through a Great Revolution," Martin Luther King Jr. said, "Let us stand up. Let us be a concerned generation. Let us remain awake through a great revolution. And we will speed up that great day when the American Dream will be a reality."

To be concerned—woke, if you will—is the responsibility of no single group or generation. There's much work to do. Let those who mock enjoy their slumber.

'Tis the Season
of That Rude Christmas Song

It's a pleasant evening before Christmas. Outside Jack Frost has kissed the air, but inside it's toasty as the fireplace snaps, crackles and pops like a bowl of Rice Krispies. Your daughter, lifted by you, has just completed the family decorating of the Christmas tree by placing a silver star on top. Your home, smelling like fresh pine and freshly baked cookies, is filled with Christmas cheer when the doorbell rings.

You open the door, and standing there are five smiling people in red and green Christmas sweaters adorned with cotton ball reindeer tails and jingling bells. They begin singing: "We wish you a merry Christmas, we wish you a merry Christmas, we wish you a merry Christmas and a happy new year. Good tidings we bring to you and your kin, we wish you a merry Christmas and a happy new year."

You smile and call to your wife and children. "Honey, kids, come here! Some people in funny Christmas sweaters are singing and wishing us a merry Christmas. Could y'all repeat that?"

They do. "We wish you a merry Christmas, we wish you a merry Christmas, we wish you a merry Christmas and a happy new year. Good tidings we bring to you and your kin, we wish you a merry Christmas and a happy new year."

You and your wife and children flash Christmas-lit smiles.

But things are about to take a dark and ugly turn. The carolers continue singing: "Oh, bring us some figgy pudding. Oh, bring us some figgy pudding. Oh, bring us some figgy pudding and bring it right here."

You stop smiling. "What?"

They repeat the verse: "Oh, bring us some figgy pudding. Oh, bring us some figgy pudding. Oh, bring us some figgy pudding and bring it right here."

"What the [expletive] is figgy pudding?" you ask.

Your wife says, "Ah, we don't have figgy pudding, but I do have a banana—"

"No, baby," you say, and cut her off. "These people can't just show up here, ask for something and then order me to 'bring it right here.' "

Your family isn't the first and it certainly won't be the last, but you are being attacked by the rudest and most threatening Christmas song in history.

Some Christmas songs and traditions are problematic. Let's be honest—Santa Claus doesn't come out looking good in the 1964 classic "Rudolph the Red-Nosed Reindeer." He and the other reindeer want nothing to do with Rudolph's red nose until they need him to bail them out that foggy Christmas Eve. Then everybody loves him as they shout out with glee.

"We Wish You a Merry Christmas," a problematic song I have written about before, is one of the oldest and most beloved of Christmas songs, dating back to sixteenth-century England. The composer is unknown, but we can confidently guess that the writer had boundary issues and a profound sense of entitlement. The song is insidiously deceptive with its pleasant, sing-along melody, which begins cheerily and well-meaning enough in wishing you and your family a merry Christmas and happy new year.

So warm and loving. People going door to door spreading holiday cheer to neighbors and strangers. But then it gets weird with the insistent begging for figgy pudding: "Oh, bring us some figgy pudding. Oh, bring us some figgy pudding. Oh, bring us some figgy pudding and bring it right here."

You're standing in your doorway, still trying to figure out what figgy pudding is and stunned that five people in awful Christmas sweaters are not asking but telling you to bring it to them. And then they lose their minds, singing: "We won't go until we get some, we won't go until we get some, we won't go until we get some, so bring some out here!"

"Wha— what!" you stutter in disbelief, now thinking only of your family's safety. "No, you didn't. You didn't show up singing at my house, demanding figgy pudding and saying you won't go until you get some?"

There was no violence, but things got a little shaky, neighbors intervened and misunderstandings were ironed out. Later that evening, dozing on the sofa, you hear your son singing "I Saw Mommy Kissing Santa Claus."

Opening your eyes, you say to yourself, "Wait, I don't have a Santa costume."

Hope Perseveres like a Lost
Butterfly in Winter

Everyone had left but her. Miss Monarch had overslept and missed the flight south and would now die. It was that simple and clear. If she didn't get to Texas—faster than fast—and then to Mexico, she'd be dead. That's what happens when it's early November and you're the last monarch butterfly in Iowa.

Because they can't survive cold temperatures, every year monarchs in eastern North America migrate to the Sierra Madre Mountains in Mexico for the winter. It's one of the most remarkable annual traditions of nature as hundreds of thousands of butterflies, which have never made the journey south, travel up to three thousand miles to winter.

But as they flew through Iowa, Miss Monarch was left behind. She was discovered in early November by seventh-grade students at the Jester Park Nature Center in Granger, Iowa. When she was found, she was a caterpillar nearing the pupa stage, soon to transform into a butterfly. She'd hatched later than usual. On November 2 the center, where she was named Miss Monarch, posted on Facebook: "We have a newly emerged female Monarch butterfly who desperately needs to hitch a ride to Texas ASAP. If you happen to be heading that way and willing to transport her, please message us."

Patty Loving, a Texan who used to raise and release monarch butterflies before she moved to Iowa, saw the post. By chance or fate, she was flying to Texas the next day, so after getting permission from Southwest Airlines she contacted Jester Park. After being put into an envelope with her wings spread, the butterfly was placed in a sealed container in a cooler.

After landing in Austin on November 5, Loving drove to San Antonio, where she'd arranged to release Miss Monarch, if the butterfly was still living, at Cielo Gardens, which is run by her friend Jen Yáñez-Alaniz. Cielo offers gardening opportunities for recently resettled refugees.

I was one of about a dozen people in the gardens that afternoon, including a KENS television crew and my friend Carmen Tafolla, who'd invited me. The former poet laureate of San Antonio and Texas had cowritten a beautiful bilingual children's book with Mexican writer and artist Regina Moya titled *The Last Butterfly / La última mariposa*.

Watching Loving take the envelope out of the plastic container, I felt the same trepidation as everyone else watching. In those seconds, as she peeked in, the fate of that butterfly seemed like the most important thing in the world. "It's alive," Loving said, with a relieved smile.

Miss Monarch took flight to oohs, aahs, applause and joy. We watched for about fifteen minutes as she flew around the gardens, stopping at several plants to dine before eventually flying to Mexico.

"This butterfly, born late and trying to begin its pilgrimage to Mexico in twenty-degree weather, would have never survived had it not been for the intercession of Pat Loving, the nature refuge, Southwest Airlines, Jen Yáñez-Alaniz and many others. It's just one butterfly, but everyone adds up to influence so many others," Tafolla said.

On Christmas Eve morning I found myself thinking about Miss Monarch while attending an outdoor interfaith vigil for Lina Khil at Saint Francis Episcopal Church. The three-year-old child, an Afghan refugee, had been missing since December 20.

As of this writing she is still missing, and for all the problems in this country, her disappearance feels like the most important thing at this moment.

On this cloudy, gloomy morning, under a pavilion sheltered by a black oak tree, her father lit a large purple candle called Lina's Candle. As the service ended at 10:31 a.m., a light drizzle made it appear and sound as if the oak were weeping. That's when I thought of the butterfly and her impossible journey, and though it took longer than it was supposed to, she eventually ended up where she was supposed to be.

May Lina's Candle stay lit until hope and love bring her home.

On Thanksgiving, Concern for Others Merits Gratitude Too

It was said of Ebenezer Scrooge that he knew how to keep Christmas well. But he also knew how to keep Thanksgiving well.

As a native of London, Scrooge never celebrated the American holiday. Charles Dickens created the miser-turned-benefactor twenty years before President Abraham Lincoln, in 1863, proclaimed Thanksgiving an official US holiday.

The Scrooge who woke up Christmas morning feeling "light as a feather" and "happy as an angel" did so because he was struck by how much he had to be grateful for and how much he could share with others. We should allow no day to slip into darkness without taking the time to reflect on those things we should be thankful for. But we've set aside the Thanksgiving holiday as a nation to give thanks, so that we do not spend so much time thinking about what's missing from our lives that we deny ourselves the time to appreciate what's present.

This week we take time to give thanks for what we cherish, for the bounty of our lives, including the gifts of love, family, home and health. But we should also give thanks for the gifts of outrage, empathy and compassion for those people who don't have those gifts and whose lives are a bounty of pain and disappointments.

When I was a student at Saint Mary's University I took a class on the Old Testament taught by the venerable Father John G. Leies. One sleepy Tuesday morning, Father Leies began talking about starvation, especially among children. We rode along on his mellifluous voice, with a hint of a German accent, as he carried us to Africa and Asia and spoke about the suffering.

Sitting back in our chairs, we were quiet, but it wasn't the kind of quiet of a classroom captivated by Father Leies's words so much as the quiet of students whose minds were wandering, our eyes glazing over as we listened to his soft and soothing voice. A voice soft and soothing, that is, until he shouted, "And you don't give a [expletive] about them!"

We jolted upright, shocked to hear this septuagenarian cherubic priest with the snow-white hair shout a profanity. Looking at us looking at him, relishing our surprise, Father Leies smiled with twinkling eyes and said, "You see. You get more agitated about a dirty word than you do about suffering people."

It was a lesson in misplaced priorities and complacency, a reminder of how easily we accommodate ourselves to what we know to be wrong, be it suffering, injustice, evil. But it was also a lesson in outrage and being indignant by anything that visits undeserved pain on someone. It's when we're no longer moved by the suffering of others, are apathetic to injustice, and have lost the will and ability to try to imagine the lives different from our own that our souls wither and our humanity diminishes.

Outrage is a gift because it's an expression of the soul that reminds us of our obligation to each other. It's a gift because it moves us to act and reconnect not just with other people but with the loving and helping neighbor we aspire to be.

One more thing: Lincoln's proclamation of Thanksgiving as a national holiday was issued during the Civil War. A few weeks after the proclamation he was in Gettysburg, on November 19, 1863, to deliver his most famous speech. On a battlefield he noted that it was for us, the living, to ensure "that the nation shall have a new birth of freedom, and that government of the people, by the people, for the people, shall not perish from the earth."

On the eve of this Thanksgiving the state of our democracy seems as perilous as it has at any time since the eve of the Civil War, and we must be wary of anyone who threatens it with violence or the intimations of violence. On this Thanksgiving we should be as thankful as Scrooge on Christmas morning, as outraged as Father Leies about suffering and as vigilant as Lincoln in preserving our nation.

To Be American
Is to See That US Ideals Can Die

When I was a high school sophomore in 1976, during the bicentennial of my country's birth, I stopped reciting the last six words of the pledge of allegiance. Thomas Jefferson's composition of the Declaration of Independence from Francis Bellamy's writing of the pledge are separated by 116 years, but a photograph I saw when I was fifteen made them both ring hollow for me.

The Pulitzer Prize–winning picture, taken by Stanley Forman in April 1976 during the Boston busing desegregation crisis, shows a young white man thrusting a flagpole, an American flag attached, at a Black man in a three-piece suit. Shortly after seeing the picture, I recited the pledge with my classmates until the last six words: "with liberty and justice for all." I knew enough of my country's history and the discrepancies between ideals and deeds to have the photograph bring home to me that those words didn't apply to me.

It was a silent, personal protest I continued into my twenties when I realized that more constructive than refraining from saying "with liberty and justice for all" was to be a better citizen and work to narrow the distance between our nation's ideals and deeds—the duty of us all. No country has ever withheld disappointment and heartbreak from its citizens. And for all my disappointments and heartbreak with my country, the United States of America, I've never ceased loving it or believing in its possibilities, even as progress came achingly slow.

Except for the attacks on 9/11, I've never felt more American than I did one year ago today when I saw a mob of my fellow citizens, incited by the lie of a stolen election, attack and desecrate the US Capitol, destroy and steal property, look for elected officials of both parties to assault and try to overturn an election. But when I saw some of them using American flags to beat police officers, reminding me of the 1976 photo, I had two thoughts. The first: This was the kind of behavior that kept me from saying "and liberty and justice for all" because it was exactly that behavior that prevented "liberty and justice for all." The second: The preservation of this democracy isn't guaranteed, and it can't be ceded to people who would cancel the outcome of elections that don't go their way and think nothing of using violence to get it done.

To be an American is not a talent. It's not a craft. It's not a skill discovered early in life that is honed and mastered to the amazement of others. We didn't align the stars or our bloodlines so we would be born in the United States of America.

To be an American and enjoy its freedoms is a gift of fortune, and it must never be forgotten that but for the grace of God, Allah, Jehovah or whatever power one believes put us here, life could have been less fortunate. But for forces we don't possess the power to change, we could just as easily be the Rohingya dissident targeted by the Myanmar government or the Haitian or Guatemalan family trying to cross the US border.

In Albert Camus's *First Letter to a German Friend*, the Noble laureate wrote of France, "This country is worthy of the difficult and demanding love that is mine. I believe she is worth fighting for since she is worthy of a higher love." The United States is worthy of the difficult and demanding love that is ours.

I, like many others, I suspect, had taken for granted the democracy that is our responsibility to expand, not restrict. But it must first be preserved. One year ago, through the smoke and yelling, we caught a glimpse and felt the tremors of what it would be like to lose something we always assumed would endure.

Being an American is to continue to fight for liberty and justice for all, and to protect each other from those seeking to harm us and our democracy.

Haunted by Voices in the Dark

It was close to 10 p.m. when I pulled up in front of my house. "If This World Were Mine" by Marvin Gaye and Tammi Terrell flowed from the CD, wrapping me in layers of nostalgia and longing.

In what has become a COVID-era routine, after being stuck inside all day working, or trying to work, I'd get in the car and, if I had no destination or invitation, go for a long nighttime musical drive, DJ'ing my moods to the appropriate soundtracks. As I came to a stop, I thought I heard yelling over Marvin and Tammi's harmonizing. I paid it no mind as I checked texts with the car running. But then I heard what sounded like moaning.

Getting out of the car, I realized it was coming from next door, from my neighbor J., a man in his early to mid-thirties with several problems, including Parkinson's. He once alluded to abuse he'd received as a child. I don't know if it was abuse or something congenital that accounted for his disabilities. Even if you can't see him, you'd recognize the rhythm of his gait and the dragging of ripped sneakers on his damaged left foot. He also uses a brace for his right arm, which was of little use to him.

He is missing several teeth, talks fast and is hard to understand. People in the neighborhood say he's "not all there," but you can hold a conversation with him, and he's self-aware enough to be embarrassed to ask for a couple of dollars, or food, or to tie his shoe, something nearly physically impossible for him to do.

He walks everywhere, at all hours of the day and night, and is an easy mark for ridicule and abuse. Once, near downtown, my brother, seeing that J. was being picked on by a group of guys, intervened to save him.

Occasionally, seeing him walking while struggling with bags of laundry, I'd drop him off at a laundromat. Sometimes, usually at night, you could hear the wails of what sounded like an animal in pain. It was J. inside his house, his body "frozen" or locked in place from the Parkinson's. Somebody would call EMS. Recently, in what was becoming a several-times-a-week occurrence, probably because of medications or lack thereof, he could be heard screaming profanities over and over, banging on the walls, throwing stuff and breaking windows. One night he was yelling, "Make it stop!" He had a caretaker but lived alone.

On this night his moaning wasn't coming from the house. I looked over his gate into his yard. I couldn't see him in the darkness but assumed he was on the ground or driveway. His three large dogs, who I feed every morning, were sitting quietly in the yard. A homeless woman walked up to me and asked, "Do you hear that? Somebody's yelling. It's loud!"

"Yeah," I said, knowing she was probably heading to my house to hit me up for money. We walked up to J.'s house. He was lying in his yard, near the white and rusted gate, and stopped moaning when he saw us. I could tell he was self-conscious about his situation.

"Can you help me up, buddy?" he asked. It's what he called me, because in the three years we'd been neighbors, I'd never told him my name. I reached over the gate and pulled him up. I picked up a crumbled $5 bill he'd been clutching and gave it back to him.

"Thank you, buddy," he said, turning and limping to his house.

The homeless lady asked me for bus fare. I gave her the $1.03 in my pocket.

"You don't have another thirty cents?" she asked.

Not long ago, we realized that J. was no longer living there, that he had moved.

We (I) shouldn't need the misfortune of others to remind us (me) of our (my) good fortune, to shake us (me) out of being so self-absorbed. Their lives have greater value than as a measure of the things we have that they need. Until I better learn those lessons, I'll continue to be haunted by voices in the dark.

Something about Court Promise Ignites Bias

This old riddle has stumped people for years: A father and son are in a car accident that kills the father and seriously injures the son, who is rushed to the hospital. In the operating room, the surgeon looks at him and says, "I can't operate—this boy is my son!"

Explain.

The surgeon was the boy's mother. It's an obvious answer—once you're told what it is. That so many don't answer it correctly speaks to a subconscious gender bias that doesn't imagine women as surgeons.

I was in my twenties when I failed in answering the riddle, and it still embarrasses me, someone who was raised by three women—three Black women—and who saw daily what they overcame and what they could do, the magic they could create, if given the opportunity.

Last week, upon Supreme Court Justice Stephen Breyer's retirement announcement, President Joe Biden repeated his campaign promise to nominate a Black woman to the high court. The negative reaction to Biden's pledge suggests some naysayers may want to examine their unconscious biases.

On Fox News alone, Sean Hannity said Biden's promise was "illegal"; Gregg Jarrett alleged that Biden is violating the Civil Rights Act of 1964; a deeply offended Maria Bartiromo said, "I mean, what kind of a qualification is that being a Black woman?";

and Tucker Carlson suggested Biden choose George Floyd's sister, saying, "She is not a judge or a lawyer or whatever, but in this case, who cares?" They have no objections that before two of the white women who have served on the court—Sandra Day O'Connor and Amy Coney Barrett—were chosen, the Republican presidents announced they would be selecting a woman.

At a news conference on October 15, 1980, Ronald Reagan said: "I am announcing today that one of the first Supreme Court vacancies in my administration will be filled by the most qualified woman I can possibly find, one who meets the high standards I will demand for all court appointments." Less than six months into his presidency Reagan kept his promise, naming O'Connor as the first woman to the court. During a September 19, 2020, political rally, President Donald Trump said, "I will be putting forth a nominee next week. It will be a woman." Were Reagan and Trump "woke" affirmative action merchants discriminating against men, or were they making admirable attempts to correct an imbalance?

Of the 115 US Supreme Court justices, chosen over forty-five presidencies, 108 have been white men. One president—not even the Black one—vows to nominate one Black woman for the first time and some folk on the right lose their minds. It's telling that they're not responding to a specific Black woman being named to the Supreme Court but to the general idea of a Black woman taking her seat there.

In a tweet, which he has since deleted and apologized for, conservative legal scholar Ilya Shapiro referred to the not-yet-named Biden pick as a "lesser black woman" than the candidate of his choice. Lesser Black woman?

Senator Roger Wicker, R-Miss., said Biden's selection would be a "beneficiary" of affirmative action. But when Trump chose Barrett, Wicker said, "I have five granddaughters; the oldest one is ten. I think Justice Amy Coney Barrett will prove to be an inspiration to these five granddaughters and to my grown daughters." Why wouldn't they also be inspired by the first Black woman ascending to the court?

Implicit in Biden's promise to choose a Black woman is the knowledge that he has a pool of talented and qualified Black women to choose from, just as Reagan and Trump knew they had a pool of talented and qualified women to choose from.

Implicit in some of the reflexive criticism of Biden's pledge is that any Black woman is less qualified than any white male. How can someone not imagine a Barbara Jordan on the Supreme Court? Or Constance Baker Motley, who in 1966 became the first Black woman appointed federal judge?

The first person of any group to achieve something significant is not the first member of that particular group to be qualified or worthy. The person is the first to not be overlooked and not denied an opportunity.

Zelenskyy Is an Authentic Hero

When he delivered his inaugural address as president of Ukraine on May 20, 2019, Volodymyr Zelenskyy said: "And, please, I really don't want you to hang my portraits on your office walls. Because a president is not an icon and not an idol. A president is not a portrait. Hang pictures of your children. And before you make any decision, look into their eyes."

If Zelenskyy was as little known now as he was three years ago, if he and the nation he leads weren't in the line of Vladimir Putin's fire and delusions, this modest request would be easily honored. But because of forces beyond his control and through the force of his character, portraits and pictures of the forty-four-year-old lawyer-actor-comedian-turned-politician will be found on walls and in history books for generations to come.

Putin's murderous invasion of Ukraine has created a stage on which Zelenskyy is inhabiting a role never played before: that of an individual well-known only to his own country, who, during war, is transformed into an authentic heroic figure as billions watch on television and social media. Zelenskyy's emergence as the most popular and inspiring person on earth, emblematic of the courage and fight of his countrymen and -women, isn't the result of marketing campaigns or urban legends. It's because the world is watching in real time as he and his nation defy Putin and his military might.

For weeks Zelenskyy and Ukrainians were skeptical of warnings from US intelligence that a Russian invasion was imminent, and they were unprepared when it began on February 24. All of which makes it that more remarkable that they refused to go gently into that night and the nights that have followed.

John Wooden, the legendary UCLA basketball coach, famously said that the true test of a man's character is what he does when no one is watching. But it's with the world watching that Zelenskyy is enduring and passing a test no one could imagine or prepare for. Robert Coles, in *Lives of Moral Leadership*, writes of the ability of any one person to change history's course: "We need heroes, people who can inspire us, help shape us morally, spur us on to purposeful action—and from time to time we are called on to be those heroes, leaders for others, either in a small, day-to-day way, or on the world's larger stage."

Beginning the night of the invasion, Zelenskyy demonstrated his ability to lead and inspire not only with his physical courage but through his moral leadership and linguistic prowess. Hours before Putin's invasion, Zelenskyy appealed to the Russian people: "If they try to take our country away from us, our freedom, our lives, the lives of our children, we will defend ourselves. Not attack, but defend ourselves. And when you will be attacking us, you will see our faces, not our backs, but our faces."

The night after the attack began, when his whereabouts were unknown, he recorded a video in front of the presidency building. With his top advisers around him, he said, "We are here. We are in Kyiv. We are protecting Ukraine." Last weekend, when the United States offered to evacuate Zelenskyy and his family out of Ukraine, he told them, "The fight is here; I need ammunition, not a ride."

Go back to his 2019 inaugural address and it's clear that the hero Zelenskyy has become is the man he already was. "I've often been asked what I'm prepared to do in order to stop fire," he said. "It's a strange question. What are you, the Ukrainians, prepared to lose for the lives of the people close to you, what? I can assure that in order for our heroes to stop dying I am ready to do everything. And I am definitely not afraid to make difficult decisions, not afraid to lose my own popularity, my ratings. And if there's a need I'm prepared to give up my own position—as long as peace arrives. But without giving up our territories—ever!"

There's also something heroic about a man who tells you to look into your children's eyes before you make a decision.

Jackson Serves Up Grace
to Make History

On April 22, 1947, one week after Jackie Robinson became the first Black player in modern Major League Baseball, the Brooklyn Dodgers began hosting the Philadelphia Phillies for a three-game series. Throughout that first game the Phillies, led by manager Ben Chapman, assaulted Robinson with racist bile.

Before signing Robinson, Dodgers owner Branch Rickey told Robinson he wanted him, during his rookie year, to have the courage not to fight back against the verbal and physical abuse he would receive. Doing so would jeopardize this "noble experiment" to integrate baseball. So Robinson listened to Chapman's taunts and remained silent. But his teammate, Alabama-born Eddie Stanky, did not, yelling at Chapman and the Phillies, "Why don't you guys go to work on somebody who can fight back? There isn't one of you has the guts of a louse."

Robinson's temperament was to fight back, and he was more than capable of doing so—and would from 1948 on. But for one year he had to take the abuse so he would not live down to a stereotype and deny opportunities to other players of color.

The Jackie Robinsons in life, trailblazers who look different from those who came before them, those who are the first of their ethnicity, gender, religion, sexual preference to accomplish something, are asked to be more humane than those who preceded them when treated poorly. They're asked to serve portions of grace in exchange for slices of opportunity. When their talent is undeniable, their temperament is explored as reason to disqualify them.

Stanky's words—"Why don't you guys go to work on somebody who can fight back?"—came to mind while I was watching the confirmation hearings for Supreme Court nominee Judge Ketanji Brown Jackson, who, if confirmed, would be the first Black woman on the court. They echoed while I listened to the interruptions, and the bellowing soliloquies, misrepresentations and interrogations from senators Ted Cruz, Lindsey Graham, Tom Cotton and Josh Hawley. They weren't there for a vigorous and respectful intellectual exchange with Jackson or to examine legitimate criticisms of her record, but rather to perform for those who enjoy the stylings of these Four Horsemen of the Apocalypse.

No, none of these senators did or said anything resembling Chapman's treatment of Robinson. But in the manner and tone they addressed Jackson, they exploited and enjoyed a double standard not allowed Amy Coney Barrett during her 2020 confirmation hearings and not allowed Jackson. That double standard is the display of anger and emotion that Brett Kavanaugh could indulge during his 2018 confirmation and that these senators deployed against Jackson. Any woman—white, Black, Latina—who behaved like Kavanaugh would have been dismissed as hysterical or emotional.

Jackson would have been seen as an "angry Black woman," and among the lessons Black parents teach their children is the spoken and unspoken caution about showing anger. "The angry Black man" and "angry Black woman" are centuries-old stereotypes rooted in fear and used to dismiss, condescend and demean. The problem has never been with those deemed angry but with those uncomfortable with Black people if they weren't always smiling, courteous and complying.

So Jackson, poised and more qualified than anyone on the

Senate Judiciary Committee, or any sitting justice, to serve on the Supreme Court, listened as Hawley painted her as soft on child sexual abuse even though the conservative *National Review* defended her and called this a "smear." She listened as a shrill and emotional Graham asked her about hearings and organizations with which she had no association. She listened as Cotton said he didn't believe her. And she listened as Cruz bellowed about critical race theory, which has nothing to do with her work, but, hey, she's Black.

There were times when Jackson looked as if she'd had enough and was ready to let loose, but she'd pause, collect herself and respond with another serving of grace. And let the record show that it wasn't the smallness of Cruz, Graham, Cotton or Hawley that brought Jackson to tears. It was the largeness of Senator Cory Booker, D-NJ, who, among other things, told her, "You have earned this spot. You are worthy. You are a great American."

It's Jackie Robinson we remember, not Ben Chapman.

Ketanji Brown Jackson is history. Her loud, emotional detractors are footnotes.

Precious Lord, Take Our Hands

On the chilly evening of April 4, 1968, Martin Luther King Jr. stood on the balcony of the Lorraine Motel in Memphis, Tennessee. He was preparing to leave for dinner, and looking down in the parking lot, he saw saxophonist Ben Branch, who was going to perform at the dinner.

Seconds before a bullet struck, King spoke his last words. "Ben, make sure you play 'Precious Lord, Take My Hand' at the meeting tonight," he said. "Play it real pretty."

It wasn't the first time King had asked for his favorite song. He often requested that his friend, gospel legend Mahalia Jackson, sing it at civil rights rallies. As a teenager, Jackson was a protégé to the song's writer, Thomas A. Dorsey. Five days after King's assassination, she performed "Precious Lord" at his nationally televised funeral. When Jackson died in 1972, Aretha Franklin sang the song at her funeral. When Franklin died in 2018, Fantasia sang it at hers.

There is no song performed more often at African American funerals than "Precious Lord," no song more guaranteed to wring out pent-up grief and give release to tears while also giving flight to expectations of better times, lifting the church with its promise of comfort and strength.

For several days last week, "Precious Lord" played in my head. That was before I saw Twitter postings of a 2014 performance by the Kyiv Symphony Orchestra and Chorus in Ukraine. Knowing what was happening in Ukraine in 2014, the annexation of

Crimea, and knowing what that nation is now enduring, it was moving to hear the chorus:

When my way grows drear
Precious Lord, linger near
When my light is almost gone
Hear my cry, hear my call
Hold my hand lest I fall
Take my hand, precious Lord
Lead me on
Precious Lord, take my hand.

"Precious Lord" has come to be known as a funeral song, and while it was composed in the deepest sorrow, it's ultimately a song of refuge and hope. The song's composer, Dorsey, is known as the "Father of Gospel Music." Before turning to gospel, the Georgia-born songwriter and pianist was a blues writer and performer known as Georgia Tom who wrote and recorded hundreds of records. He wrote, arranged and played for Ma Rainey, the "Mother of the Blues."

The tension between sacred and secular music in the Black church is mirrored in the fact that before Dorsey wrote gospel classics like "Precious Lord" and "Peace in the Valley," he wrote blues numbers with titles like "It's Tight Like that," "Pat That Bread" and "Somebody's Been Using That Thing."

In August 1932, Dorsey's wife and child died in childbirth. Heavy with grief, Dorsey sat at a piano, playing with the keys when, as he put it, "the words like drops of water from the crevice of a rock above seemed to drop in line. With me on the piano, 'Precious Lord, take my hand, lead me on, let me stand; I'm tired, I'm weak, I'm worn. Through the storm, through the night, lead me on to the light. Take my hand, precious Lord, and lead me home.'"

This was gospel blues. In his superb book *Boogaloo: The*

Quintessence of American Popular Music, Arthur Kempton writes, "Dorsey's great accomplishment was to make 'precious Lord, take my hand' feel the same way as 'baby, please don't go.'"

The song's title is "Take My Hand, Precious Lord," but most people call it "Precious Lord" or, as King did, "Precious Lord, Take My Hand." Whatever it's called, it's said to be the most recorded gospel song in history and was selected by the Recording Industry Association of America for its 365 Songs of the Century for the twentieth century.

Whether one is of faith, little faith or no faith, the song asks us to believe that even the longest and darkest of nights won't last, that the most treacherous of storms will end and that when we are at our weakest we'll discover our strength. Somehow we'll find our way home.

Without Confronting Hate, There Is No Stopping It

"We cannot let hateful people tell you otherwise, to scapegoat and deflect from the fact they aren't doing anything to fix the real issues that impact people's lives. And I know that hate will only win if people like me stand by and let it happen. . . . We will not let hate win." With these words from an eloquent and righteously indignant speech last week, Michigan state senator Mallory McMorrow went viral.

McMorrow, a Democrat, was responding to a fundraising email from a Republican colleague claiming children were under assault from "gender-bending indoctrination" and "race-based education." The letter accused McMorrow of being among progressives who "are outraged they can't teach can't groom and sexualize kindergartners or that eight-year-olds are responsible for slavery." The accusations are lies and disgusting, aligning with the sick QAnon obsession with recklessly labeling political opponents as pedophiles and child traffickers.

Hating is violence. This hatred, left unchecked, will lead to physical violence, one reason McMorrow was right to vow, "We will not let hate win."

But let's not underestimate hate's chances. Unlike Father Time, Uncle Hate isn't unbeaten but has chalked up a centuries-long record of wins and is remarkably durable. Of all the diseases that have inflicted humanity, hate is the oldest, most infectious and most virulent. It's also the most preventable since we choose if we hate. When it's not prevented, called out and challenged, hate is a fuse that runs through history and leaves destruction in its wake. Hate doesn't have a political orientation but will happily go wherever it's invited and stoked, and where it can blind its hosts to their own culpability of inviting it to stay.

Hate deflects responsibility for its existence and projects its moral failings onto those we're asked to hate. In George Orwell's *1984* there is a period during the day when party members gather for Two Minutes Hate, in which they are driven into a frenzy by watching a film of the people who are supposed to be their enemies. Their frenzy rages until the image of Big Brother, their leader, appears on the screen to "comfort" them, followed by party slogans:

WAR IS PEACE
FREEDOM IS SLAVERY
IGNORANCE IS STRENGTH

We're living in a twenty-four-hour news cycle of Two Minutes Hate. The mindset and tactics McMorrow spoke against encourage fear of critical race theory, transgender kids and immigrants, and glibly dismiss political opponents as "woke," "socialists" and "leftists" out to destroy America. It's a mindset that sees other Americans as worthier of contempt and condemnation than Russian president Vladimir Putin.

To hate someone is to deny their humanity, their dignity, their right to exist. To falsely accuse someone of vile actions is to invite not only hatred but also violence upon that person. This is why hate cannot be met with hate, because it perpetuates.

McMorrow demonstrated that refusing to answer hate and lies with more hate and lies doesn't mean running away. It means confronting the spewers of hate, looking them in the eyes and calling them out.

It's not transgender kids or people who want a full and accurate teaching of our nation's history who will ruin our country. It's those who make them objects to be feared and hated. It's those who shun and stereotype people who are different. It's those who want us to remain a nation of shadow boxers, sparring with images and reflections while never having contact with what is real. It's those who want to divide us, make us a nation of strangers to our history and the lives of others. And it's those who incite us to be afraid of each other, to always be peeping around the corners of our fears.

In Carlos Fuentes's novella *Constancia*, a character says, "How long a vigil, I ask myself, does historical violence impose on us?" The answer is until we choose to end it, beginning with confronting those who want it to continue.

Trump's Fear of Fruit Comes Flying onto Political Stage

At a rally in Florida during the 2016 presidential campaign, Donald Trump said the election would decide whether the United States would remain a free country or "we become a corrupt banana republic controlled by large donors and foreign governments."

Throughout his presidency, critics assailed Trump's leadership style as that of an authoritarian running a banana republic. But thanks to an October 2021 videotaped deposition released last week, we know how terribly wrong his critics were. Trump could never be associated with a banana republic because he's afraid of bananas, tomatoes, pineapples and other fruit being thrown at him.

Federal guidelines recommend that adults eat at least four to five servings of fruits and vegetables per day. Like each of us, Trump doesn't want those servings hurled at him. But it's his obsession with flying fruit as deadly projectiles that sounds fruit loopy. The testimony comes from a civil lawsuit brought by protesters alleging to have been assaulted by Trump's security detail outside his New York offices in 2015.

Pointing to a pattern of candidate Trump encouraging violence at his rallies, the lawyers focused on a February 1, 2016, campaign speech in Cedar Rapids, Iowa, where Trump told supporters, "If you see someone getting ready to throw a tomato, just knock the crap out of them, would you?" In the deposition, that comment led to this exchange between an attorney and Trump:

Q: "That was your statement."

Trump: "Oh, yeah. It was very dangerous."

Q: "What was very dangerous?"

Trump: "We were threatened."

Q: "With what?"

Trump: "They were going to throw fruit. We were threatened, we had a threat."

When Trump was asked how he became aware that people were going to throw fruit, he answered that they were told, and "you get hit with fruit, it's—no, it's very violent stuff."

After attorneys agreed that a tomato was a fruit, Trump said, "It's worse than tomato, it's other things also. But tomato, when they start doing that stuff, it's very dangerous. There was an alert out that day."

Later, the once-most-powerful man in the world said that "we were put on alert they were going to do fruit."

"And some fruit is a lot worse than—tomatoes are bad, by the way," he said. "But it's very dangerous. No, I wanted them to watch. They were on alert. I remember that specific event because everybody was on alert. They were going to hit—they were going to hit hard."

Asked if it was all right for his security or audience members to use physical force to stop the assault of flying fruit, Trump, the most feared Republican in the country, answered, "To stop somebody from throwing pineapples, tomatoes, bananas, stuff like that, yeah, it's dangerous stuff."

Those of you tempted to laugh have never seen the damage a perfectly thrown kumquat can do to the human body. And well-aimed plums have done more to topple governments and alter the course of history than all the armies led by kings and generals.

What's important to grasp is that ahead of the Cedar Rapids rally, Trump's security detail had picked up—ahem—"intelligence" that plotters were stocking up on produce so they could infiltrate his rally and "hit hard."

One of the most chilling scenes in the movie *Malcolm X* is when the assassins sit around a table piled with guns they are preparing and loading. The vision terrifying Trump was of protesters sitting around a kitchen table divvying up the arsenal of tomatoes, bananas, pineapples and other dangerous fruit they were going to attack him with.

Twice in his deposition, Trump mentioned pineapples, which, given their size, may truly be one of the most dangerous fruits. But other than Patrick Mahomes and Aaron Rodgers, who has the arm strength and accuracy to use a pineapple to take out a presidential candidate?

It should be noted that no tomatoes, bananas, pineapples or other dangerous fruit were confiscated from protesters at the February 1, 2016, Cedar Rapids rally. It should also be noted that tomatoes, bananas and pineapples were not among the weapons used by Trump supporters on January 6, 2021, when they attacked the Capitol.

Babies Suffer; Abbott, Ever Cynical, Sees a Wedge

Luke 18:15–17 of the King James Bible reads: "And they brought unto him also infants, that he would touch them: but when his disciples saw it, they rebuked them.

"But Jesus called them unto him, and said, suffer little children to come unto me, and forbid them not: for of such is the kingdom of God.

"Verily I say unto you, whosoever shall not receive the kingdom of God as a little child shall in no wise enter therein."

However wrong the disciples were in rebuking mothers for bringing their infants to Jesus to receive his blessing, their objections weren't rooted in a fear that if he possessed a finite number of blessings, they should be reserved for a certain kind of infant. They didn't insist that the Lord's healing touch be denied to one infant so that another could receive it because of where the child was from.

If Jesus could do for baby formula what he did for fishes and loaves, there would be no shortage. And if the United States weren't going through its worst baby formula shortage in decades, this wouldn't be an issue Governor Greg Abbott could exploit. Instead we have a joint statement Abbott released Thursday with the National Border Patrol Council.

From the Book of Abbott 5:12–22: "Children are our most vulnerable, precious Texans and deserve to be put first. Yet President Biden has turned a blind eye to parents across America who are facing the nightmare of a nationwide baby formula short-age. While mothers and fathers stare at empty grocery store shelves in a panic, the Biden Administration is happy to provide baby formula to illegal immigrants coming across our southern border. This is yet another one in a long line of reckless, out-of-touch priorities from the Biden Administration when it comes to securing our border and protecting Americans. Our children deserve a president who puts their needs and survival first—not one who gives critical supplies to illegal immigrants before the very people he took an oath to serve."

This isn't a statement of genuine concern for children during a national crisis. It's political dodgeball in which children are props hurled against the Biden administration.

The *Wall Street Journal* reported last month that 40 percent of the most popular baby formula is out of stock across the country. The shortage goes back to February when Abbott Nutri-tion (no connection to the governor) recalled baby formula and closed two manufacturing plants after two infants died from bacterial infections after consuming the formula. The *New York Times* noted that San Antonio has the highest rate of shortages in the country, with 56 percent of its normal supply gone.

As with any crisis, this shortage especially hurts people with low incomes. Baby formula is given to immigrant infants be-cause they and their families are in custody in the United States, and US law and simple morality commands they be fed.

A nuanced, compassionate statement by Abbott counseling patience and cooperation as the nation finds a way to feed all of God's babies would have been principled leadership. Instead he wants Texans to know the federal government is not providing for your children because it's providing for their children. "Our most vulnerable precious Texans" will suffer because of them.

Children anywhere are the most vulnerable and precious, and they should come first, not because they're Texans but because they're children. Does Abbott not want immigrant children to have access to baby formula? He didn't answer that question because he's not that cruel. But he posed the shortage the way he did because he is that cynical.

On Thursday it was announced the Food and Drug Administration will outline specific actions to increase formula imports. As that crisis abates, Abbott can reflect on the first sentence of his statement: "Children are our most vulnerable, precious Texans and deserve to be put first."

If that's true, why is Texas first in uninsured children and the number of children living in poverty?

Brewing Hatred in Buffalo Shatters Trust

From the day we're born, our lives are in the hands of others. Not just the doctors who bring us into this world and the families who raise us, but people we may never see or know. We depend on the judgment and decency of strangers, trusting that they will honor our shared humanity by honoring our right to live in dignity and peace. We cross streets trusting that drivers will stop at red lights. We eat in restaurants trusting that those who prepare our food won't poison it. We board planes trusting that the pilots are qualified.

And we trust that a night at the movies, a day in school, a morning in a house of worship or a Saturday afternoon in the grocery store won't be violently interrupted by a gunman agitated by hate. Until the latest gunman shatters that trust, violating the sanctuaries of our public spaces. In the most recent violation of this trust, an eighteen-year-old self-proclaimed white supremacist is accused of killing ten Black people in a Buffalo, NY, supermarket he chose because it was in a predominantly Black neighborhood.

There's little reason to trust that lessons, caution or regret will be drawn from this latest act of orchestrated white supremacist violence any more than they have been drawn from decades, generations, centuries of orchestrated white supremacist violence. Not when it's not taken seriously. Not when our national security agencies repeatedly warn us that white supremacists and other far-right extremists are our most significant domestic terrorism threat, yet the rage in the country is to avoid talking about racism by stuffing a boogeyman with straw, calling it critical race theory and blaming it for the state of the country.

The accused Buffalo shooter wrote a racist and antisemitic screed echoing the "great replacement" lie white supremacists, some anti-immigration groups and Fox News's Tucker Carlson espouse: that nonwhite people are being brought into the United States to replace white people and dilute the white vote. The shooter also reportedly denounced critical race theory, which is consistent with a *Buffalo News* story that the day before his rampage he talked for ninety minutes with a Black man named Grady Lewis on a wide range of topics. Lewis said the young man said that critical race theory "teaches that all whites are violent."

That's not what critical race theory teaches. No doubt the accused shooter had never heard of it before 2021, because the loudest objectors to critical race theory had never heard of it before 2021—and still don't know what it is in 2022. They lie about it being taught in K–12 schools and are unable to cite specific writers or books that embody the theory. If they mention the *New York Times* 1619 Project and are asked which of the more than fifty separate entries they find objectionable, they're silent because they've not read it. Critical race theory is used to avoid candid discussions about American history and race, and about how the powerful repercussions of racism still rock this land, as they did, again, in Buffalo.

The accused shooter doesn't hate Black people, immigrants and Jews because he was born white. No one is born to hate. That eighteen-year-old was taught to hate them because they were Black, immigrants and Jews. To not only hate them as groups because they were different, but to hate them enough to demonize, slander and accuse them of taking something from him that he thinks they aren't entitled to have. To hate them enough to wish them harm, do them harm and eliminate them from this earth.

Critical race theory, unarmed and not taught in any schools attended by the accused Buffalo shooter, killed no one last weekend. The finger of hatred, born of ignorance and in service to white supremacy, pulled the trigger.

The shadows of hate darkening this nation may never lift. But we must use the light we have to seek out those we can trust to hold back the darkness. We have no choice but to try, because other triggers are waiting to be pulled.

Again and Again,
We Bear Witness to Tragedy

Through devotion
Blessed are the children
Praise the teacher
That brings true love to many
—"Devotion," Earth, Wind, and Fire

At the entrance of Uvalde Memorial Park off Main Street is a plaque dedicated to the young men from Uvalde County who lost their lives in World War I. During the war, which lasted from 1914 to 1918, thirty-five soldiers from Uvalde were killed. These men gave what President Abraham Lincoln, in his Gettysburg Address, said of the men killed in that Civil War battle: "the last full measure of devotion."

On Tuesday at Robb Elementary School, a mile from the park, twenty-one people were shot to death. More than half the number of those who'd been killed in four years of war were massacred by a weapon unimagined by men in combat then or our Founding Fathers, all within one horrific hour. Of the slain, nineteen were children ranging from eight to eleven years old. The other two, Eva Mireles and Irma Garcia, were teachers who, attempting to save the lives of children, gave their last full measure of devotion at a school to which Getty Street will lead you.

Along Main Street were reminders of the normal progression of a child's school years. A banner announced that pre-K enrollment was under way; a yellow school bus across from H-E-B advertised the need for bus drivers; graduation pictures of Uvalde High School's Class of 2022 were displayed in front of city offices.

Turn left at Main and Getty, followed by a couple of other turns, and you'll arrive at the school where all expectations of the normal progression of nineteen children's school years, and the remaining years of their teachers, were shattered.

On Wednesday the world gathered across the street from Robb Elementary School, at the corners of Old Carrizo Road and Geraldine. That's where the world's media camped to report on a unique but frequent American spectacle: a mass shooting, a school shooting with multiple fatalities.

Being played out—this time in Uvalde—is the heartbreaking ritual of strangers saying goodbye to children they never had the chance to say hello to and looking back on lives not given the time to go forward.

In a house directly across from the school, a "no trespassing" sign and a yellow sign with "Respect for Life" stood in a yard shaded by a velvet ash tree surrounded by a rose of Sharon bush. Throughout the day, the media tread across the yard, as did mourners who reached across the yellow police tape to hand flowers and stuffed animals to Department of Public Safety officers, who placed them at the growing memorial below the school's sign.

There will be other memorials in the days, weeks and years to come for the nineteen children and two women murdered in that school. There will be a plaque engraved with their names, just as there is a plaque engraved with the names of the men killed in war. Memorial Day will forever have deeper and tragic meaning for Uvalde. To memorialize is to remember, and memory begins with bearing witness to lives and events. And to listen to those who bear witness.

On Wednesday, reluctantly at first but with growing confidence, Adalynn Garza began bearing witness. The nine-year-old third grader was hiding with her teacher and other students in a dark second-grade classroom during the shooting. "We did level zero," she said. Asked what that was, she answered, "Stay quiet and be still." They'd practiced active shooting drills.

At least three children she was close to died, including ten-year-old Tess Mata. "I couldn't sleep last night," Adalynn said on Wednesday. "It kept coming to my head."

And while it's a silly thing to ask a child who was in the middle of a deadly mass shooting, it must be asked: How was she feeling now?

"I feel scared," Adalynn said, as she twirled the long hair of her six-year-old sister, Kinsley, "because what happened in this grade will happen again."

The child didn't say "can." She said "will."

The Fairy Tale America Tells Itself about Our Gun Nightmare

Once upon a time, in a land of oak trees and honey, a place once called Encina, there lived princesses and princes who ruled the hearts of that land, which they brightened with the dazzling colors of their joy and laughter.

Once upon a time, like princesses and princes everywhere, there were summer nights when they would gaze upon the glittering sky and sing:

> Twinkle, twinkle little star
> How I wonder what you are
> Up above the sky so high
> Like a diamond in the sky.

Once upon a time, like princesses and princes everywhere, they would go to bed with stuffed animals and fall asleep to fairy tales, which began with "Once upon a time" and ended with "happily ever after."

Once upon a time, in a land once called Encina but now known as Uvalde, time and "happily ever after" were assumed for princesses and princes, who would grow into their dreams and become queens and kings.

Princesses and princes happily spent their time playing softball and basketball, doing gymnastics, catching footballs from grandfathers, cheerleading, running, swimming, learning dances from TikTok, learning to sew from YouTube, doing photography, singing with fathers, saving money to go to Disney World, watching *Encanto*, enjoying Ariana Grande perform, cheering for the Houston Astros, being with family. All while planning to be an artist, a teacher, a marine biologist, a lawyer or a police officer. Once upon a time it was all possible. Until time stopped and took away these princesses and princes. Now there is no happily ever after.

Stuffed animals like the ones they once cuddled populate a memorial in Uvalde's town square, reminding us that this time a billion loving kisses from their parents and grandparents won't open the eyes of these sleeping beauties.

Fairy tales are often stories of how to behave. We tell children fairy tales to entertain and educate. But we also tell fairy tales to deceive ourselves, to pretend we're better than we are and we're doing all the things we should be doing. There is no bigger fairy tale we tell ourselves in the United States than that children are our most precious resource and we do all we can to protect them. Not when the leading cause of death of children in this nation is firearms. Protect the Second Amendment, fine. But protect second graders, and third and fourth graders, and all young people.

Once upon a time we believed we'd do something more to protect them after we lost so many in Sandy Hook, then Parkland, then Santa Fe. Instead we watched the repeated assassinations of our youth, as happily ever after, ever after, ever after, ever after was shattered.

We call children angels, but we want that to be metaphorical. We don't want them to be given angel's wings before they receive their graduation rings, before their time on this earth has taken flight and they've had the chance to navigate full lives, to have a chance at happily ever after, ever after, ever after.

Once upon a time, in a land of oak trees and honey, a place once called Encina but now known as Uvalde, there lived princesses and princes who ruled the hearts of that land, which they brightened with the dazzling colors of their joy and laughter. Their names were Navaeh, José, Jacklyn, Annabell, Jayce, Makenna, Jailah, Lexi, Tess, Xavier, Amerie, Maranda, Eliahana, Rogelio, Layla, Alithia, Maite, Uziyah, Eliana. Their queen-protectors were named Irma and Eva.

After Uvalde, What Will "Truly Good of Heart" Do?

On June 12, 1942, a red-and-white checkered diary became one of the most famous birthday gifts in history. The recipient was a Jewish girl from Germany living in Amsterdam with her family. She wanted to be a writer, and for about two years she filled her diary with her thoughts, observations and dreams, not knowing she was writing her masterwork, the only book she'd have the time to write.

Less than a month after receiving the diary, Anne Frank, her parents and older sister, and four other Jews went into hiding in a secret annex at the back of her father's company building. They remained there until August 4, 1944, when Nazi police, tipped off, found and arrested them. The only survivors from that annex and the concentration camps they were sent to were Anne's father, Otto, and her diary. *The Diary of Anne Frank* is the most celebrated book written by a child—because it was written by a child, with a precocious talent, hiding for her life.

On June 20, 1944, she wrote: "Writing in a diary is a really strange experience for someone like me. Not only because I've never written anything before, but also because it seems to me that later on neither I nor anyone else will be interested in the musings of a thirteen-year-old schoolgirl. Oh well, it doesn't matter. I feel like writing, and I have an even greater need to get all kinds of things off my chest."

Decades later we still care about the musings of this

thirteen-year-old girl. The most famous is from July 15, 1944, the third-to-last passage. "It's difficult in times like these: ideals, dreams and cherished hopes rise within us, only to be crushed by grim reality," she wrote. "It's a wonder I haven't abandoned all my ideals, they seem so absurd and impractical. Yet I cling to them because I still believe, in spite of everything, that people are truly good at heart."

Those last words—"I still believe, in spite of everything, that people are truly good at heart"—have been used for decades as a feel-good affirmation, often accompanied by a picture of a smiling Anne holding a pencil. But it was a belief grounded in hope, and we should never forget that the most important pages of *The Diary of Anne Frank* are the ones never written. Her last entry was August 1, 1944. She was arrested three days later.

What would she have written about the horrors she suffered and witnessed in the Bergen-Belsen concentration camp, before dying from typhus fever, in February 1945, at fifteen?

One sentence after Anne states her belief in people's goodness is this one: "I see the world being slowly transformed into a wilderness, I hear the approaching thunder that, one day, will destroy us too, I feel the suffering of millions." I cannot read that without thinking of the children of Uvalde because, like most of you, I can't read or hear anything these days without thinking of the children of Uvalde.

The children in Robb Elementary who heard the approaching thunder of an AR-15-style rifle, and who hid in classrooms and under desks for what may have seemed to them like two years; the children who were destroyed; the children who, according to pediatrician Roy Guerrero, were "pulverized" and "decapitated" by gunfire.

And I can't understand the people, no doubt good of heart, who aren't moved enough to make such a weapon less accessible. I always return to what the legendary columnist Murray

Kempton wrote of Martin Luther King Jr.: "A great man knows he wasn't put on this earth to be part of a process through which a child can be hurt." That should guide personal behavior and public policy.

Like Anne Frank, I believe (most) people are truly good at heart. But there weren't any great people to save her life. Today there aren't enough great people among elected officials trying to save the lives of other children.

No Moving on from Uvalde

On Thursday morning, the last hearse carrying the last casket, holding the last victim, for the last funeral in Uvalde for the shooting victims pulled in front of Sacred Heart Catholic Church. Across the street a small orange butterfly alighted on the grass beneath a pecan tree standing between two houses.

Staring at the butterfly, I tried to appreciate its beauty and be lifted by its spiritual symbolism of transformation, hope and rebirth. But it was just a butterfly, and I was reminded of the ridiculously brief life span of butterflies as I watched the white and yellow casket of eleven-year-old Layla Salazar taken into the church.

Next Saturday's funeral for ten-year-old Uziyah Garcia in San Angelo will conclude the funerals for the nineteen students and two teachers murdered in a mass shooting in Robb Elementary School on May 24.

For one month we've absorbed every heartbreaking detail of the victims' lives, the chronology of events and the baffling decisions of law enforcement, all the while thinking we can't handle any new information about the shooting. For one month we've felt an exhausting, heavy and astonishing sadness that has now settled deep into our bones. For one month we've come to know people who weren't allowed to introduce themselves on their own terms but whose introductions were forced on us by an eighteen-year-old with an AR-style weapon and the unconscionable legalized madness that allows someone that age to own such guns.

Layla's and Uziyah's funerals mark a transition for most of us. We will slowly begin to turn our attention elsewhere, because there has never been a tragedy, no matter how awful and how many lives were stolen, where we didn't turn our attention elsewhere, whether to our own problems or the other maladies of our nation and world. Yet even as we begin to shift our attention, Uvalde feels different. It feels as if it won't allow us to completely turn away and forget. Not when the pain is this deep and raw, not when there remain too many unanswered questions as officials use the families of the victims to hide and deflect accountability.

For South Texans, part of this is because of Uvalde's proximity and heritage, but that's not all. Other mass shootings have shaken us to grief and anger. Parkland shook us mightily, and Sandy Hook shook us foolishly into thinking that the murder of twenty first graders would lead to significant gun safety reform. Uvalde began to seem different once we learned that the gunman had more than an hour to taunt and murder his victims—it took that long for law enforcement on the scene to stop him.

We can't find weak solace in hoping they all went as quickly as possible when we now have the accounts of survivors, including children and a teacher, painting images in our minds we can't erase. Forced to think longer of the final moments of twenty-one faces and names we've come to know so well, they're forever bound to our memories, as are thoughts of their families' pain.

On June 4 a man knelt in front of one of Ellie Garcia's memorials in the town square which, like Robb Elementary, has bloomed into a large memorial. After placing a purple teddy bear, he stayed on his right knee as his sad and weary eyes took in the dolls, stuffed animals, flags and messages. He slowly rose and sat on the bench directly in front of Ellie's memorial, hunched over, and continued staring at the tribute for a child who died at nine. He sometimes looked around at the other people in the square. He was someplace deeper and more sacred, a place that shouldn't be violated with words of condolences.

It was what would have been Ellie's tenth birthday, and after spending half an hour at her memorial, her grandfather rose from his seat and drifted through and away from the square, across a street and to a parking lot and the vehicle where his fishing sidekick and princess would not be waiting.

Today, as we turn toward Juneteenth, Father's Day and summer activities, let's remember the fathers and grandfathers and their beautiful butterflies no longer within their loving haunted gaze.

A Saint Who Worked
Miracles with the 'Fro

The patron saint of the Afro has died. Okay, that's not quite true. And when I write "that's not quite true," I mean that I made that up and there is no patron saint of the Afro. If there were, he would have had to die long before he could be declared a saint of anything.

But I did Google "patron saint of the Afro," and the first name that came up was Saint Benedict the Moor. (Kids, whenever "the Moor" is attached to a name like Saint Benedict or Othello, that means someone with a surprised look on their face is pointing while loudly whispering "He's Black!") Benedict was born to enslaved Africans—or what some Texans would call involuntarily relocated Africans—in Sicily.

There's no mention of Afros in any of Benedict's bios, but in some artistic renderings he does appear to be working a little 'fro. Benedict is the patron saint of, among other things, African missions, African Americans, Black missions and Black people. It's as if the Catholic Church said, "Let's just give everything Black to Benedict until we get some more Black saints up in here."

But if there were a patron saint of the Afro, it should be Willie Lee Morrow, who died last month at eighty-two. Born in Tuscaloosa, Alabama, Morrow moved to San Diego, where he opened a barber shop and created a multimillion-dollar Black hair care empire, including inventing the Afro pick. (Just writing the words "Afro pick" excited the few remaining follicles on my scalp to leap and aspire to an ascension once enjoyed but now impossible.) Morrow was also a pioneer of the Jheri curl, but the less said about that, the better. Afro picks were essential for teasing out hair by digging down to the scalp to stretch it from the roots so an Afro could be shaped. Sporting an Afro wasn't simply about letting your hair grow out. It had to be cared for, nourished with the right products, trimmed and sculpted by good barbers.

Reading Morrow's obituaries took me back to the 1970s and *Soul Train*. One of the show's main sponsors was Johnson Products, the makers of Afro Sheen, which had a hilarious commercial in which a young man who hadn't combed out his hair is visited by the ghost of Frederick Douglass, who chides him about leaving the house with his Afro looking a mess. The young man squirts some Afro Sheen Comb Easy on his hair, shapes it with his Afro pick and is ready to go.

As a kid, I wanted an Afro, but my maternal grandmother was against it. When my mother, aunt and other grandmother talked her into it, I started wearing one at twelve. A few months later my uncle married into a Mexican American family, and when my brother and I went to the reception in Hondo, the other kids thought we were members of the Jackson Five. My Afro was never as big as peak Jackie, Jermaine and Michael but somewhere between Marlon and early Michael.

Because my hair was very thick (I hate talking about my hair in the past tense)—so thick I'd get it braided to loosen it up—I could put pencils, pens, coins and folded-up dollar bills in my Afro and forget about them until the next morning. When I took off a baseball cap, I'd have ring around the 'fro.

I owned an assortment of steel and plastic prong Afro picks, including foldable ones with red and green handles representing Africa and others with handles the shape of a Black Power fist. I also had steel rakes, which we called cake cutters because they were weapons. Each morning, after applying Afro Sheen Comb Easy and using the Afro pick and cake cutter, I topped off my hair with coconut-scented hairspray. All of these products were purchased at an Afro shop in Alamo Plaza.

I miss my Afro. I even wrote a love letter to it once. But I don't miss the maintenance. But Saint Morrow—yeah, I've canonized him—made that maintenance easy. If I ever visit his grave, I'll pour out a little Afro Sheen in tribute to him and in memory of my beloved 'fro.

This July Fourth Rededicate Ourselves to Democracy

I, too, am America.
—Langston Hughes, "I, Too"

The first rendition of the Fourth of July, sung in 1776 from the script that was the Declaration of Independence, was written for a small choir. Not included in the vocal arrangements and never intending to be given any leads were the voices of darker brothers and sisters, the Indigenous brothers and sisters, and the white sisters.

Brilliant men capable of imagining an ingenious, if imperfect, form of government couldn't imagine the richness and talent of the voices they were excluding or that races and genders different from their own should be heard. But such was the system they created that through suffering and struggle, resistance and revolution, tenacity and talent, those voices forced their way on stage, expanding and making better and more equitable the democratic chorus that is America. These voices ringing out across the land have accents, lilts, brogues and inflections carrying the melodies of regions and the shadings of culture and heritage.

Yet having to suffer, struggle and resist so often, seeing so many heroes, heroines and allies die to be included in the choir, is tiring and tests your allegiances and desire to sing. Decisions made by presidents, governors, legislatures and courts that put restrictions on your voice, encroach on your freedom and endanger you can shake you till you fall on your knees—and keep you kneeling on one in protest.

Still, we rise and still we sing, finding new and creative ways to interpret and expand the two great American songbooks of democracy so their lyrics have deeper meaning for all our lives. Before a 1968 World Series game in Detroit, the Puerto Rican singer-songwriter José Feliciano sang a Latin-infused version of "The Star-Spangled Banner," performing it with soulful and aching emotion. His performance was meant as a tribute and show of gratitude to a nation that had given him the opportunities to become a star, but it generated outrage, condemnation and death threats from those believing their national anthem should only be performed in the conventional way.

Before the 1983 NBA All-Star Game Marvin Gaye delivered the greatest rendition of the national anthem, layering the song with a Caribbean rhythm that transformed it into a sensual hymn, a love song to America, which had the players swaying and fans clapping with joy. It was less controversial than Feliciano's but still off-putting to those who believed the anthem should be performed only one way.

The Fourth of July is about the many different voices that make up the democratic chorus of America. Voices that interpret the country's history, tell its many stories—good and bad— through their own experiences, melodies and rhythms. But this year it arrives as many Americans feel that their voices are being ignored or targeted for silence. The democracy we celebrate has never seemed so fragile, literally under attack. It arrives with knowledge of how far a sitting president of the United States and his mob were willing to go to overturn an election and the collective voice of American voters. It arrives with a continued assault on voting rights. It arrives with women, more than half of the population of the United States, having fewer rights and say over their bodies than they did last Fourth of July.

This is a Fourth of July not only for celebration but for reflection and rededicating ourselves to what it is we're supposed to be celebrating, for finding and raising our voices and securing our inclusion in America's democratic chorus.

Laugh Was the Profanity, Not O'Rourke's Word Choice

When your intent to interrupt, mock and ridicule someone back-fires, and you become the mocked and ridiculed, neither you nor your defenders can complain about your treatment or *tsk* be-cause someone used bad words and called you a bad name. When you laugh during the recounting of a murderous mass shooting, no verbal response can come close to being as grotesque as what you found funny.

Since his 2018 campaign for the US Senate, Beto O'Rourke is known for his propensity for profanity. Some think it's re-freshing and real because it reflects his passion. Some find it off-putting and juvenile. Others consider it calculated and part of his stump speech. But on Wednesday evening during a town hall in Mineral Wells, O'Rourke, the Democratic nominee for governor, let loose an epithet that has gone viral for its morally outraged spontaneity.

Supporters of Governor Greg Abbott, identified by their T-shirts, who appeared not to be disruptive, just standing and listening, were in the back of the room where O'Rourke was speaking. When he talked about Uvalde and the AR-15-style gun used to murder nineteen children and two teachers, a male Ab-bott supporter is heard laughing—loud enough to suggest that he wanted to be heard.

In midsentence O'Rourke turned toward the man, pointed and

said, "It may be funny to you, MF, but it's not funny to me, okay!" His supporters jumped to their feet with raucous cheers and applause. It may have been the most exquisitely indignant use of "MF" ever in American politics. Not gratuitous or planned but a human reaction to the inhumane action of someone laughing about the murders of children and their teachers.

This is the second time in less than three months that O'Rourke, Uvalde and profanity have intersected. On the day after the shooting, as Abbott was speaking at a press conference, O'Rourke stood up from the audience to confront him. "The time to stop this was after Santa Fe High School. The time to stop this was after El Paso. The time to stop the next shooting is right now and you are doing nothing," he said. "You are all doing nothing. You said this is not predictable; this is totally predictable."

Uvalde mayor Don McLaughlin yelled at O'Rourke, "I can't believe you're a sick son of a b—— that would come to a deal like this to make a political issue."

O'Rourke's supporters didn't like him being called an SOB, but given the emotions, the mayor's response and language was understandable. In retrospect, given the incompetent and corrupt handling of Uvalde by state leaders and law enforcement agencies, O'Rourke was more correct than he could have known.

Cruelty and the degradation of people you disagree with crosses ideological and party lines. Laughing at the death of children, reveling in anyone's pain, isn't a reflection of a person's party and politics but of their character and the person they choose to be. Yet such laughing isn't surprising at a time when a bombastic profiteer such as Alex Jones has convinced millions of Americans that another school shooting in which children and teachers were murdered, Sandy Hook, is a hoax.

There are millions of Texans who think about May 24, Robb

Elementary and the children and women of Uvalde who died there. When we think of them, it's not mirth or merriment that we feel or laughing we want to do.

There's some clutching of pearls by people with misplaced priorities who have the vapors because O'Rourke said a naughty world. The true profanity of the moment was a man laughing about dead children and teachers—and the ultimate profanity is how they died. Maybe you don't want your children hearing a famous politician saying a bad word. But think of the families who'd give anything to have their children be alive to hear those words and to have two teachers be alive to tell them not to repeat them.

Anyone upset with O'Rourke's authentic response to callousness should aim their outrage at those who enable weapons of war to be aimed and discharged at nineteen babies and two teachers. Don't cry over a twelve-letter profanity spoken. Weep, don't laugh, over twenty-one lives stolen.

Fruitcakes Have Fillings, Too

It starts with a craving around Halloween. As the days get shorter and the nights longer I find myself thinking about it more, picturing it, tasting it in my imagination. By the end of Thanksgiving I'm jonesing for it, gots to have it. Not "got" but "gots," as in, "I gots to have some fruitcake."

Okay, go ahead. I hear the fusillade of jokes, the barrage of mockery, the disdain, the pure hatred for a dessert that has done nothing except serve the pleasures of those who love it. Fruitcake is the most falsely mocked of foods. The mere mention of it starts people making fun of it.

What's so funny about the word "fruitcake"? If that gets folks to laughing, wait till they hear the word "snickerdoodle." That cookie, by its very name, snickerdoodle, invites you to laugh at it, but we leave it alone at the expense of fruitcake.

And what is fruitcake? It is what its name says it is. It's a cake made with fruit. The word "fruit" isn't funny nor is the word "cake," but put them together and we've got a punchline. What's so hilarious about a delicacy made with fruits, nuts, raisins, spices and brown sugar? Brown sugar, people! Ain't nothing wrong with brown sugar! Brown sugar keeps you smiling and feeling good! Brown sugar makes everything better! Brown sugar will save this country and the world! Brown sugar— (Editor's note: "We get it, Cary. Move on.")

Sorry about that. By the way, bourbon is often an important ingredient in fruitcake. The point is, where is the funny in all of this? What did fruitcake do to become the most maligned food in history? All foods are disliked by some people, but fruitcake is the only one for which scorn is openly encouraged.

Fruitcakes can be traced back to ancient Rome, whose troops ate, for sustained energy, a type of bread or bar called Satura made with raisins, pomegranate seeds, pine nuts and wine.

The enduring (no pun intended) joke about fruitcakes is their durability. They do last a long time because the ingredients have low-water activity—their low moisture keeps microorganisms from reproducing. In 2016 conservators in Antarctica discovered a 106-year-old fruitcake that had been brought over during the 1910 Terra Nova expedition of Robert Falcon Scott. (If your great-great-grandfather had bet on that fruitcake lasting longer than the *Titanic*, which sunk in 1912, you'd be a trust fund baby now.) The oldest known fruitcake is 144 years old. I jones for fruitcake, but I'm not eating a fruitcake baked during Reconstruction.

Let me be clear: I love fruitcake. I love the sight of it, the smell of it, the taste of it and the fact that I can eat the same cake for twelve years. See, so pervasive is the mockery of fruitcake that even fruitcakeophiles like me will joke.

My love of fruitcake goes back to childhood. I grew up with fruitcakes. Let me rephrase that. I grew up in a house full of fruitcakes. Still, not good.

This time of year my grandmother would make incredible fruitcakes—more than a dozen of them—swaddle them in cheesecloth soaked in bourbon and wrap them in foil. Many she'd send to relatives and friends around the country, and the others she'd keep refrigerated. It wasn't unusual to eat fruitcake months after the holidays. I was raised on fruitcake. To paraphrase President John F. Kennedy, "Ich bin ein fruitcake."

My only reason for returning to the paper three years ago was to be a voice for fruitcakes everywhere. Let me rephrase that. When people think of fruitcakes, I want them to think of me.

I'm not thinking straight because my mind is on a tin from Collins Street Bakery.

If you haven't tried fruitcake, give it a try before you judge. If you don't like it, fine, but no need to mock it. Fruitcakes have fillings, too.

The Heartbreak of Being a Cowboys Fan

For the twenty-seventh year in a row I will awake on the morning of the NFC Championship game without the familiar mix of excitement and nerves as I wonder if my Dallas Cowboys will advance to the Super Bowl. Honestly, that mix of excitement and nerves about the Cowboys advancing to the Super Bowl is no longer so familiar because it's been nearly three decades since I've experienced it.

Last Sunday, for the second consecutive year, the Cowboys season ended ignominiously on a "What the hell was that?" last play against the San Francisco 49ers. A few Cowboys fans mindlessly destroyed their TVs and burned their Dak Prescott jerseys. Those less impulsive of us took our cues from two characters on the Island of Misfit Toys, from the animated classic *Rudolph the Red-Nosed Reindeer*, who thought that Santa Claus was once again passing them by.

Some, like me, were Charlie-in-the-Box, who said he was going to bed to start dreaming about next year. Others echoed Dolly the doll, who said, "I haven't any dreams left to dream." And since I'm on the subject, let me pause and ask a question that has perplexed me longer than the Dallas Cowboys: Why is Dolly on the Island of the Misfit Toys? I understand a Charlie-in-the-Box not named Jack, a spotted elephant and a bird that can't fly (who, despite this, gets tossed off Santa's sleigh without an umbrella by an elf). But what's wrong with Dolly?

I digress, which I wouldn't have done had the Cowboys won

Sunday. To be a Cowboys fan is to be like any fan of a sports franchise or collegiate team. You're disappointed more often than satisfied. But it's the mixture of uncertainty, fun and frustration that makes sports fascinating and maddening.

To be a Cowboys fan when the going was good, like during the Tom Landry and Jimmy Johnson heydays, was glorious. It also made for insufferable Cowboys fans, which in turn made the team the most loved and hated sports franchise in the nation. It's the most valuable sports franchise in the world (worth $8 billion, according to *Forbes*), and whatever their record, the Cowboys have unmatched TV drawing power. But to be a Cowboys fan when they're bad or just not quite good enough is to be mocked and to see the Cowboys treated as a laughingstock by other fans, most of whose teams haven't come close to Dallas's eight Super Bowl appearances and five Super Bowl wins.

There was a time when the Cowboys had the record for Super Bowl appearances and the team was tied for Super Bowl wins, but it's been so long since they've played in one that Tom Brady alone has eclipsed those marks.

I've grown up with the Cowboys. We were both born in 1960. Because of them I've had my heart lifted as well as broken countless times—off the field as well as on. In 1971 Cowboys quarterback Roger Staubach spoke at an engagement in San Antonio. This was ahead of what would be his breakout season and Dallas's first Super Bowl appearance. My father saw him at the airport and asked for an autograph for me. Staubach, who will always be a god among men in my eyes, signed a small piece of notebook paper. The next day, during class at school, I showed off the autograph to my friends. It was confiscated by a substitute teacher named Mrs. Baldwin. At the end of the day I asked for it back, but she wouldn't return it. That was the last time I saw her or my Staubach autograph.

In the 1980s my aunt dated Dallas superstar running back

Tony Dorsett, my all-time favorite football player. When she broke up with him, I don't know how Tony felt, but I was devastated. "How could you do this to Uncle Tony?" I asked my aunt.

"He wasn't your uncle!" she answered.

"No thanks to you!" I said.

As I write this, the Cowboys have fired five assistant coaches. Just what Santa Jerry needs to have Dak guide him to the Super Bowl, right? Like Charlie-in-the Box, I'll start dreaming about next year.

Some Voices Lift, Others Divide

In late September 2001 I sat in Yankee Stadium behind more than three dozen Sikh men. We weren't there for a baseball game but for an interfaith memorial service for the victims killed, twelve days earlier, in the 9/11 attacks.

During the service, the Boys and Girls Choir of Harlem sang a beautiful rendition of "Lift Every Voice and Sing." Their performance elicited no pockets of manufactured outrage; no opportunistic politicians accused the service's organizers of being "woke"; no one claimed the song's purpose was to make white people feel guilty.

When the choir finished, the Sikhs, along with thousands of others, stood, applauded and proudly waved American flags.

Last Sunday, for the first time, "Lift Every Voice and Sing" was performed, by Sheryl Lee Ralph, before the Super Bowl. "America the Beautiful" was performed by Babyface, and, of course, "The Star-Spangled Banner," our national anthem, as always, was performed by Chris Stapleton.

The performance of "Lift Every Voice and Sing" might have escaped controversy were it not also known by its unofficial name—the "Black national anthem." Two leading voices on the American far right quickly tweeted their objections. Colorado Republican representative Lauren Boebert chirped, "America only has ONE NATIONAL ANTHEM. Why is the NFL trying to divide us by playing multiple!? Do football, not wokeness." Not to be out-anti-woked, her colleague Georgia Republican

representative Marjorie Taylor Greene wrote, "Chris Stapleton just sang the most beautiful national anthem at the Super
Bowl. But we could have gone without the rest of the wokeness."
They and their ilk are trying to do to the song what they've done
with "woke," which is to hijack and distort it for their nefarious
purposes.

The irony is that the song was first performed in 1900 to celebrate the birthday of Abraham Lincoln, the Republican president who wouldn't be able to win a presidential primary in today's Republican Party. Super Bowl Sunday, February 12, was
Lincoln's birthday.

The poem "Lift Every Voice and Sing" was written by James
Weldon Johnson, future leader of the National Association for
the Advancement of Colored People, a writer and leading figure of the Harlem Renaissance. Set to music composed by his
brother J. Rosamond Johnson, it became a song the NAACP,
after World War I, promoted as the "Negro national anthem" before it evolved into the "Black national anthem."

For generations, wherever African Americans have gathered
in churches, schools and ceremonies, it has been sung. It is a
cultural tradition, the most frequently recited—or sung—poem
written by an African American. It is a song about the history of
a people and the history of a nation. It's about the trans-Atlantic
slave trade, Reconstruction and Jim Crow, and it's about emancipation and fighting to expand democracy. It's about pain and
progress, tragedy and triumph, being pushed back while still
pushing on. It's about resistance, resiliency and reconciliation.
It's about getting knocked down but getting back up to march
until victory is won.

From the first verse:

Sing a song full of the faith that the dark past has taught us,
Sing a song full of the hope that the present has brought us.

Like many things and institutions featuring the names "Black" or "Mexican American" or "Native American" or "Women's," Black History Month was created out of exclusion, out of not being accepted or recognized by the dominant culture and power.

"Lift Every Voice and Sing" is about faith and hope and overcoming the dark past. But first that dark past must be acknowledged and reckoned with, not ignored. It is an inclusive song, asking that all voices be lifted and heard.

"Woke" isn't a divisive state of mind. It's been made divisive by those who have misappropriated its use to mock it and turn it into a buzzword. "Lift Every Voice and Sing" isn't a divisive song. It's been made divisive by those who hear a different song in their heads. It's first three lines are:

> Lift every voice and sing
> Till earth and heaven ring,
> Ring with the harmonies of Liberty.

Ignore the discordant notes warbled by its critics. Ring with the harmonies of liberty.

A Dance Party with a Side of Produce

I've learned several things while shopping in the Olmos Park H-E-B. If Marvin Gaye is singing, you should know when to accompany the Marvelous One and when to let him go solo. Sing out loud to "What's Going On" but not to "Let's Get it On."

The husband of the woman you don't see behind you in the cereal aisle may not take kindly to you crooning,

> There's nothing wrong with me
> Loving you, baby no no,
> And giving yourself to me can never be wrong
> If the love is true, oh baby.

You may think that KC and the Sunshine Band is cheesy, but let "Shake Your Booty" start playing while you're browsing the cheese section and see what starts shaking; try standing still to "That's the Way (I Like It)" when it comes on. Aha, aha.

What did I tell you?

If you're in the produce section and Linda Ronstadt is reflecting your troubled mind and lonesomeness with "Blue Bayou," by the time you're in the bakery, Gladys Knight could be telling you that "You're the Best Thing That's Ever Happened to Me," and the Five Stairsteps will be assuring you that, "O-o-h Child," things are going to get easier.

Over the past three years I've stumbled into being the unofficial correspondent of the Olmos Park H-E-B's music playlist. Before then I liked the store, and I was attracted to its Healthy

Living section and that it sold the *New York Times*. I live no-where near the store, but during the COVID-19 lockdown, with few places open, I began going every day, even if only to pick up the *Times*. After a while I began moving to the music, sing-ing with the music, paying attention to the music, and posting about the music on social media. It could be surreal staring at empty shelves as Lou Rawls sang "You'll Never Find (Another Love Like Mine)."

The store's playlist was as eclectic as my eClacktic musical tastes with a bent toward the R&B that was the first music I heard and fell in love with as a child. And the Olmos Park H-E-B's R&B game can be ridiculous. When they play "Slide" by Slave or "Flashlight" by Parliament Funkadelic, they have me looking for my roller skates. When they play "If I Could Turn Back the Hands of Time" by Tyrone Davis, it's a Saturday night and my grandfather and great-uncle are outside drinking, laughing, playing dominoes and having a good time. Once, after hearing "Me and Mrs. Jones" meeting "every day in the same café" I thought that Billy Paul should take Mrs. Jones to "Hotel Cali-fornia," which the Eagles had referred to in the previous song.

The social media posts became a thing, and soon I had people writing me and commenting about the music they were hearing in their H-E-Bs, which, they usually said, wasn't as good as the music being played at the Olmos Park H-E-B. People began post-ing from Olmos Park about what songs were being played. One morning about a year and a half into this, the store's excellent and affable manager, Mario, introduced himself to me and said people were now coming to the store because of the music. In posts I began calling the Olmos Park H-E-B the OP H-E-B or just the OP.

People seeing me in another store act as if I'm being unfaith-ful. One morning I was in Central Market when a couple saw me and asked, "What are you doing here?"

"I'm not cheating on OP," I said, feeling guilty. "I'm going there afterward. Listen to this music. Would I cheat for that?"

Less than a minute later I ran into a friend with a quizzical look in her eyes; she was also surprised to see me there. I felt like an actor too closely identified with a particular role.

Last year KENS 5 ultra-talented duo reporter Marvin Hurst and photographer Mike Humphries wanted to do a story on my musical shopping excursion and the OP. I (and I confess to Marvin and Mike now) kept coming up with excuses, because I'm shy and cameras scare me. I finally gave in and they did a great story, or so I'm told because I've yet to look at it. But it was nominated for an Emmy Award.

In the aisles of the OP H-E-B, I've seen H-E-B employees and customers dancing and singing to songs, sometimes together and sometimes in different parts of the store. I've stopped in my tracks at the heartbreaking beauty of Michael Martin Murphy's "Wildfire" and found myself dancing to Aretha Franklin's "Rock Steady," which is my favorite song to dance to. I've been melancholy listening to the Chi-Lites' "Have You Seen Her," and I've been moved to activism by McFadden & Whitehead's "Ain't No Stopping Us Now."

In August Wilson's play *Ma Rainey's Black Bottom*, Ma Rainey says, "I always got to have music going on in my head somewhere. It keeps things balanced. Music will do that. It fills things up. The more music you got in the world, the fuller it is."

The OP keeps the music going on. But don't sing "Let's Get it On" out loud to strangers.

Somebody's Child Was Helped

Somebody's child was playing chicken in the street. She may not have known it. There was never a look in her face as if this was a game, never a look of mischievous joy and daring, never a look of defiance.

The child, somebody's child, looked to be in her twenties. It was about 8:45 on a Tuesday morning, and she was on the sidewalk on South Flores Street by the H-E-B Market. Nothing stood out about her except that she was on the sidewalk wrapped in a purple blanket.

Nothing stood out until she was running across South Flores, weaving, stopping, running as cars blared their horns, hit the brakes and swerved. Making it to the other side of the street, where there was a bus stop, the young woman turned around on the curb, looked up and down South Flores and, with traffic flowing, dashed back into the street, running, weaving, stopping, running as cars blared their horns, hit the brakes and swerved.

There was a desperate, panicked look in her eyes, but she made it to the other side and turned around, ready to run again. An older woman in front of the store, visibly upset, said, "What's wrong with her? What is she doing? She's going to get killed! Where's the security guard?" Someone went inside to get the guard. The young woman was still on the H-E-B side of the street as a couple of people spoke with her to keep her from running back into the street.

The security guard talked softly to her, asking if she was all right and if she needed anything. Her eyes flitted back and forth with suspicion. She was a young Latina adult, but she could have also been a teenager. Under the purple blanket she wore a long-sleeve rust-colored shirt, black pants and black sandals.

She began crying as she spoke, addressing the guard but looking at the ground, saying, "Sir, if I have offended you in any way, that was not my intention, please forgive me. That was not my intent, and I am sorry." The way she spoke, her sincere, clear, almost formal enunciation was beautiful yet heartbreaking.

The guard told her not to worry about him, that she hadn't offended him but that he was concerned about her. Still looking down and crying, she lifted her hands, palms to the sky, and said, "God has prepared me to accept anything but, sir, if I have offended you, in any way, I'm sorry."

Along the way, it came out that she'd been to Haven for Hope. Sometimes she was addressing the security guard, sometimes God, other times a family member, "But Tío didn't know—he wasn't even—" It was hard to follow, but the way she spoke was mesmerizing.

Two police cars arrived. Like the security guard, the officers spoke to her gently, telling her they wanted to help her.

"Everybody's doing good except for me," she cried.

They continued to engage with her, asking questions in ways that were reassuring and not threatening.

Crying, she told them, "I was smoking dope, I was smoking dope, right now, and then I started running back and forth."

When the officers said they were going to call an ambulance, she begged them not to, saying, "I feel so, so free out here! I feel so, so free out here!"

When asked why she didn't like EMS, she said, "I'm sorry if I called you any names, disregard that."

EMS came, her vitals were taken and EMS left. By then the young woman had calmed down. An officer went across the street to get a small plastic bag that belonged to her. Someone who'd gone into the store to buy her some food handed it to the officer, who helped the young woman into the backseat. She was not in handcuffs.

Somebody's child had a rough day. Whoever that somebody is, know that others treated your child as if she were their own.

Keep Marching, Children

It's 1951 and R.R. Moton High School is a dump. Pre–*Brown v. Board of Education*, the Black high school in Farmville, Virginia, is evidence that separate isn't equal. The white high school across town, Farmville High, has all the resources needed for the education and comfort of its students, but on rainy days at Moton students use umbrellas to keep dry in classrooms because of the porous roofs.

On April 23, 1951, the principal of Moton High receives a phone call that two of his students are going to be arrested at the bus station, so he leaves to go help them. It's a trick, and in his absence a note written in his name is sent to each of the classrooms calling for everyone to gather for a general assembly. Not knowing their reason for gathering, the 450 students and 25 teachers wait for their principal to explain.

But when the curtain opens, standing on stage isn't the principal but Barbara Johns, a sixteen-year-old junior, who had manipulated the principal's absence so she could call on the student body to protest the second-class conditions of their school. She asks, then demands, that the teachers leave the auditorium. Those who don't are politely escorted out by students.

Moton High lacks, among other things, a cafeteria, lockers, a science lab, a gym and an infirmary. Johns tells her fellow students that since their parents and other Black adults haven't been listened to by the white establishment, it's time for the Black students to act. She calls for a strike and leads all the students on a march out of school to the county courthouse and into the offices of the school superintendent. All day, the students demand better schools.

When their demands are rebuffed, Johns reaches out to NAACP lawyers. In a mass rally the lawyers warn Farmville's Black community of the dangers involved with filing a lawsuit, but the students respond that there aren't enough jails to hold them.

Over the next few months Johns is harassed. The Ku Klux Klan burns a cross in her family's front yard. Fearing for their daughter's safety, her parents send her to Montgomery, Alabama, to live with her uncle, Rev. Vernon Johns, the pastor of Dexter Avenue Baptist Church.

Now it's 1963 and the man who succeeded Vernon Johns at Dexter Avenue Baptist Church, Martin Luther King Jr., is leading a civil rights campaign in Birmingham to desegregate public facilities. King spends Easter weekend in jail. After his release protests continue but the campaign isn't capturing the nation's attention. That changes on May 2 when Black youth, more than a thousand and some as young as six years old, pour out of the Sixteenth Street Baptist Church singing freedom songs. Police use paddy wagons, squad cars and buses to ferry the children to jail. The next day, when another thousand-plus students roll out of church and down the street, Bull Connor orders high pressure water hoses, dogs and batons be turned on them. Birmingham now has the attention of the world.

It's 2023, and last Wednesday thousands of students across the nation, including in Uvalde, walked out of school protesting gun violence and the callousness and cowardice of lawmakers who do little to stop it. One of the Uvalde students was Jazmin Cazares, a senior at Uvalde High School. Her nine-year-old sister, Jacklyn, was one of the twenty-one people murdered at Robb Elementary. Jazmin was part of what she described on Twitter as a seventy-seven-minute sit-in, explaining, "That's how long it took for police to enter rooms 111 and 112 at Robb Elementary."

Students have been marching with urgency since the 2018 school shooting in Parkland, Florida, stole seventeen lives. The name of the student-led movement arising from that massacre, March for Our Lives, is an indictment of a nation whose leaders leave children with no option but to march for their lives. Their marching and activism make many uncomfortable because marching and activism always make people uncomfortable. Nonviolent protest is supposed to make people uncomfortable.

While imprisoned in Birmingham on Easter weekend, sixty years ago, King began composing his "Letter from a Birmingham Jail" as a response to clergy critical of him and the protests. "You may well ask," he wrote, "'Why direct action, why sit-ins, marches, and so forth? Isn't negotiation a better path?' You are exactly right in your call for negotiation. Indeed, this is the purpose of direct action. Nonviolent direct action seeks to create such a crisis and establish such creative tension that a community that has consistently refused to negotiate is forced to confront the issue. It seeks so to dramatize the issue that it can no longer be ignored."

And it works.

Because of Barbara Johns and her schoolmates, their lawsuit was one of the five cases of the *Brown v. Board of Education* decision in which the US Supreme Court ruled that separate wasn't equal. A statue of Barbara Johns will replace that of Robert E. Lee in the US Capitol. Because of children marching in Birmingham, city leaders and business owners desegregated public facilities.

There is a direct line between Barbara Johns's generation and Jazmin Cazares's generation. So walk together children. Don't you get weary.

Love of "Our Theresa" Endures

She had dimples deep enough to swim in.

The phone call telling me Theresa was gone came when I was in a Dallas church for my aunt's rosary. Wandering around the church in a daze, I told my brother and my nephew, who asked, "Our Theresa?"

Our Theresa.

"Our" is the pronoun of community, of belonging, of responsibility. Few people felt as strong a responsibility to her community as Theresa Canales, whether it was the community of her neighborhood or the community of her world. Humanity was her community.

Theresa wasn't a public figure in the sense that she was famous or a household name, but the extent of her reach in so many communities and in the lives she touched through her presence, teaching, and engaged citizenship was as meaningful as any celebrity. Wide is the community that will always consider her "our Theresa."

Theresa died unexpectedly on May 25. She was fifty-one. She wasn't ready to leave, and the many who loved her weren't prepared to let "our Theresa" go.

At the time of her death, she was director of community engagement for Saint Mary's University. In her short life Theresa—or Teresa or T or TC—was a schoolteacher. She taught reading and language arts, English as a second language and

English. She was a community activist, public intellectual, writer, political organizer, strategist and so much more.

Among the local elected officials Theresa worked with in some capacity were US representative Charlie Gonzalez, Mayor Ed Garza, state representative Mike Villarreal, Bexar County Precinct 4 commissioner Tommy Calvert Jr., District 3 city councilwomen Rebecca and Phyllis Viagran, and Mayor Ron Nirenberg. On Thursday Phyllis offered a moment of silence for Theresa at the beginning of the city council meeting. She had a special relationship with former Texas House speaker Joe Straus and his wife, Julie, whose two daughters she nannied.

She was a talented cook, writer, musician, artist and dancer who also could do construction work and home repairs, develop websites, and design, code and build databases. She radiated joy and beamed gratitude at life's simplest pleasures, like planting bluebonnets.

I can't do justice writing about this amazing woman who understood me better than anyone. She once told me, "We don't have to put a name to what we mean to each other as long as we know what we mean to each other." Whatever the changing status of our relationship, she was my closest friend for ten and a half years.

I first saw Theresa on October 21, 2012, in an art gallery for a tribute to Gonzalez, who was retiring from Congress. I was on the second floor, leaning on the railing, when this beautiful wisp of a woman in a dark brown dress with tiny white dots walked in, signed in and took a seat. As the program started and I went to take a seat, she introduced herself.

Three weeks later we went to lunch and learned our fathers were from Gonzales, about seventy-five minutes east of San Antonio. She came from a family of musicians, which included her father, Margarito Canales.

As in everything, her taste in music was eclectic. She said her childhood was defined by Tejano music, George Jones and the Commodores.

Theresa was Mexican American, but she was often mistaken for other ethnicities. Once, while we were driving in Atlanta, she said, "Wherever I go, they think I'm something different." Truth be told, Theresa was a young Latina with the soul of an eighty-five-year-old Black woman, because only an eighty-five-year-old Black woman could enunciate "Chiiiiiild!" as she did. She also did the best Jerry Lewis "hey, lady!" I've ever heard.

Her sense of humor could be sharp to the point. We sometimes read the same novel at the same time, taking turns reading chapters to each other. One of our trips to New Orleans was spurred by reading Attica Locke's wonderful novel *The Cutting Season*, which took place on an old slave plantation based on the Oak Alley plantation between New Orleans and Baton Rouge.

When we visited Oak Alley, Theresa asked the lady behind the ticket counter, "Do Black people get a discount?" As we walked the grounds in the July heat, thinking about slaves forced to work sunup to sundown, Theresa asked me, "Do you want to go stand in the shade just because we can?"

She could speak knowledgeably about gardening, calligraphy, astronomy, botany, religious practices of various cultures, science, languages, art, literature, music, Shakespeare and history. I never looked at dandelions the same after she schooled me on their health benefits and profitability as a crop.

Children centered her world and were the greatest inspiration for her work. My thirteen-year-old niece Laiana was three when she met Theresa, and it was love at first sight.

The most amazing gifts of this Renaissance woman were her ability to love, and her relentless cheer and optimism, no matter the difficulties she endured or the slights thrown at her. I've never known anyone who went so out of her way to help others and relieve them of their pain. She saw beauty and made beauty where she could.

A few years ago, her friend poet Naomi Shihab Nye captured Theresa in a poem, "You Are Your Own State Department."

> When your country does not feel cozy, what do you do?
> Theresa walks more now, to feel closer to her
> ground. If destination within two miles, she must
> hike or take the bus. Carries apples,
> extra bottles of chilled water to give away.

Several times since her passing I've asked Theresa to send me a sign that she's happy. Last Sunday night, standing outside my mother's house, where I'd last seen Theresa on Mother's Day, I thought about asking God for that sign. At that moment, 9:35 p.m., something small, white and feathery drifted down inches from my face. I waited for more to fall, but when none did I took out a flashlight to check the ground. I saw nothing.

I thanked our Dandelion Angel. Our Theresa.

The girl with dimples deep enough to fill with tears and drown in.

ACKNOWLEDGMENTS

This is the part of the book that is the most daunting because I can't possibly include all the people who have supported me throughout my life and career. I thank all of my family and all of my friends. If you know you're one or the other or both, know this includes you.

Of course, there's no single institution I'm more thankful to than the *San Antonio Express-News*, without which this book and my career would not have been possible.

For my first stint at the paper, special thanks to Maury Maverick Jr., Bob Richter, Lynnell Burkett, Sterlin Holmesly, Craig "Mr. T" Thomason, Robert Rivard, Larry Walker, Raul Reyes, Linda Vaughan, Bruce Davidson, Veronica Flores-Paniagua, Terry Bertling, Brett Thacker, Rick Casey, Roddy Stinson and Carlos Guerra.

My second act at the *Express-News* begins with the indefatigable and talented editorial page editor, Josh Brodesky, who in bringing me back to the paper in 2019 offered me a gift I never thought possible. Most of the pieces in this collection, written after my return, were edited by him.

Years before I came back, my former colleagues at the paper were raving about Marc Duvoisin, the *Express-News*'s superb and immensely kind editor-in-chief and senior vice president. It's been my pleasure to learn that it wasn't just hype. He's the real deal.

Mark Medici, the publisher of the *Express-News*, is a

marvelous (and loud) force of nature unlike any newspaper publisher most of us have known. When I was sick with COVID-19 in May 2020 (and lying about how sick I was), I had to talk him out of sending an ambulance to my house to take me to the hospital. So what if we disagree about whether MJ (Mark) or LeBron (me) is the greatest basketball player of all time.

I was humbled when I learned that Joe Holley, one of my favorite journalists and people, would write the foreword for this collection. I was a fan of his before he joined the *Express-News* and we became colleagues. I was awestruck, but his humility and sheer decency and humanity melted away the "struck" part; I continue to be in awe of his way with words. Thank you, Joe, for endorsing this collection.

I thank all of my *Express-News* colleagues and friends, past and present, for always making the *Express-News* feel like home.

Thank you, Tom Payton, and the staff at Trinity University Press for doing this collection thing a second time with me. I appreciate your ideas and vision.

Thank you, Gabriela Poyo, for your time, work, and talent in helping me prepare this manuscript. You will be one of your generation's leaders who will get us closer to those finish lines. You certainly made it possible for me to cross this one.

These books and my career would not have been possible were it not for readers. To everyone who's taken the time to read me just once or over the decades, I can't thank you enough for your support.